THE
CHALLENGE
TO THE
SOUTH

Members of the Commission

Chairman: Julius K. Nyerere (Tanzania)
Secretary-General: Manmohan Singh (India)

Ismail Sabri Abdalla	(Egypt)
Abdlatif Al-Hamad	(Kuwait)
Paulo Evaristo Arns	(Brazil)
Solita Collas-Monsod	(Philippines)
Eneas Da Conceiçao Comiche	(Mozambique)
Gamani Corea	(Sri Lanka)
Aboubakar Diaby-Ouattara	(Ivory Coast)
Aldo Ferrer	(Argentina)
Celso Furtado	(Brazil)
Enrique Iglesias	(Uruguay)
Devaki Jain	(India)
Simba Makoni	(Zimbabwe)
Michael Manley	(Jamaica)
Jorge Eduardo Navarrete	(Mexico)
Pius Okigbo	(Nigeria)
Augustin Papic	(Yugoslavia)
Carlos Andrés Pérez	(Venezuela)
Qian Jiadong	(China)
Shridath Ramphal	(Guyana)
Carlos Rafael Rodríguez	(Cuba)
Abdus Salam	(Pakistan)
Marie-Angélique Savané	(Senegal)
Tan Sri Ghazali Shafie	(Malaysia)
Tupua Tamasese Tupuola Efi	(Western Samoa)
Nitisastro Widjojo	(Indonesia)
Layachi Yaker	(Algeria)

THE
CHALLENGE
TO THE
SOUTH

The Report of the
South Commission

OXFORD UNIVERSITY PRESS
1990

Oxford University Press, Walton Street, Oxford OX2 6DP

Oxford New York Toronto
Delhi Bombay Calcutta Madras Karachi
Petaling Jaya Singapore Hong Kong Tokyo
Nairobi Dar es Salaam Cape Town
Melbourne Auckland
and associated companies in
Berlin Ibadan

Oxford is a trade mark of Oxford University Press

Published in the United States
by Oxford University Press, New York

British Library Cataloguing in Publication Data
Data available
ISBN 0–19–877311–0

Library of Congress Cataloging in Publication Data
Data available
ISBN 0–19–877311–0

Typeset by The South Commission
Printed Great Britain by
Biddles Ltd
Guildford & King's Lynn

Chairman's Preface

The South Commission is made up of individuals from all the continents of the South, acting in their personal capacity. It has its origins in a recognition within the South that developing countries have many problems and much experience in common, but that no one in the South was responsible for looking at these things in a comprehensive manner, or at the lessons about appropriate development strategies which could be drawn from them. Political leaders are naturally preoccupied with the particular problems of their own countries and the urgent needs of their own citizens; individual intellectuals deal with particular aspects of an all-encompassing problem and again usually concentrate on their own country or region. Further, the South does not know the South–what goes on in its countries, what are the ideas of its peoples, what its potential is, and the manner in which South-South co-operation can widen development options for all countries. Instead each country is forced to make its own mistakes, without being able to learn from the experience of others in a similar situation, and to benefit from the experience of their successes.

In the light of these facts the South Commission was formally established in 1987, following years of informal discussion among intellectual and political leaders from the South. The final initiative was taken by Prime Minister Mahathir Mohamad of Malaysia after a meeting organised in Kuala Lumpur by the Third World Foundation and the Malaysian Institute of Strategic and International Studies. It is he who came to see me in Dar-es-Salaam, and who announced to the Non-Aligned Movement Summit Meeting in Harare in 1986 the intention to establish the South Commission under my Chairmanship. But Prime Minister Mahathir bears no responsibility for the contents of this Report; that is the sole responsiblity of the members of the Commission, acting jointly.

In agreeing to serve on the South Commission, my colleagues and myself undertook the work of together looking at the South, analysing the problems its countries face, the strategies they have adopted for dealing with them, and the lessons which could be drawn from past experience in the light of current and anticipated international conditions. All of us, from the beginning to the end, had a single purpose in mind. That purpose was to help the peoples and governments of the South to be more effective in overcoming their numerous problems, in achieving their ambition of developing their countries in freedom, and in improving the lives and living conditions of their peoples.

This Report is the result of our work. Those who encouraged us to undertake this task hoped that we would make practical recommendations which could usefully be carried out by those concerned. This we have tried our best to do, and believe that we have done. Despite the very different backgrounds, experience, interests, faiths, and ideologies of the members of the Commission, it is a unanimous Report. We have made recommendations on strategies appropriate for and conducive to development in the countries of the South in the 1990s and beyond. We believe that our proposals are practical ones, and suggest steps which can be taken by the countries of the South. It is certainly true that they usually demand hard work and some willingness to sacrifice, as well as dedication and commitment by peoples and governments; but they offer hope for the future–which the present equally difficult strategies in many cases fail to do.

It will be up to each government and people to work out the tactics needed if its own country is to move in the directions we suggest–and also to determine its own timetable in so far as external circumstances allow flexibility. We neither are nor have pretences to be omniscient beings, who have the local knowledge and understanding necessary to arrange the effective application of a strategy in all the different countries of the South. We do, however, recommend an expansion of South-South co-operation, and it is obvious that when a group of countries have decided to work together within an agreed framework they need to give continuing political support and to allocate sufficient human and material resources for the work to be carried through efficiently and expeditiously.

Underlying all the Report's recommendations is our recognition, and clear statement, that responsibility for the development of the South lies in the South, and in the hands of the peoples of the South.

The publication of this Report is a sign that the work of the South Commission, as a Commission, is coming to an end. The work which has to be done to fulfill the needs and common purposes of the South is, however, only just beginning. We, the Commission's members, will only regard ourselves as having succeeded in our efforts to be of service if the recommendations of this Report, and of the Statements we have issued, are given serious consideration by the governments and peoples of the South–and by their friends in the North.

We have been led to believe that this consideration will be given. For in persisting with our work since 1987, all members of the Commission have been encouraged by the interest shown in what we were doing and the support given to us. One vitally important evidence of this has been that the Commission and its basic work have been financed by countries, institutions, and a private business, of the South. From the South, and despite the intense financial crises facing most developing countries and institutions, the Commission has collected over seven and a half million US dollars for its three years of work. These contributions are listed in the Annexe to the Report. In addition, governments of the South have hosted meetings of the Commission in their countries, and in a number of cases have facilitated the activities of members from their countries.

The Commission also benefited from some support from the North, notably from the Government of Switzerland which enabled the Commission to set up its Secretariat in Geneva with the status of an international organization and provided an annual grant for three years to cover the rent for its office and certain operational expenses.

But money is not enough. We in the Commission have reason to express our own heavy debt to the individuals who have constituted our Secretariat, and the team they became under the exemplary leadership of our fellow–member, Dr. Manmohan Singh. Few in number but high in quality, the Secretariat staff have worked long hours and at high intensity to service the Commission with technical papers of superb quality. They have sought, and received, co-operation from many other individuals, from research institutes and development institutions of the South, and from United Nations bodies–in particular UNCTAD and UNESCO. To all of these people and organizations we are most grateful. Further, the Secretariat has made of our small Geneva office a place which welcomed other workers in the development field, for consultation and mutual assistance. In addition, there are many other individuals and groups whom I myself, other Commissioners, or members of the Secretariat have met on our extensive travels in the countries of the South and who have helped to shape our thinking and have thus contributed to the ideas in this Report.

The names of the Secretariat staff are listed, together with information about some of the people who have helped us and about the mechanics of the Commission's work, in the Annexe. But although the responsibility for the contents of this Report rests only with the Commission members, I want to emphasize that it is the existence and the quality of the Secretariat which have enabled us to fulfill our self-appointed responsibility to the peoples and countries of the South in preparing it. I thank them all very much indeed.

Dar-es-Salaam, May 1990

Contents

List of Figures

List of Acronyms

ACP	African, Caribbean, and Pacific States
ADB	African Development Bank
ALADI	Latin American Integration Association (*Asociación Latinoamericana de Integración*)
AsDB	Asian Development Bank
ASEAN	Association of South East Asian Nations
ASTRO	International Association of State Trading Organisations of Developing Countries
BLADEX	Latin American Export Bank (*Banco Latinoamericano de Exportaciones*)
CACM	Central American Common Market
CARICOM	Caribbean Community
CCFF	Compensatory and Contingency Financing Facility
CEAO	West African Economic Community (*Communauté économique de l'Afrique occidentale*)
CEEAC	Economic Community of Central African States (*Communauté économique des états d'Afrique centrale*)
CFCs	chlorofluorocarbons
CFF	Compensatory Financing Facility
DAWN	Development Alternatives for Women in a New Era
EC	European Community
ECDC	economic co-operation among developing countries
ECOWAS	Economic Community of West African States
ESAF	Enhanced Structural Adjustment Facility
FAO	Food and Agricultural Organization
GATT	General Agreement on Tariffs and Trade
GCC	Co-operation Council for the Arab States of the Gulf
CGIAR	Consultative Group on International Agricultural Research
GDP	gross domestic product
GNP	gross national product
GSP	Generalized System of Preferences
GSTP	Global System of Trade Preferences
IBRD	International Bank for Reconstruction and Development (World Bank)

ICTP	International Centre for Theoretical Physics
IDA	International Development Association
IDB	Inter-American Development Bank
IFAD	International Fund for Agricultural Development
IMF	International Monetary Fund
ITC	International Trade Centre
ITO	International Trade Organization
LAFTA	Latin American Free Trade Association
NGO	non-governmental organization
OAU	Organization of African Unity
ODA	official development assistance
OECD	Organisation for Economic Co-operation and Development
OPEC	Organization of Petroleum Exporting Countries
PTA	Preferential Trade Area
R&D	research and development
SAARC	South Asian Association for Regional Co-operation
SADCC	Southern African Development Co-ordination Conference
SAFICO	Andean Trade Financing System (*Sistema Andino de Financiamiento del Comercio*)
SDRs	Special Drawing Rights
SELA	Latin American Economic System (*Sistema Económico Latinoamericano*)
SUNFED	Special United Nations Fund for Economic Development
TCDC	Technical Co-operation among Developing Countries
TRIMs	trade-related investment measures
TRIPs	trade-related aspects of intellectual property rights
UDEAC	Central African Customs and Economic Union (*Union douanière et économique d'Afrique centrale*)
UNCTAD	United Nations Conference on Trade and Development
UNDP	United Nations Development Programme
UNESCO	United Nations Educational, Scientific and Cultural Organization
UNICEF	United Nations Children's Fund
UNIDO	United Nations Industrial Development Organization

| WHO | World Health Organization |
| WIPO | World Intellectual Property Organization |

The South and Its Tasks

1

A WORLD DIVIDED

Three and a half billion people, three quarters of all humanity, live in the developing countries. By the year 2000, the proportion will probably have risen to four fifths. Together the developing countries–accounting for more than two thirds of the earth's land surface area–are often called the Third World.

We refer to them as the South. Largely bypassed by the benefits of prosperity and progress, they exist on the periphery of the developed countries of the North. While most of the people of the North are affluent, most of the people of the South are poor; while the economies of the North are generally strong and resilient, those of the South are mostly weak and defenceless; while the countries in the North are, by and large, in control of their destinies, those of the South are very vulnerable to external factors and lacking in functional sovereignty.

The countries of the South vary greatly in size, in natural resource endowment, in the structure of their economies, in the level of economic, social, and technological development. They also differ in their cultures, in their political systems, and in the ideologies they profess. Their economic and technological diversity has become more marked in recent years, making the South of today even less homogeneous than the South of yesterday.

Yet in this diversity there is a basic unity. What the countries of the South have in common transcends their differences; it gives them a shared identity and a reason to work together for common objectives. And their economic diversity offers opportunities for co-operation that can benefit them all.

The primary bond that links the countries and peoples of the South is their desire to escape from poverty and underdevelopment and secure a better life for their citizens. This shared aspiration is a foundation for their solidarity, expressed through such organizations as the Group of 77–of which all countries of the South except China are members–and the Non-Aligned Movement, with a large and growing membership from all continents in the South.

The decision-making processes that govern the international flows of trade, capital, and technology are controlled by the major developed countries of the North and by the international institutions they dominate. The countries of the South are unfavourably placed in the world economic system; they are individually powerless to influence these processes and institutions and, hence, the global economic environment which vitally affects their development. For this reason they have made a collective demand for the reform of the international economic system so as to make it more equitable and responsive to the needs of the vast majority of humanity–the people of the South. The struggle for a fairer international system has consolidated their cohesion and strengthened their resolve to pursue united action.

Were all humanity a single nation-state, the present North-South divide would make it an unviable, semi-feudal entity, split by internal conflicts. Its small part is advanced, prosperous, powerful; its much bigger part is underdeveloped, poor, powerless. A nation so divided within itself would be recognized as unstable. A world so divided should likewise be recognized as inherently unstable. And the position is worsening, not improving. During the 1970s, there was hope that a New International Economic Order would be generally accepted as an objective and that the North-South gap would narrow. But for most countries of the South that gap has been widening. The world is becoming, not less, but more disparate in the basic conditions of human life. For many in the South, the hope has faded; the prospects have become gloomier than they were perceived to be only a decade ago.

In the three decades after the Second World War, most developing countries made significant economic and social progress. Indeed in the 1960s and 1970s, the developing countries as a group did better than the developed countries in rates of economic growth–and also better than the developed countries in their early stages of development.

The mid-1970s witnessed a shift towards continuing disarray in the world economy. The consequence of this disarray was eventually the world recession of 1980-83. Industrialized countries have since then enjoyed a period of recovery and uninterrupted growth, though at a slower pace than in the previous post-war phases of recovery, but an acute economic crisis continues in many parts of the developing world. In the decade of the

1980s, a large majority of developing countries suffered severe blows to their economic growth and living standards; countries with a heavy burden of external debt suffered most. Retrogression, persistent instability and uncertainty, and recurring financial crises troubled the developing world–although with some important exceptions, notably in Asia–throughout the 1980s.

The impact of these setbacks has been pervasive, and has been reflected in such indicators of public well-being as infant mortality, life expectancy, levels of nutrition, incidence of disease, and school enrolment. As a result, social discontent and political unrest have been building up, especially among the poorer groups in the population; these, notably women, have borne a disproportionate part of the effect of cuts in social services and employment. Young people, facing reduced opportunities for employment and training, are becoming increasingly disaffected.

The widening disparities between South and North are attributable not merely to differences in economic progress, but also to an enlargement of the North's power vis-à-vis the rest of the world. The leading countries of the North now more readily use that power in pursuit of their objectives. The ' gunboat' diplomacy of the nineteenth century still has its economic and political counterpart in the closing years of the twentieth. The fate of the South is increasingly dictated by the perceptions and policies of governments in the North, of the multilateral institutions which a few of those governments control, and of the network of private institutions that are increasingly prominent. Domination has been reinforced where partnership was needed and hoped for by the South.

Yet, the North too is not homogeneous. There are economic, social, and cultural differences among the developed countries of the West. They also differ in their approach to global issues and, to some extent, in their attitude towards the countries of the South.

The South remains economically linked mainly to the market economy countries of the North–both a legacy of the colonial past sustained by the North's relative economic strength and a consequence of the development strategies sometimes adopted in the South. However, our notion of the North also includes the countries of Eastern Europe, whose attitude towards the South has differed from that of the West. So far, these countries, while strongly supporting the aspirations of the South, have not played a major role in North-South negotiations on economic matters. Links of co-operation between them and the South have not been fully developed. Conditions in these countries are changing very fast and a new basis for co-operation will need to be evolved as they seek to redefine their position in the global economy.

A WORLD IN TRANSITION

In this last decade of the century, the world is in a process of rapid transition. Political alignments, economic systems, and social values are being transformed. The conventional notions, familiar since the end of the Second World War, are less and less applicable to the changing international environment. These momentous changes present opportunities from which the South should seek to benefit, but they also entail the risk of a less propitious climate for development.

At the base of these changes is the acceleration of scientific and technological advance. The science and technology revolution is fundamentally affecting societies, economies, and international relations. It has given a strong impetus to the trend towards globalization, which has been induced by such institutional changes as deregulation and privatization undertaken by the leading countries of the North.

Lessening of International Tensions

Among the important political changes which began to materialize in the late 1980s is the progress being made in bridging the military and political divide between East and West. The superpowers and their military alliances have summoned up a vision of a world in which their nations can live in peace. They have opened a dialogue for political accommodation; this has cooled the passions of conflict and set their governments moving towards disarmament.

From the earliest post-war years, through the efforts of the developing countries, the goal of disarmament has been coupled at the international level with that of development. The objective of eliminating poverty and distress world-wide, and reducing the tensions that global economic disparities generate, could now move up on the world agenda. Progress towards disarmament should allow the world community to give greater attention to urgent development needs; saving on military expenditure also enlarges the ability of the international system to meet these needs. As the disarmament process gains momentum, an early decision to link it effectively with the provision of resources for development would be timely and appropriate. The easing of East-West tensions may, in addition, contribute to reducing the incidence and scale of armed conflict in the South, and as a consequence allow the South to economize on military expenditure and concentrate on development.

Increasing Globalization

A prominent feature of the last two decades has been the increasing globalization of the world economy, particularly of production and finance. The role of transnational companies has grown. Take-overs and mergers of companies across national boundaries have multiplied, helped by the explosive growth of international private financial flows. The spread of the deregulation of financial movements and electronic trading in developed countries has opened the way for massive transfers of funds and trading in securities–stocks and shares, bonds and other financial instruments–among the major financial centres as well as facilitated capital flight from the South. Private financial flows have become a substantial multiple of world merchandise trade. These very large cross-border movements of assets tend to cause more frequent shifts in exchange and interest rates, affecting the competitive position of individual countries.

A network of relationships has been built up among private entities–banks, investment houses, transnational companies–in the leading developed countries. This has served to strengthen the influence of decisions made by private bodies on world economic activity, and to that extent to limit the effectiveness of governmental policy decisions. For the South the result is even further marginalization and greater powerlessness.

One feature of globalization is the trend towards the formation of stronger regional groupings to cope with shifts in the balance of economic power. The single market in the European Community and the US-Canada free trade area undoubtedly represent attempts to create larger economic spaces in order to regain international competitiveness, e.g. vis-à-vis the fast growing Japanese and newly industrializing economies of East Asia, particularly in the context of the emerging links of co-operation in the Asia-Pacific region.

Culturally too the world is increasingly interlinked. The communications revolution is steadily enlarging the access to information for the peoples of the South. Statements are made in the North about the effect on patterns of living of immigration from the South. But in the South cultural influences from the North are much stronger, more pervasive, and in some respects pernicious. They are transmitted through the media–whose impact has been intensified by the spread of television, through the advertising of consumer products associated with affluent life-styles, through education patterned on Northern models, and through tourism.

International movements of people are also a growing form of interlinkage in the world today. Economic, social, and political factors are responsible for migratory movements; some migrants seek refuge from fighting or persecution, some hope to escape from poverty, looking for employment or leaving behind a situation offering little or no prospect of betterment. At the same time, the expansion of transnational corporations, notably in the area of services, involves a growing movement of nationals of Northern countries to the South, for whom the North demands special treatment. This could be a much more significant phenomenon in economic terms than South-North migration.

Similarly, the current intense concern about environmental degradation has highlighted the close interrelationships of nations and peoples. The effects of environmental damage do not stop at national frontiers. The thinning of the ozone layer, the greenhouse effect, marine pollution, and nuclear radiation are global phenomena. While these result primarily from patterns of growth and consumption in the North, the South cannot escape their impact. In addition, the environment in the South is increasingly being harmed by the North through such direct acts as the dumping of hazardous wastes and the relocation of polluting industries. These aggravate the South's own environmental deterioration, such as deforestation, desertification, soil and water degradation, air pollution, and urban squalor.

The damage to the environment is increasingly viewed with concern by decision-makers and public opinion. This concern could be a powerful motive for harnessing the collective energies of the international community for the removal of poverty and underdevelopment, which are the principal causes of environmental stress in the South.

World health is also indivisible. Smallpox had to be eradicated everywhere before any country could be immune from it; AIDS is now spreading relentlessly despite attempts to stop it at national borders.

Another phenomenon with global ramifications that compel international co-operation is the illicit traffic in narcotic drugs. The principal incentive for the growth of this international traffic is the rising demand in certain developed countries. This aspect has been given insufficient attention vis-à-vis the supply side of the problem. Much greater attention should be devoted to curbing the consumption of drugs in the North. The traffic has become highly organized, involving a variety of criminal or shady activities, such as bribery, corruption, tax evasion, the abuse of the international banking system for laundering profits, the smuggling of weapons, violence, and terrorism. In some developing countries such activities have become a serious threat to social stability and public safety; indeed, social and political systems there are in danger of being destroyed.

Globalization has been significantly assisted by technology, which has been an important influence on the pace of social and economic change the world over. The speed of scientific and technological advance has far-reaching implications for all aspects of society and all spheres of human relations. New technologies offer dramatic new capabilities to humanity, which could be used to remove some of the most stubborn obstacles to the South's development. But scientific and technological innovation is not necessarily benign, as is proved by its military applications and by some of its consequences in the biosphere. Also, the uneven distribution of scientific capability could accentuate global inequities and the powerlessness and dependence of those who do not have control of its potential.

From Subordination to Interdependence

All the world is linked together, inextricably. But it is linked in an asymmetrical and skewed manner. There are links between the North and the South, but the countries of the South are politically, economically, and culturally subordinate to the much stronger and better-organized North. This is true even of the larger countries of the South in almost all exchanges; the relationship is one of dependence much more than interdependence.

There is interdependence between the countries of the North; but there is at present no generalized South-South interdependence. At most, there are some relatively recent and fragile links among countries in a particular region. For persons or goods to move from one region or continent, or from one part of a continent of the South to another, it is often necessary to pass through one or more Northern countries. Even intra-South telecommunications links usually pass through the North or via satellites controlled or owned by companies or bodies in the North.

This dependence inevitably restricts domestic and external freedom in the South and its legally sovereign States. Interdependence strengthens; but dependence implies a diminution of freedom and of the capacity for autonomous action for any nation or for any group of nations working together.

Thus, having for the most part won the struggle for political independence, the countries of the South have been increasingly hampered by its limitations; it has not given them the power to determine their own policies and their own future.

The conviction has therefore steadily grown in the South that there is a need to continue the struggle for independence, political and economic, through self-reliant development and South-South co-operation, and for equitable participation in international decision-making. The peoples of the South must by their own exertions free themselves from poverty, underdevelopment, and dependency and gain control of their economies and polities. History shows that domination is never surrendered voluntarily; it has to be brought to an end by the self-reliant actions of those who are dominated. History also shows that even greatly superior power can be defeated if people are determined not to accept it and to act together to weaken and eventually overcome it.

Colonialism was overthrown when the colonized refused to accept it. Using their own slender resources they organized them-

selves for struggle against foreign domination. They did this separately within each colonial territory, while supporting each
other's struggles even when following different strategies, and ac-
cepting whatever outside help was offered on satisfactory terms.
The economic domination now experienced by the countries of
the South in varying degrees can begin to be overcome only
through similar determined, self-reliant action.

A decision by the South to reject subordination, and to act on
that repudiation, does not imply a desire for confrontation. The
confrontation already inherent in the current domination by the
North must be replaced by a more balanced and equitable management of global affairs which satisfies the interests of developed
and developing countries alike and recognizes the interdependence of the world's people.

THE SOUTH AND ITS VISION

It is in this spirit that the South Commission's work has been
done. It is a spirit of concern for the people of the developing
countries, but of concern as well that the world should become a
more just and secure habitation for all countries and all people.
We have believed throughout our work that the world is at a mo-
ment of historic challenge and opportunity–and that the South
has an obligation to help to ensure, by its own response, that global responses too become worthy of humanity. The purpose of
this Report is to contribute to the success of this endeavour so that
the countries of the South may determine their own destinies
while playing a full part in humanity's development and in enhancing the security of its common heritage–the planet Earth.

A Truly Interdependent World

The South's vision has to embrace the whole world, for it is part
of that world. It cannot isolate itself; nor should it wish to isolate
itself from the rest of the world.

On the contrary, the South seeks an undivided world in which
there would be no 'South' and no 'North'; in which there would
not be one part developed, rich, and dominating, and the other
underdeveloped, poor, and dominated. The South's goal is a
world of equal opportunities in which criss-crossing lines of

interaction–political, economic, social, cultural, scientific–may sustain global interdependence; in which nations in their variety would work together in pursuit of jointly agreed goals; in which peace, security, and dignity would be the birthright of all persons and all peoples; in which all can take advantage of the advances of science; and in which the world's resources may be prudently used to satisfy the needs of all and not merely the narrow self-interest of a few.

This vision of the world can be made real only through a very long series of steps in a consistent and deliberate movement. Its attainment may demand that all countries accept trimming of the scope of national decision-making and move to greater co-operation as a human society.

Despite recent moves towards the assertion of national identities, the trend of human history has been towards ever closer integration. In the past this movement was propelled by scientific and technological advance, but its objectives were achieved through conflict and war. Today such use of naked power is unacceptable, and science has made conflict immensely more destructive and war a threat to the survival of humankind. If the world's people are to secure their future, they have now to move towards global unity through widening co-operation on an equitable basis. And because it is the people of the South who most urgently need change in the present world order, it is they who have to take the initiative to make this vision of the world a reality.

Development Defined

The South's vision must also embrace a notion of what development ultimately signifies. In our view, development is a process which enables human beings to realize their potential, build self-confidence, and lead lives of dignity and fulfilment. It is a process which frees people from the fear of want and exploitation. It is a movement away from political, economic, or social oppression. Through development, political independence acquires its true significance. And it is a process of growth, a movement essentially springing from within the society that is developing.

Development therefore implies growing self-reliance, both individual and collective. The base for a nation's development must be its own resources, both human and material, fully used to meet its own needs. External assistance can promote development. But to have this effect, this assistance has to be integrated into the national effort and applied to the purposes of those it is meant to benefit. Development is based on self-reliance and is self-directed; without these characteristics there can be no genuine development.

But a nation is its people. Development has therefore to be an effort of, by, and for the people. True development has to be people-centred. It has to be directed at the fulfilment of human potential and the improvement of the social and economic well-being of the people. And it has to be designed to secure what the people themselves perceive to be their social and economic interests.

People are both individuals and members of society. To articulate their interests–and to influence the course of national development–they have to be free members of their society. They have to be free to learn, to say what they think and know what others think, to organize in furtherance of their common interests. They have to be able to choose freely those who govern them, and those who govern must be accountable to the people.

Development at the same time takes place in the context of social, economic, and political organization, with the consequence that citizens owe obligations to society. For development means growth of the individual and of the community of which the individual is a part. In the modern world, that community ranges from the family, the village, town, or city to the nation and the world as a whole. At all these levels, and through means appropriate to them, individuals must be able to influence decisions and also join in their implementation and the control of activities which affect them. But their involvement has to conform to a framework of rules set by themselves as a part of that larger community and enforced on their behalf by those chosen to govern.

Thus, development necessarily implies political freedom, for individuals as for nations. The interests and desires of the South could not be expressed–or known–until the former colonial territories attained independence. Similarly, the people's interests and desires can only be known when they are free–and have the channels– to express them.

Democratic institutions and popular participation in decision-making are therefore essential to genuine development. Only when there is effective political freedom can the people's interests become paramount within nations. The people must be able to determine the system of government, who forms their government, and in broad terms what the government does in their name and on their behalf. Respect for human rights, the rule of law, and the possibility to change governments through peaceful means are among the basic constituents of a democratic polity.

The form of democracy–its machinery–must be appropriate to the nation's history, size, and cultural diversity. Other nations do not necessarily provide models which can be directly transplanted. Political systems need to be understood by the people they serve and suited to their own value systems. What is vital is that governments should be, through nationally appropriate mechanisms, accountable to the people and responsive to their freely expressed views.

Periodic elections, however free and fair, are insufficient by themselves to secure action tending to achieve genuine development. If a government is to be able to mobilize a country's human and material resources for development and to ensure that the path of development continues to respond to the interests of its people, it needs a system of constant interaction with the people it represents. What that system is, and how it is organized, must again depend on the nature of the society. Nevertheless, continual questioning by citizens, whose freedom of expression should be unencumbered, and by independent observers can stimulate the reforms necessary to maintain the system's democratic effectiveness as the national society develops and changes.

Rapid and sustained economic growth is indispensable for the South's development. Hunger, disease, and ignorance cannot be overcome unless the production of goods and services is greatly increased. Nor can the South's nations be really independent if they have to continue to rely on external aid for such basic needs as food or other vital economic requirements.

It is only a rapidly expanding economy that can create the resources for the improvement of human well-being and of the public services which contribute to it. A fast-growing labour force can also be assured of jobs only if the economy is growing vigorously. Moreover, the social and economic tensions which inevitably arise over the distribution of income and wealth can hardly be resolved unless total output is expanding and productive employment is provided.

Yet it must be emphasized that economic growth as measured by the gross national product (GNP) is not synonymous with development. Not only the growth of the national product but what is produced, how and at what social and environmental cost, by whom and for whom—all this is relevant to people-centred development and should be taken into account in the formulation of policy. A broad assessment of the pace and direction of change and of its impact on the well-being of the people would provide the necessary guidance.

In a development process defined in these broad terms, social questions and social relations are as important as economic matters. Freedom for individuals, or for family and neighbourhood initiative and activities, or for the practice of religious beliefs, are among values for which many people show themselves willing to make large economic sacrifices. Such matters are therefore relevant to our notion of development.

Gross injustices are clearly incompatible with development. Personal insecurity, whether it arises from widespread crime or government action, is incompatible with freedom and therefore with development. So too is the denial of human dignity and equality. Discrimination on the grounds of sex, colour, race, religion, or political belief cannot be justified by economic or social advances which spill over to those who suffer such discrimination. Apartheid would remain the antithesis of development even if black South Africans were able to enjoy a larger share in South Africa's wealth.

To sum up: development is a process of self-reliant growth, achieved through the participation of the people acting in their own interests as they see them, and under their own control. Its first objective must be to end poverty, provide productive employment, and satisfy the basic needs of all the people, any surplus being fairly shared. This implies that basic goods and services such as food and shelter, basic education and health facilities, and clean water must be accessible to all. In addition, development presupposes a democratic structure of government, together with its supporting individual freedoms of speech, organization, and publication, as well as a system of justice which protects all the people from actions inconsistent with just laws that are known and publicly accepted.

THE TASKS OF THE SOUTH

The National Dimension

As the countries of the South differ from one another, they will have to take different routes to the common goal of development. They differ in, for example, the level of national income and its distribution, the quantity and quality of infrastructure and productive capacity, levels of education and skills and managerial capacity, and the degree of public participation in political and social life. In addition, a country's culture, homogeneity, and history will affect the priorities and the speed of movement towards the goal.

Three factors will, however, have an important bearing on the success of the development efforts of all countries of the South. First, each country will need to organize itself for a united and sustained internal effort to overcome underdevelopment and dependency, achieve economic growth with distributive justice, and modernize its society in a manner appropriate to its culture and the aspirations of its people. The responsibility for the South's development lies in the South. Sustained development cannot simply be imported. The structural transformation implicit in development can materialize only if the efforts, ingenuity, and resources of the people of the South are fully mobilized in its support. The key to success is the incorporation of the people in the process of development; this means both recognizing them as the purpose of development and assigning them the central role in designing development strategies and in implementing them.

Second, the harnessing of the national potential calls for a clear definition of the long-term and interim objectives, of the strategy to be adopted, and of the policies to be followed. It calls for determined action but also for flexibility in tactics.

Third, all developing countries will find their progress affected by external factors, including the functioning of the international economy, and some economic or political decisions made by individual developed countries in their own interests. A hostile international environment will be a hindrance–perhaps a major hindrance. External influences that could arise from the North-South divide must be taken into account. They will affect the direction in which a government can move as well as the speed at which it can move. But a developing country's government must also take into account its present and potential strength, internally and externally. If it is confident of full public support for a course of action, a government will be much freer to take it. If it can expect wide international support, its position will be similarly stronger. Solidarity among the countries of the South therefore becomes of critical importance.

The crisis which affected a large majority of developing countries in the 1980s makes it necessary that past development strategies should be reappraised. The various structural, institutional, and behavioural changes which have taken place in the world economy over the past few decades should also be examined, and the theoretical basis of development strategies and economic policies reviewed in the light of this examination.

Nearly all countries caught up in the crisis are now undertaking programmes of economic adjustment. The question for them is not the need for reform but its content– and the conditions in which it has to be undertaken in relation to the external environment, and the level of financial support as well as its social costs.

The search for improved domestic policies has to be pursued and the mix of policies must depend on a country's particular circumstances. However, it is clear that much greater emphasis has to be placed on efficiency and on systems that more fully utilize the talents and enterprise of the people. Innovative approaches have to be evolved to reconcile the demands of efficiency and equity. The development of human resources has to be a key element of new strategies. Employment policies need to be framed in the light of trends in the demographic structure and of the size and composition of the labour force. There is also a need for a careful appraisal of the role of the State, of planning, and of the market in efforts to achieve development objectives. Much development experience is now available and greater efforts should be made to compare and share it.

The recent dramatic advances in the field of science and technology pose an especially daunting challenge to the developing countries. They open new opportunities, but to take advantage of them, these countries need very rapidly to build up their capabilities to apply new technologies to their own development and to make informed choices between the technologies on offer. Difficult as this is, especially in the least developed countries, it is an essential undertaking. For the countries of the South have to harness the new technologies to their development requirements, leap-frogging over earlier technologies. Beyond assimilation of imported technologies and their adaptation to local socio-cultural and environmental conditions, the countries of the South should have a longer-term objective of building a national (or subregional) science and technology capacity. This implies investment in basic sciences, research and development, and technological innovation. The cultures of the South should regain the capacity to generate scientific and technological knowledge.

South-South Co-operation

The variety of levels of development and the diversity of resource endowments among developing countries, which call for different routes towards liberation from underdevelopment, also provide expanded scope for South-South co-operation. By joint endeavours to use to the maximum their different resources of expertise, capital, or markets, all would be able to address their separate and differing needs more effectively, thereby widening their development options. South-South co-operation can provide important new opportunities for development based on geographical proximity, on similarities in demand and tastes, on relevance of respective development experience, know-how, and skills, and on availability of complementary natural and financial resources and management and technical skills. Additional possibilities for trading are also offered by the greater diversity in levels of development. By exploiting these openings for co-operation, the South as a group can also become stronger in its negotiations with the North.

In the prevailing world environment, South-South co-operation offers developing countries a strategic means for pursuing relatively autonomous paths to development suited to the needs and aspirations of their people. On their own, most countries of the South are unlikely to be able to exploit fully the economies of scale necessary for success in a large number of industries. Nor will they be able to devote the critical minimum of resources necessary for research and development and for strengthening their scientific and technological capabilities. Acting separately, Third World countries will also be in an extremely weak bargaining position in dealing with the well-organized groupings of developed countries or with transnational corporations. Hence, solidarity and co-operation are imperative for the countries of the South.

The South has to take note of the fact that developed countries are themselves expanding their efforts at economic integration. That the developed countries, whose economies are already large, are moving in this direction only emphasizes the need for collaboration among developing countries in a changing world in which size of economy and economic and political power are assuming greater significance. Developing countries must therefore seek to take full advantage of the economies of aggregation. Subregional, regional, and interregional co-operation has now become indispensable for their sustained growth. The fact that transnational corporations exercise a dominant influence both on the generation of new technologies and on the flows of international trade makes such co-operation even more vital. The hold of these corporations on the world economy would further tighten if the type of rules contained in the General Agreement on Tariffs and Trade (GATT) were extended to services, investment, and intellectual property rights.

Geographical proximity is one basis for co-operation, leading to bilateral, subregional, or regional action. Another situation in which countries may find it advantageous to work together is that where they can advance their common interest in a certain commodity or in developing a joint industry. In addition, political or cultural affinity can provide a rationale for co-operation. And in chosen fields co-operation can embrace the whole of the South. It is important that co-operation should not only take place between government agencies. Trading, industrial, and financial enterprises, trade unions, research organizations, non-governmental organizations, and the media of the South should all be encouraged and helped to contribute to the advancement of the collective cause of the South and its solidarity in action.

The rewards of co-operation can, in time, become considerable. But they have to be earned; resources and effort have to be invested, and it takes time to produce results. In particular, co-operation will succeed only if it benefits all the participants fairly. South-South links must avoid reproducing within the South the exploitative patterns which have characterized North-South relationships. As economic levels vary greatly within the South, special arrangements have to be made for the benefit of the least developed and poorest countries and of others in special situations, e.g. landlocked or small island States.

Steps towards South-South co-operation—towards collective self-reliance, solidarity, regional integration, and effective organization in support of these objectives— are necessary steps on the road to development and a better future for the South's people. They must be part of the vision of the South, for it is through links that bring the nations of the South closer in active partnership that it will draw the strength to secure a world without divisions.

North-South Relations

The growth and diversification of the South's economies and the expansion of South-South exchanges could, in time, help to blunt the impact of the North's domination of the international economic system and reduce the South's dependence on the North for markets, capital, and technology. Meanwhile, as emphasized by the proposals for the New International Economic Order, it is only through a reform of the international system governing flows of trade, capital, and technology that the global environment for development can be improved. It is precisely this reform that is the object of the South's demand for a comprehensive dialogue with the North. And it should determine the South's position in the various North-South discussions which are now under way.

In the course of the 1980s the international processes of development co-operation that had begun to take shape in earlier post-war decades virtually collapsed. For one thing, the large impact that changes in the level of economic activity in the North exert on the developing countries and on the prices and volume of their exports of primary commodities have been given no attention in policy co-ordination among major developed countries. Their anti-inflationary policies have been among the factors responsible for depressing real commodity prices to the lowest level since the Great Depression of the 1930s, but they have done nothing to mitigate the adverse effects of the decline on the developing countries. In fact, they have welcomed the benefits that low commodity prices have given them, including the transfer of resources from the South implicit in the deterioration of the terms of trade.

The changed environment is also reflected in the international trade and financial institutions, in which, the interests and objectives of the developing countries are grossly neglected because of their weak position. Thus, after several rounds of multilateral trade negotiations in the GATT, the developing countries continue to face many discriminatory barriers to their exports in the industrialized countries. In the Uruguay Round, their long-standing grievances were pushed into second place by issues of greater interest to the developed countries.

Nor has the International Monetary Fund (IMF) paid much attention to the reserve position and liquidity needs of developing countries in considering the issue of allocations of Special Drawing Rights (SDRs). And the international financial system has failed to provide the positive flows of capital to developing countries that have traditionally been accepted as vital for development. By contrast, in recent years, developing countries have had to make net debt-related transfers of nearly $40 billion per year to developed countries, and there is little prospect of a reversal of this perverse flow of capital from poor to rich.

Recent initiatives to secure debt reduction and to increase the finance available for adjustment might ease the situation, but they are not on a sufficient scale to halt this debilitating drain of resources to rich countries. The likelihood is that, in the absence of effective remedial action, stagnation and retrogression in most countries of the South will persist in the 1990s. The 'lost decade' may thus well be extended.

The opportunities for a genuine global dialogue on key issues of development have been extremely limited in recent years. When exchanges have taken place, some Northern countries have tended to engage in protestations of goodwill and support, while offering gratuitous advice about policy errors in the South. For their part, the Southern countries are often ill-prepared for these discussions. In the multilateral financial institutions, where a small number of developed countries determine in practice both the agenda and the outcome of meetings, the developing countries are relegated to a subsidiary role, limited principally to proposing minor textual changes to formulations worked out by the leading countries.

The international community should define a programme for a global dialogue on key development issues during the 1990s. Both sides should approach the dialogue with the political will needed to achieve concrete, mutually beneficial results, favouring development of the South. The South should be better prepared for this endeavour.

An Organized South for Meaningful North-South Negotiations

There must be no illusions regarding the enormity of the task of reversing the present unfavourable trends. International economic relations are in the final analysis power relations. Thus, the countries that dominate the international economic system are unlikely to agree easily to reforms designed to redress the inequities in the world distribution of income and wealth. Only a determined collective effort by the South could advance the prospect of meaningful North-South negotiations to restructure the present system of world economic relations.

Despite their sometimes divergent interests and views, the market economy countries of the North have until now almost always formed a common front when involved in North-South negotiations of any kind. They have even adopted common positions in confronting individual developing countries on issues such as debt. The South, by contrast, has failed to act together with sufficient determination.

As mentioned earlier, the countries of Eastern Europe have not played a major role in North-South negotiations, although in the international debate they have often voiced support for the South. Improving East-West relations and events in Eastern Europe are changing the attitudes of these countries; they are giving priority to improving economic relations with the West rather than to negotiations in favour of greater justice for the South. It would be unwise for the South to assume that there will be an automatic improvement in the North's approach to North-South relations as a result of better East-West relations. In fact, another situation is emerging: one in which both attention and technical and financial resources are being diverted from development in the South to economic reconstruction in Eastern Europe. In the first, wholly appropriate, flush of enthusiasm over political and economic reform in that part of the North, the South might be further forgotten and marginalized. That would be a blow struck against the interests of three quarters of the world's people and ultimately against the interests of the world community as a whole.

The South does have organizations and structures designed to build a common stand vis-à-vis the North. Politically these have achieved considerable success, especially in the anti-colonial struggle. But they have been less effective in dealing with economic issues.

There are two basic reasons for this. First, though the South has recognized the need for solidarity in North-South negotiations, individual developing countries have not always been able to sustain that solidarity in the face of the temptation separately to seek remedies for pressing national situations. With different national priorities, individual countries are often unable to withstand the pressures selectively exerted upon them by the North. Furthermore, inadequate appreciation of the long-term implications of matters under negotiation leads some of them to break ranks with other countries of the South without realizing that this would harm the broader interests of all—including their own.

Secondly, the South has failed to organize itself effectively for complex, collective negotiations. Most countries of the South do not individually have the capacity to deal with the detailed, technical negotiations in the many forums and on the multitude of subjects involved in present-day North-South economic relations. Each of these countries tends eventually to spread its very limited resources of skilled negotiators so thin that it is not fully effective in any area.

In this situation, well-organized collective action could benefit all countries, with little, if any, significant sacrifice of national advantage. However, the countries of the South have failed to achieve this solidarity. They have not been able to establish common priorities in keeping with the development interests of all, or to share technical and negotiating expertise, or to hold constructive South-South discussions in advance of negotiations, or even to develop a shared professional service to support them on matters under negotiation. This failure has greatly reduced the South's effectiveness in North-South negotiations.

Clearly, meaningful negotiations on North-South issues are essential for a co-operative and equitable management of growing global interdependence. But before such negotiations can be conducted, it is necessary for the South to strengthen its collective position and update its negotiating agenda. The basic, and oft-reiterated, objectives of the South retain their validity. But the issues and the priorities within and among them, and the South's specific proposals, need to be reviewed in the light of changes and experiences in the 1980s as seen from the South.

Pending a resumption of a comprehensive North-South dialogue, the South must continue to take an active part in the efforts to extend the application of rules to global economic relations and to strengthen their enforcement. For in the absence of rules, the weakest—i.e. the countries of the South—are always losers. Movement towards a just international system (with laws, codes, norms, standards, and regulatory practices) is therefore of great importance to the South. It needs to strengthen the growth of international rule-making and rule enforcement. Consistent support for the United Nations and for efforts to make it more effective has to be part of the South's strategy.

Another objective has to be to press for changes in the main international institutions concerned with finance and trade. These are now controlled by the rich nations and are not therefore truly international in their functioning. They were designed to meet the needs of the developed countries at the end of the Second World War; their membership was subsequently enlarged to include more countries from the South but without any basic change in their structures. Their concept and potential as global institutions are undermined by the way in which their current structures are used; this state of affairs needs to be changed so that these institutions may more effectively promote global development and become truly international.

THE CHALLENGE TO THE SOUTH

The South covers the larger part of the Earth's surface. Its people are the vast majority of the world's inhabitants. But they have a very much smaller proportion of the world's income than the people of the North. Hundreds of millions of the people living in the South suffer from hunger, malnutrition, and preventable disease, and are illiterate or lack education and modern skills. The 1990s threaten even 'more hardship for the people of the South and even greater instability for their countries.

The peoples of the South have begun to say that these conditions are unacceptable. They must now make that rejection effective.

The challenge to the South is to reaffirm, in words and action, that the purpose of development is the promotion of the well-being of its people, with economic growth directed at satisfying their needs and fulfilling their purposes.

The challenge to the South is to strengthen democratic institutions so that its people may live in freedom and chart their own path to development in harmony with their culture and values.

The challenge to the South is to use its own resources more effectively to accelerate its development, giving priority to meeting the basic needs of its people and freeing them from poverty, disease, ignorance, and fear.

The challenge to the South is to enable its people to realize the full potential of their talents and creativity, and to develop self-confidence, and to mobilize their contribution to the well-being and progress of their societies.

The challenge to the South is to enlarge its capacity to benefit from advances in science and technology in securing a better life for its people.

The challenge to the South is to pursue its development with due concern for the protection of the natural environment so that it may sustain the present and future generations.

The challenge to the South is to organize itself effectively and to seek strength through wide-ranging joint undertakings of South-South co-operation which benefit from complementary resources and increase collective self-reliance.

The challenge to the South is to use its unity and solidarity in efforts to make the world a more just and more secure home for all its people, through a restructuring of global relationships that responds to the growing intimations of the interdependence of the world's nations and people: members of one human family living in one world.

These challenges are formidable. But they must be met.

If the South, its nations, governments, peoples, and non-governmental organizations act, and act together, the South has the ability to transform itself and move the world towards its vision of the future—one undivided world. The process will be slow and difficult. There will be many set-backs and even retreats. But each step forward, each improvement in the condition of the South's people, will be a gain worth having.

There are and will be individuals and groups, and even governments, in the North who share the South's vision of the direction in which the world should move. The South must welcome these allies and seek to enlarge their ranks.

But it is the South's people who suffer most from the poverty and failings of the South, as well as from the present world order with its maldistribution and misuse of the world's resources. The responsibility to work for change in the present conditions therefore lies firmly with the South.

The State of the South

2

THE DEVELOPMENT RECORD OF THE SOUTH, 1950-80

The Difficult Inheritance, Hopes, and Achievements

Since becoming independent between 1945 and 1965, over fifty countries of Asia, Africa, and the Caribbean have begun to make painful but decided movement away from dependence on subsistence agriculture and the export of a few cash crops or minerals towards more balanced economic structures. Far-reaching social and economic changes have also taken place in some of the older nations of the South. Many of them, including some of the most populous nations like China, have significantly altered the structure of their economies. Industrial, scientific, and technological advances have been made in several developing countries, especially in Latin America and Asia; in an increasing range of industrial products, some countries of the South are today challenging the dominant industrial powers in world markets.

The countries of the South have followed different paths, and their speed of advance has varied. But the economic and social progress they have made has been impressive and should not be underestimated by comparison with the great distance they still have to travel. Their gains, often overlooked or taken for granted, indicate what the peoples and countries of the South can achieve. They are now better equipped for the future because of the past achievements.

Internal obstacles

In all cases, economic and social transformation in the countries of the South faced immense internal and external obstacles in the period after 1950. The economies of the newly independent countries were weak and fragmented, reflecting centuries of colonial subjugation and exploitation. Few foundations had been laid for accelerated development. This was especially so in certain parts of Africa, where industries and an economic infrastructure–

power, transport, communications–were virtually non-existent. Both in Africa and Asia, most countries had suffered from a colonial policy that deliberately inhibited industrial development and promoted heavy reliance on the export of primary products. Even in the countries of Latin America, which had expelled their colonial masters in the nineteenth century and made greater progress in industrialization, primary products continued to provide the bulk of export earnings in the late 1940s. Primary products have throughout been subject to violent fluctuations in world prices, and in the post-war period the trend in the terms of trade has generally been adverse to the primary producers. Communications and transport links were rudimentary, except to some extent in parts of Latin America, and apart from those connecting mining and plantation centres to ports.

The infrastructure for developing the resources of the people through education and training was also grossly inadequate. Levels of literacy, education, and skills were woefully low. In most parts of Africa, many countries in Asia, and even in parts of Latin America, 20 per cent literacy was normal, and 50 per cent primary school enrolment was regarded as good.

These economic and social deficiencies were exacerbated by rapidly increasing populations and by fast-spreading urbanization, as people flocked to the towns in the hope of a better life. There was overwhelming pressure for expanded public utilities and welfare services; but these countries possessed neither the productive base nor the funds to support them. Nor did they have the administrative capacity or financial institutions to tap such resources as did exist and channel them to meet the public need.

Inherited social structures also hindered the conduct of the publicly declared war on poverty. In Latin America, rigid class divisions–largely based on the concentration of land ownership–were still evident in many countries, and income inequalities were marked everywhere. This was the case in pre-independent Asia too, where in addition such modern political structures as existed were modelled on those of the colonial rulers, and political and economic control was effectively in the hands of a small elite. In Africa, the fragile political institutions of most of the newly independent countries faced the formidable task of forging national unity. Their borders had been established when European leaders drew frontier lines on a map of Africa at the

Berlin Congress in 1884-85, ignoring natural geographical boundaries as well as cultural and linguistic links. Within many countries of Africa (and some of Asia) social tensions were therefore aggravated by ethnic and cultural claims and counter-claims. Arbitrary or unclear borders imposed for the convenience of colonial rulers left a heritage of potential conflict among many new nation-states.

External environment

To these difficulties were added in the post-war period international arrangements for the world economy designed basically to serve the interests of the developed countries.

The objective of the Bretton Woods Conference of 1944 was to establish a global monetary and financial system. The institutions created there–the World Bank and the International Monetary Fund–were thus intended to promote stable exchange rates, foster the growth of world trade, and facilitate international movements of capital. But its main participants–the industrialized countries–were guided by the desire to avoid what they perceived as the disastrous shortcomings of their pre-war system of external economic relations. Paramount among these were beggar-thy-neighbour trading and exchange rate policies, involving protectionism and competitive devaluations, and inadequate arrangements for financial liquidity.

There was an almost inevitable lack of concern for the interests of developing countries. Most of them were still colonies and therefore not represented at Bretton Woods. India's forthcoming independence was recognized; but like those Third World countries that had been independent for a long time, India was only marginally involved in the proceedings. Thus the Third World was largely ignored and its interests received scant consideration. And its subordinate position was perpetuated by the decision-making structures established for the new institutions; the voting systems gave clear control to the larger contributors–the leading industrialized countries.

Concern for developing countries was not completely absent; the mandate of the World Bank included the provision of development assistance. But in the early post-war years this was clearly secondary to its role in financing the reconstruction of war-devastated Europe and Japan. Indeed, the proposal for a

Special United Nations Fund for Economic Development (SUNFED), which would offer large-scale aid on easy terms to developing countries, was rejected in the 1950s, mainly because developed countries objected to the United Nations becoming involved in financial aid to developing countries.

Further, the idea of concluding international arrangements for stabilizing commodity prices was killed when the US Congress refused to ratify the Havana Charter, which would have established an International Trade Organization (ITO). The General Agreement on Tariffs and Trade, which came into being as an interim arrangement, was a poor substitute for the ITO. It had little authority to deal with questions concerning the development of Third World countries.

Also ignored in these new institutional arrangements was the view that in the international management of balance-of-payments disequilibria, there should be pressure to adjust on both surplus countries and deficit countries, rather than only on those in deficit.

However, the Bretton Woods system did make an important contribution to what was to be an unprecedented period of growth in world production and trade during the first two postwar decades. This growth was supported by the high degree of co-operation among the developed countries of the West in the context of the Cold War, which quickly followed the end of the Second World War. The 1950s and 1960s became 'Golden Years' for the industrialized countries; they enjoyed one of the strongest and most sustained booms in recent history, with full employment and negligible inflation.

This dynamic international economic environment in many ways contributed to the growth of world trade and supported the development efforts of a number of countries of the South, old and new. However, many developing countries, because of narrowly based and rigid economic structures, were unable to take advantage of expanding opportunities in world markets. By and large, developing countries exporting primary products continued to feel the impact of general sluggishness and considerable instability in this segment of world trade. World demand for manufactures grew much more rapidly, and some developing countries took full advantage of this buoyancy. However, a number of important manufactured products exported by developing countries faced discriminatory trade barriers imposed by developed countries, often in violation of GATT principles. Textiles are the most obvious, though not the only, example.

There were also increased flows of capital from the developed to the developing countries during that period. As part of an emerging international consensus for development, the developed countries accepted some responsibility for assisting the developing countries. As a result, there was a considerable expansion of official flows of capital to the developing countries, often on concessional terms. However, the increase in development assistance fell far short of internationally accepted targets. Moreover, aid was not allocated among recipient countries according to objective economic criteria but was often governed by political and security considerations. In any case, private flows, consisting of direct investment, export credits, and bank loans, soon overtook aid flows; by the mid-1970s private flows represented nearly 70 per cent of total net bilateral flows from industrialized to developing countries.

In so far as increased private flows reflected the growth and spread of transnational corporations, they were a mixed blessing. Within the Third World, the now familiar debates began to take shape about the true financial contribution of foreign investment after allowing for reverse flows of profits, royalties and fees, imported inputs, and transfer pricing. There is no doubt, however, that foreign direct investment did stimulate modernization and growth in some areas; in some cases its influence extended outwards through linkages with the rest of the economy, but in many others the areas receiving such investment remained isolated enclaves without a wider beneficial impact.

The hopes

Thus, while generally ignoring–or even being unfavourable to–the interests of the countries of the South, the workings of the international economy were, in the early post-war years, in some ways helpful to their development efforts. The most important positive element, however, was their sense of confidence and enthusiasm.

For many, there was the hope born of success in their liberation struggles. Everywhere there was talk of equality and progress, and of building national identities on indigenous cultural traditions and values.

By the mid-1950s, however, the post-war distribution of global economic and political power, heavily concentrated in a few developed countries, began to appear to many countries of the South as inequitable and a danger to world stability. Again, the experience of the liberation struggles of the Afro-Asian peoples generated hopes that, through appropriate collective action, this global system could be made accommodative of the interests of the South. The Afro-Asian Conference at Bandung in 1955 was both an expression of the growing confidence of the South in its collective strength and an assertion of its determination to influence global relations in a truly internationalist direction. The Conference sowed the seeds of the Non-Aligned Movement, whose first meeting was held in 1961 and which has grown to include most countries of the South, including many in Latin America. The major concerns of the Movement have been the struggle against colonialism and imperialism, the protection of the sovereignty and rights of small and underdeveloped states, and their development in freedom.

At the international level, poverty and backwardness came gradually to be be perceived as worthy of global concern. The United Nations and its various agencies fostered the growth of this awareness, though practical efforts and the resources mobilized for world development fell far short of needs. The World Bank set up the International Development Association (IDA) in 1960 with a mandate to give loans on easy terms to the poorest developing countries. The IMF set up its Compensatory Financing Facility (CFF) in 1963 with the object of supporting the efforts of developing countries to deal with foreign exchange crises caused by sharp falls in earnings from exports of primary commodities due to reasons beyond their control.

The United Nations Conference on Trade and Development (UNCTAD) was established in 1964. Its declared purpose was to promote development and trade, enhance economic co-operation among developing countries, and help to redress the inequity in North-South economic relations. The formation of the Group of 77–now the negotiating instrument of the developing countries on many economic issues–was a recognition by the South of the need for more organized solidarity.

The establishment of UNCTAD reflected an awareness of the need for structural reforms in the world trading system so as to make it conducive to rapid development in the South. However, it was soon realized that developed countries were willing to consider only marginal changes in trading arrangements which would not disturb the basic framework of the system.

Also during the 1950s and 1960s, a number of developing countries initiated arrangements for regional and subregional cooperation within the South. Some were primarily political in nature, but others had direct economic objectives. Latin America led the way in establishing regional and subregional groupings designed to liberalize and expand trade among members, and to promote industrial development by taking advantage of economies of scale. This lead was soon followed by similar moves in Africa, West Asia, and South-East Asia.

In addition, regional and subregional development banks were set up in Africa, Asia, and Latin America in order to channel multilateral assistance with greater sensitivity to regional needs, and to encourage efforts towards collective self-reliance. And within UNCTAD, the Generalized System of Preferences (GSP) was negotiated; under this system the countries of the North accorded preferential tariff treatment to imports of selected manufactures from the South. However, the system was subject to so many restrictions and exceptions that its impact was at best only marginal.

All in all, hope remained alive in the South. Progress had been made, and there seemed to be reason to expect further advances.

This chapter will review in what ways the hope of the immediate post-war period was maintained and partly fulfilled in the 1950s and 1960s, albeit in a manner which was unsustainable. It will show how progress was increasingly hampered in the 1970s; and how and why it was halted in the generalized development crisis of the 1980s. The remainder of this Report will suggest ways of rekindling hope in the South through a self-reliant and people-centred development effort, through intensified South-South co-operation, and through a restructuring of international economic relations.

The achievements

There was impressive economic growth in almost all the developing countries until the closing years of the 1970s; many of them sustained high rates of growth year after year. For the South as a whole, the mobilization of domestic savings and resources from abroad resulted in a dynamic process of capital accumulation. Domestic investment rose from 10-12 per cent of gross domestic product (GDP) in the early 1950s to 18 per cent in the 1960s and 24 per cent in the 1970s. The increase of per capita incomes after 1950–they are estimated to have more than doubled over the next thirty years–compares favourably with the past development experience in industrial countries, as well as with previous experience within the South.

In the 1960s, the rate of growth of the developing countries' GDP averaged close to 6 per cent per year. After the period of international monetary instability, which began in the early 1970s, and the rise in oil prices of 1973, growth was slower; developing countries, particularly the oil importers among them, suffered a significant deterioration in the external environment. In sub-Saharan Africa, where climatic disasters aggravated the parlous situation, the growth rate fell sharply during the second half of the 1970s. Nevertheless, owing partly to the improved financial position of oil-exporting developing countries, the South as a whole grew at an average of over 5 per cent per year in the 1970s. Average per capita and total GDP growth rates for the South since 1960 are illustrated in Fig.2.1.

The three decades of rapid growth led to important economic changes and social achievements in very many developing countries. The proportion of people living in absolute poverty, though not their number, was reduced. In many countries traditional methods of farming were improved; in some, agricultural modernization made vast strides. As discussed in more detail in the concluding section of this chapter, investments in public health and education and progressive government policies improved the levels of public well-being. Some of the poorest countries participated in these advances, which is evidence of the remarkable results that can be achieved through public policy and social action, despite low levels of national income. This is one of the most encouraging lessons of the past development record.

Figure 2.1

Per Capita and Total GDP Growth Rates in the South, 1960-87

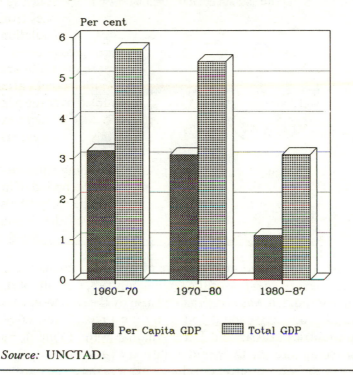

Source: UNCTAD.

The growth of the industrial sector transformed the productive, and sometimes the social, structures in a number of developing countries, especially in Asia and Latin America. This facilitated–at the same time as it was served by–a large expansion in supplies of water and energy, in transport and communications networks, housing, and other infrastructure. The overall economic transformation of the South between 1960 and 1980 is illustrated in Fig.2.2.

This industrial transformation, in which transnational corporations often played a part, was everywhere actively promoted by the State through varying measures of industrial planning, trade protection, development finance, and public investments in strategic industries. In most countries the transformation was re-

Figure 2.2

Economic Transformation of the South: Sectoral
Distribution of GDP, 1960 and 1980

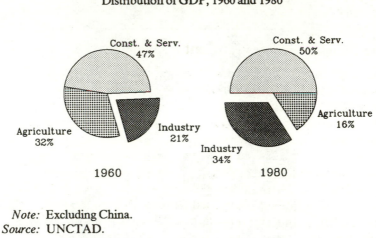

Note: Excluding China.
Source: UNCTAD.

flected in the expanded manufacture of consumer goods for the
domestic market. In a few of the larger countries, notably Brazil,
China, and India, it was accompanied also by the development of
industries producing capital goods. By the 1970s, several developing countries in Asia and Latin America were becoming significant competitors in the world trade in manufactures.

One of the most positive developments was the steady growth
and increasing activity of grass-roots organizations and movements in both rural and urban areas. These non-governmental
organizations were formed generally in response to felt
needs–economic, social, cultural, political–which official organizations had ignored or overlooked, or were unable or unwilling to
address.   Unfortunately, in some countries these groups were
perceived as a threat to the established order, resulting in unne-
cessarily adversarial relationships. Nevertheless, their endeavours have led to increased awareness and acceptance of
development designs and management based on indigenous resources, local experiences in the use of technology, and popular
participation in planning. More importantly, their efforts have
provided concrete affirmation of the concept of people-centred

development. Their work should be viewed as being complementary to, rather than conflicting with, government activity. After all, no genuine development in the South can be sustained without the participation of the people, who are both the means and the end of development.

The Flaws in the Development Experience

It is important to remember this period of progress and its atmosphere of hope now, when there is a deep pessimism in much of the Third World about the prospects for economic development. Yet, by the late 1980s it could be seen that the achievements of the South during that period had not fundamentally changed the status of most Third World countries in relation to the world economic system. They remained poor, subordinate, and powerless. In general their national self-reliance had not increased; in some countries dependence intensified as they tried to modernize. Poverty persisted and the income gap between the North and the South widened.

Further, the undoubted economic growth in the South rarely removed the structural inequalities and cleavages; despite the emergence of a middle class, in many countries the income gap between rich and poor became wider. As a result, with a few exceptions, economic growth did not produce greater national unity and stability or social cohesion. Most countries failed to improve the social and economic status of women. Growth generally led to increased imbalances, unplanned and usually chaotic urbanization, small enclaves of modern industry in uneasy coexistence with large semi-traditional sectors, rising demand for imports combined with lagging capacity in exports, and much damage to the environment.

This sweeping description of shortcomings does not, of course, apply uniformly to all developing countries; it does not apply at all to a few countries. It is, however, a valid picture of conditions in the developing countries as a group. And it is admittedly a judgement with the benefit of hindsight.

History did not offer reliable charts to guide countries starting on the road to development in the second half of the twentieth century. The circumstances in which they were setting out to change their economies differed in important respects from those which had attended today's advanced countries at a comparable stage in their economic progress. The differences were particularly marked in respect of demographic conditions, technology, and, not least, the expectations of the people.

The economics of development was itself only beginning to be a recognized subject of specialized study. Governments attempting to step up the pace of national economic activity in order to secure a better life for their people had therefore virtually to learn by trial and error.

Post-war development experience confirms that, while high rates of economic growth are necessary for the purpose of eliminating mass poverty, they are not, by themselves, sufficient. A comparative analysis of the experience of various developing countries which recorded very high rates of growth shows clearly that growth tends to reduce poverty only if combined with specific economic and social policies directed to that end. The fruits of economic growth were widely dispersed only when action had been taken earlier to redistribute scarce productive assets such as land, and to develop human resources through a balance of scientific and technical education and mass education. These experiences also suggest that growth has to be particularly strong and the growth pattern highly labour-intensive so as to achieve and sustain a rapidly rising level of employment.

A large number of developing countries did not carry out such comprehensive development strategies; the high capital intensity of investment and inadequate attention to the social dimensions led to a situation in which historically high rates of growth did not make a visible dent in poverty or in social and economic inequalities. There were other countries where growth was not high enough to trickle down. For instance, in India, growth in the first three post-war decades was much slower than the average for developing countries. The rise in India's per capita income, of the order of 1.5 per cent per year, was too small to secure a significant improvement in the living standards of the mass of the people.

In many countries, the beneficial effect on living standards of a fairly high growth rate was to a great extent neutralized by fast growth in population. During comparable stages in European development, death rates had declined gradually as living standards improved and enhanced resistance to disease; at the same time, birth rates declined. By contrast, post-war advances in medicine led to a dramatic fall in the death rate–and to longer life expectancy–in many developing countries well before the birth rate declined in response to higher living standards. The outcome was a population explosion in a large number of countries, which was aggravated by their failure to take effective measures to moderate the birth rate.

Changes in the techniques and tools used both in farming and in industry intensified the impact of demographic pressure, in that much less labour was required to produce a unit of output. Hence, it was difficult to reconcile productive efficiency with the need to provide jobs for a rapidly growing labour force. And the spread of information, through improved transport and communications linking North to South, raised the level of popular expectations–in terms of income and the standard of living–even in remote parts of the developing world.

All these factors have to be taken into account in interpreting the South's development experience, although clearly neither these factors nor any other simple explanation would do justice to its diversity and complexity. Nevertheless, lessons can be learned; there is reason to believe that, in a good number of cases, different development strategies may work better in the future.

An unequalizing pattern of development

The declared purpose of development was the eradication of poverty, ignorance, and disease. A large number of developing countries adopted as models developed countries which had by and large banished those evils. And, as these countries appeared to set great store by the rate of GDP growth, most countries in the South tended to use it as the yardstick of performance. Increases in the rate of GDP growth became almost a goal in themselves; for practical purposes they came to define development. Most developing countries failed to see that such figures could conceal the poverty, suffering, and injustices that were the very ills they were eager to cure. They did not take into account the very different circumstances in which the South was attempting to develop. Placing too much confidence in the theory that growth would trickle down, they took little direct action to improve the productivity and raise the incomes of the poor or to ensure a less unequal distribution of the benefits of growth through such programmes as land reform.

The consequences of this pattern of development are now clear. Inequalities tended to widen as the economy grew and became more industrialized. Both between the modern and the traditional sectors in the South, and within each sector, the gap in income, knowledge, and power was growing. Increasingly, the rich and powerful in the countries of the South were able to enjoy the life-style and consumption patterns of developed countries of the North. But large segments of the population experienced no significant improvement in their standard of living, while being able to see the growing affluence of the few. The worst sufferers–and almost invariably the least able to protest or otherwise protect their interests–were usually the most vulnerable of the poor: women, children, and other socially disadvantaged groups.

Dissatisfaction with these trends found different forms of expression. In Africa and Asia the sense of collective purpose and shared objectives that had marked the liberation struggles gave way in many cases to division and to social unrest, sometimes triggered by extraneous events into political eruption. In Latin America, large sections of the population became increasingly alienated from the established system, with political instability as a result.

Peasant agriculture was neglected in many countries, the consequences being particularly adverse in the least developed countries. This neglect was not always deliberate; in some cases, meeting at least a minimum of the heavy infrastructure demands of a large country and a scattered population was a pre-condition for effective direct attention to the needs of the peasants. But such neglect almost always meant stagnant or worsening conditions for the rural poor, and generally resulted in food output and peasant incomes failing to keep pace with population growth. The outcome was often a drag on all development efforts, in particular on attempts to industrialize. For industries need markets and people who can afford to buy their output, and can hardly flourish when the mass of the people remain poor.

A number of poor developing countries which used to produce enough food for domestic needs gradually became net importers of food, and inevitably their economy as a whole became more vulnerable. The result was a rising need for foreign exchange to pay for food imports, and, in a few countries, periodic famine.

In middle-income and semi-industrialized countries one consequence of the greater social and economic inequalities was inevitably that more resources were devoted to meeting the demands of the higher-income groups for goods and services ranging from luxury articles to an urban infrastructure geared to their needs. This usually meant a greatly enlarged demand for imported goods—either for the manufactured goods themselves, for which local agents act as distributors, or for the machinery or inputs to produce them domestically. There was no comparable increase in the demand for locally produced food, because the poor who needed it were less capable of buying it, and the rich spent their enlarged income on other things.

In addition, the development pattern followed had adverse effects on the natural environment. In many undertakings, the calculation of costs and returns neglected the long-term social costs of depleting non-renewable resources and of damage to the environment. In the modern sector of the economy, the exploitation of the forests, fertile land, fisheries, and mineral resources and the expansion of industrial activities went ahead without regard for the social effects, the need to replenish renewable resources, or the ecological balance. And the increase in the number of the poor added to the pressure on the environment. Trees were cut down for export, to bring new land into cultivation, or to produce firewood and timber for houses, and the trees felled were not replaced by new planting. Land was exploited until erosion and the depletion of nutrients made it completely unproductive.

Scientific and technological dependence

There was another basic weakness in the development path followed. The South's impressive achievements during the three decades until 1980 were not accompanied by a lessening of its scientific and technological dependence on the North. Insufficient financial and human resources prevented the achievement of the critical mass needed for scientific and technological development (see Figs.2.3 and 2.4). With the exception of a few countries, the growth of output and productivity relied heavily on imports of capital goods and manufacturing technology. Indeed, the large expansion of output during this period led to a much heavier dependence on the technology of the North –a heightened vulnerability which the North exploited in the crisis of the 1980s.

Figure 2.3

Expenditure on R&D as Per Cent of GNP in the North and in the South

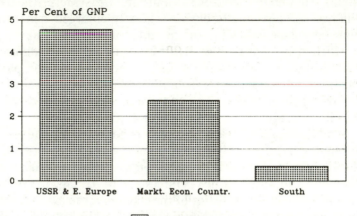

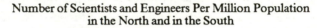

Figure 2.4

Number of Scientists and Engineers Per Million Population
in the North and in the South

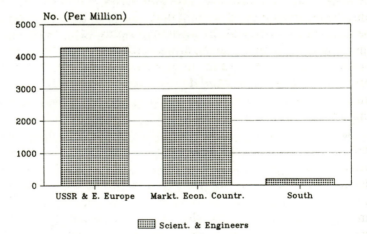

Source: UNESCO *Statistical Yearbook 1989.*

Some advances in science and technology led to production processes that were more knowledge-intensive, with considerable savings in the use of raw materials, energy, and unskilled labour–factors of production abundant in the majority of countries in the South. This trend tended to erode the South's traditional comparative advantages on the world market and weakened its economies.

The increased dependence on the North occurred in different degrees in all four of the categories in which science and technology for civilian uses can be classified, namely basic sciences, applied sciences, classical low technology, and science-based high technology.

Developing countries tended, by and large, to neglect basic sciences. These were often regarded as too abstract and costly. The assumption was that the South could rely primarily on scientific results obtained in the developed world. Owing to this attitude, the South did not train an adequate number of qualified scientists to whom countries could turn for advice on the scientific problems that are bound to arise when scientific knowledge is applied in practice.

The absence of a critical minimum effort in basic sciences in turn affected the pace of development of applied sciences. Harnessing these is essential for economic growth and development and the improvement of welfare in the South. They have a direct bearing on the ability of the economy to satisfy the basic needs of the people, particularly in the areas of food security, the provision of water and energy, and the improvement of health, as well as to preserve the environment. Yet most developing countries failed to undertake systematic efforts to develop indigenous capabilities in these areas.

In particular, far too little attention was given to applying science to improve agriculture, livestock, forestry, fishing, and food processing. Only in a few countries was a determined drive undertaken to evolve, through national research and development, a package of high-yielding seeds, water management, fertilizers, and means of pest control which suited local circumstances and was within reach of what local farmers could afford. The Green Revolution in those countries succeeded in raising output and in ensuring a measure of national food security. These breakthroughs were, however, limited mainly to maize, wheat, and rice.

They were not followed by equally determined research in other crops, especially those grown in arid or semi-arid regions. Nor were the successes achieved in one country, or in some of its parts, effectively transmitted for adaptation in other parts and countries.

The industrially more advanced developing countries laid considerable emphasis on standard industrial or classical low technologies for iron, steel, and other metals, bulk chemicals, petroleum, the generation and distribution of power, and heavy electrical machinery. No new scientific principles remain to be discovered in these areas. However, they constitute the traditional field of craftmanship and skills, where improving the design and the quality of products, and achieving efficiency gains and cost reductions through, for instance, the adaptation and modification of available technologies, are all important means of increasing competitiveness. Several countries sought to acquire competence in these areas, even though their efforts suffered from serious weaknesses. In most cases, though, these technologies were simply imported.

Only a few developing countries paid attention to the new science-based high technologies. Unlike the standard industrial technologies referred to above, mastery over new sciences and technologies requires high expertise in the relevant basic sciences. Experience has shown that high technologies cannot simply be transferred: the notion that it would be possible for the South to obtain them from abroad without the development of an indigenous broad-based scientific and technological infrastructure is mistaken.

Underlying the inadequacy of the efforts at technological development was a lack of appreciation of the contribution that science can make to development, and as a result a lack of purposeful commitment towards science, either basic or applied, including the commitment to self-reliance in technology. There was even a sense of inferiority in the field of science and technology, despite the fact that experience has conclusively shown that science and technology can be learned in a predictable manner by all people, irrespective of culture or country: a finding reinforced by the dramatic easing of physical mobility and communications, itself among the most revolutionary aspects of modern technological advance.

It should not be inferred that nothing was done to develop science and technology. But the progress was very uneven. Countries which had more favourable initial conditions in industry and education were able to move faster; in the rest of the South little movement in this direction was achieved. And in most cases there were serious weaknesses in the approach to science and technology policy which hampered, and eventually slowed down, self-sustaining progress even in the case of the more advanced countries. These weaknesses varied greatly from country to country, but there were many common elements in what have proved to be mistakes.

Policies on science and technology were usually not integrated into the national development plan, but were an isolated adjunct to it. Development plans, which frequently dealt with investment targets in great–occasionally unnecessary–detail, often referred only in very general terms to science and technology, if at all. There was often no attempt at identifying the human and financial resources needed to achieve the targets, or the contribution that the various scientific and technological programmes and projects were expected to make to national development. Clear sectoral priorities were not determined, nor were scarce resources concentrated on them, within a specified time frame.

Moreover, public-sector projects for industries and infrastructure were often financed by tied aid, which meant that the capital equipment, design and engineering, and technology had all to be purchased from the country providing the finance. At times, the technologies were already or soon obsolete, or were unsuited to local conditions. In many cases the agreements did not allow domestic firms to be associated with the construction of plants or their expansion. As a result, some technological capabilities built at great cost remained unused, or soon became outdated and unviable.

A number of countries established regulatory machinery with powers to reject, accept, or modify proposals for economic projects. The intention was admirable: to encourage the use of local resources and the development of local technology. But very often the procedures were complex, rigid, and cumbersome, and led to long delays and escalating costs. In some cases, opportunities were lost to other countries, or the promoters became discouraged.

Perhaps most important of all, a systematic relationship between scientific practice and technological application was lacking. Many scientists worked alone, without the support of productive enterprises. In many countries the productive units failed to give clear signals of their needs which the domestic science and technology establishment could be called upon to meet. The need to facilitate the conversion of scientific achievement into technological innovation–a costly process–was not sufficiently recognized.

What made matters worse was that the private sector tended to rely almost entirely on imported technologies, often linked with direct foreign investment by transnationals. While the latter were evidently not concerned with the development of a national technological capacity, their local partners, who should have been, also often resisted any idea of promoting local technology because of the additional cost. This was particularly shortsighted, for on account of the domestic technological weakness, project promoters were not always able to judge whether the technology they proposed to import was up-to-date or appropriate. Nor did they have enough information to negotiate for the right technology on the right terms and conditions.

Indeed, all these flaws were attributable essentially to structural deficiencies hampering the development and use of science and technology. Despite all the efforts devoted to expanding and improving educational and training systems, and despite undoubted achievements, in most countries, investment in education and training in science and technology was insufficient. The brain drain, that is the migration of skilled scientific and technical personnel to the developed countries, further diminished the potential of the developing countries in these areas. A vicious circle set in: under-development and its accompanying scarcities of resources, notably of foreign exchange, severely constrained the amount of resources available for science and technology; this constraint in turn affected negatively the development prospects of the countries.

A distinction must be drawn here between large, middle-income, more industrialized countries, which can plausibly undertake to make significant progress in research and development, and smaller, less developed countries for which this is not realistic. However, the creation of a scientific culture nurtured through the educational system is a realizable objective for all countries, which should recognize its vital role in development. Furthermore, South-South co-operation can enhance scientific and technological capabilities and allow the smaller countries also a part in collective research and development activities. The absence of awareness, or the belated recognition, of this requisite for scientific and technological development is a shared shortcoming in the South.

The neglect of cultural dimensions

Culture, viewed as the sum total of values, beliefs, attitudes, customs, and patterns of behaviour in a given society, is a vital pillar of social and economic transformation. Capital formation and technical progress are essential elements of development, but the broad environment for their effectiveness is a society's culture; it is only by the affirmation and enrichment of cultural identities through mass participation that development can be given strong roots and made a sustained process. For only on secure cultural foundations can a society maintain its cohesion and security during the profound changes that are the concomitants of development and economic modernization.

Development strategies which discount the importance of cultural factors have shown themselves liable to breed indifference, alienation, and social discord. In some cases where these factors have been ignored, the genuine urge for cultural autonomy and identity has been sidetracked by backward-looking and obscurantist forces.

The South did not often keep the people at the centre of its planning and development efforts; attention was concentrated on increasing physical investment and production, and it was not realized that these efforts could not be fully effective unless attitudes and values were enlisted to contribute to the achievement of these objectives. In so far as attention was paid to the formation of human capital, it was viewed largely as an instrument of economic growth. The broader conception of development as a process of enhancing human capabilities and cultural enrichment was missing.

There was another phenomenon associated with the development pattern generally adopted by the developing countries from the 1950s onwards. The adoption of the life-styles of the affluent

societies, the influence of transnational investment unrelated to
the needs of the host country, and the effects of the post-war
communications revolution led to a gradual substitution of alien
cultural values, attitudes, and social structures for those rooted in
the cultures of the South. This spread beyond the modern into the
traditional sectors of the society, further weakening the capacity
of these to cope with the effects of rapid change. For modernization came to mean imitating Western ideas, consumption patterns, and social relationships.

Had the influence of the West produced a commitment to science and to the scientific analysis of social conditions and policy
options, as well as to efficiency in the organization of production,
the results would have been beneficial. But what was copied most
extensively was some of the less estimable aspects of Western
societies–individualism, conspicuous consumption, waste, a media culture manipulated for the purposes of money-making, the
abuse of drugs. The value systems and close family and community support that are a strength of traditional societies began to
be undermined from every angle; no alternative system of public
provision of social welfare could be put in place given the lack of
resources.

By now it is clear that the uncritical imitation of Western models has weakened resilience and cohesion and given rise to social
tensions and distress among large segments of the population in
the South. As a consequence, development strategies have often
failed to utilize the enormous reserves of traditional wisdom and
of creativity and enterprise in the countries of the Third World or
allow their cultural wellsprings to feed the process of development.

Movement away from popular participation

Linked to the failure to make people central, as both the instruments and the purpose of development efforts, was the tendency
to move away from democratic government towards various
types of autocracy or dictatorships, military or civilian.

Colonies are by their nature not democratic, being ruled from
outside. The nationalist movements which led the liberation
struggles in Asia and Africa did, however, in most cases gain their
strength from grass-roots participation. They had strong leader-
ships, but these were effectively accountable to–and ultimately

controlled by–an active rank and file. In those few countries where an armed struggle was waged, there was also great decentralization of power as regards tactics and local management; there was no other way in which powerful colonial governments could have been overcome by comparatively small numbers of guerrillas.

Most Latin American countries, having gained independence in the first half of the nineteenth century, lived through successive periods of internal instability and wars, sometimes fighting foreign powers and in many cases each other. In the first two decades of the twentieth century, the oligarchic traditional structures, based on a class of large land-owners, the armies and the church, started to be challenged. The eruption of the popular masses in Mexico took the form of a radical social revolution. In several other countries, processes of political and social evolution took place, and, by the end of the Second World War, many democratic advances had been achieved throughout the region. In the 1950s social revolutions broke out in other countries, like Bolivia and Cuba, to replace outdated social structures and promote equality and popular participation.

Democracy has suffered serious set-backs in the South since those early days. In the newly independent countries the leaders of governments, as representatives of the people's aspirations, were committed to rapid development. Long processes of consultation, explanation, and discussion were felt to impede effective decision-making. Nervousness about popular participation in national affairs was in some cases due to the fragility of the nation-state itself. Where the country's population was composed of many different ethnic, tribal, or religious groups, there was an understandable fear that political parties appealing to such group loyalties would encourage disunity and put national integrity at risk. The emergence of autocratic tendencies within the leadership also discouraged popular participation in the political processes.

In a context in which trained personnel and financial resources were very scarce, the high expectations of the people could not be fulfilled solely through government action; at the same time, however, the people's own development efforts were discouraged. The failure of governments to make tangible improvements in their conditions of living led to increasing discontent, and the rulers began to see popular participation in the political process as a threat, both to their own position and even to development as they conceived it. Legitimate opposition tended to be suppressed, and there was an increasing disregard of human rights. In many countries there were military coups d'état followed by dictatorships.

Similarly, in the older countries, notably in Latin America, processes of popular mobilization generated a rise in expectations, but the improvements in growth, productivity, and patterns of income distribution were insufficient to satisfy them. The resulting dissatisfaction expressed itself in support for parties and movements that radically challenged the status quo; sometimes armed movements were formed which spurned the democratic process in their urge for rapid structural change. In several countries of Latin America, including some of the larger and more industrialized ones, these tensions led in the 1960s and early 1970s to the collapse of democracy and to the establishment of military dictatorships which repressed popular participation. Democratic systems were restored in the 1980s, but the new democracies were left to face very severe economic and social difficulties, which placed considerable strain on the smooth functioning of somewhat fragile participatory structures.

The centralizing tendencies that appeared in developing countries were often rooted in their economic circumstances. In some cases, colonial policies had been biased against the involvement of the majority of indigenous people in commercial activity, giving rise to the establishment of economic elites. These policies left a legacy of patronage, economic disparities, political contradictions, and social divisions. Some newly independent countries had no domestic entrepreneurial class that could mobilize capital and develop the economy; in others its existence was not perceived. Thus governments felt impelled to do virtually everything themselves; the more ambitious they were to establish their country's economic independence and to overcome poverty, the greater the burden they assumed in terms of regulating the economy and direct intervention in productive activities.

In the older states there was also the perception that extensive State involvement in the economy was the only way to counteract the influence of powerful external economic forces and agents, which were essentially inimical to the building of a domestic industrial base in order to conquer underdevelopment.

Most governments in the South tended to overcentralize administration and planning; indeed, in many of the countries of Africa, the shortage of highly educated citizens was so serious that they had in any case very little choice. Such centralization led often to excessive power being vested in a few senior bureaucrats, who were not always immune to the temptations inseparable from such power.

Furthermore, many goverments failed to modernize the administration and political processes in a form appropriate to the local culture. Inadequate emphasis was given to the training of qualified administrative and professional personnel inspired by an ethic of public service. There was also inadequate appreciation of the need for clear and predictable procedures for public action and intervention, for forms of disclosure and accountability to the people, and for an independent judiciary competent to settle disputes and provide redress in the event of administrative errors or arbitrariness. Reforms on these lines could help to reconcile the need for popular participation in decision-making and the need for decisive action. Such reforms cannot be carried out without the necessary human and financial resources, nor, above all, without a democratic commitment and an understanding of its implications.

All this centralization tended to lead to snail-pace decision-making and to inefficiency, and it had particularly harmful consequences for the management of public enterprises and financial systems. They could not be enterprising, nor react to external events as quickly as demanded by the fast-changing economic environment in which they operated. The result was heavy cost to the nation in both money and efficiency.

A further consequence of heavy centralization was that the authorities were unable to be duly selective in the use of either incentives or controls, particularly in industrial policy. Protection against imports, tax incentives, and subsidized credit were sometimes given in a blanket fashion to industries, without consideration of their market potential, at home or abroad, or of their subsequent performance. The result was the creation of many inefficient industrial activities of doubtful longer-term usefulness, which could survive only because the rest of the economy was in effect subsidizing them.

In many countries these trends weakened the capacity of the public sector to generate resources; they also made it possible for the private sector to earn excessive profits, which were frequently spent on conspicuous consumption rather than on productive investment. On the other hand, many governments, wishing to improve income distribution or to raise the living standards of the poor, authorized increases in wages and crop prices, inflated the budget, and expanded the money supply, without at the same time carrying out basic structural reforms designed to improve productivity and achieve greater equality. The result of these populist approaches was inflation–an inevitable by-product of attempts to buy off social unrest through soft options.

When the economies were expanding in real terms, the higher nominal incomes of the poor often brought some genuine improvement in their condition. But basically, inflation was an easy way of avoiding a choice among alternative patterns of distribution of the national product among social groups and sectors. Investment and growth were in many cases the major victims of the uncertainty which was generated when these basic choices were not made and inflation was allowed to escalate. And when economic growth slowed, or went into reverse, the ephemeral nature of the gains in nominal income became apparent; social tensions were exacerbated and the difficulties of macroeconomic management increased still further.

In some countries, excessive foreign borrowing had a similar effect. For debt-led economic booms which were not accompanied by socially just structural changes proved to be unsustainable and in the end counter-productive; they led to inequitable income distribution and inefficient resource allocation, and they blocked long-term growth. The debt-servicing obligations they left behind put immense strain on government budgets and the balance of payments, and accentuated inflationary pressures. Together these elements depressed the living standards of the poor and affected also the middle classes, while the rich were largely able to protect themselves (or even benefit) from the economic crises through financial speculation and capital flight.

The problems arising out of the deficiency of approaches to development planning, as well as the temporary and increasingly fragile solutions attempted, were all closely interlinked with the slow, erratic, and, in many ways, disappointing pace of social and political progress. For whenever the State or a few powerful and rich individuals, rather than society as a whole, are seen as the main actors of development, the result is widespread apathy within the society, alienation from organized social and political structures, and even conflict.

Further, the combination of a top-down approach to development with very weak administrative and planning capacities tended to discredit the whole concept of planning and of public intervention as a technique of social management. This is unwarranted. There is an undeniable need in the circumstances of developing countries for public intervention to speed up capital accumulation while avoiding an unfair distribution of its benefits. And it is notable that purposeful public intervention has marked the progress of those developing countries that have been most successful in terms of growth and equity. The real issue is how to match capability with intervention, making intervention effective in its purposes; efficiency, integrity, and a clear choice of priorities are essential for this. It is these qualities that have been missing so often.

Corruption

Corruption has been on the increase in many countries—in all parts of the world. Circumstances differ and so do the causes. In the West it tends to be associated with big business and such activities as manipulation of the stock markets; in socialist countries and the South, over-regulation and the absence of effective systems of public accountability make it tempting to resort to corrupt practices. Over-centralization, limited administrative capabilities, laxity of tax administration, and authoritarian tendencies have combined to provide fertile conditions for corruption in many developing countries.

In the South, the excessive concentration of economic power in the hands of the government and the corporate sector, poverty, insecurity, and the underpayment of public personnel also account for some of these undesirable practices. So do corrupting influences from Northern sources related, but not confined, to obtaining profitable contracts and to the trade in arms and the illicit traffic in drugs.

Regardless of these factors, governments must bear a large part of the responsibility for corruption in the South. By and large they have not regarded its eradication as a priority, despite its acknowledged economic, social, and political costs. Higher standards of integrity in public life could do much to strengthen the people's confidence in governments and the sense of community and civic responsibility. The issue bears not solely on venality in the public sector, but on encouragement and facilitation of corruption within society through governmental mismanagement, authoritarianism, inadequate systems of control and public accountability, and militarization. The genuine democratization of political structures can go a long way to arresting these harmful activities. Sustained progress must rely on the effective functioning of democratic processes. It is also necessary to minimize the scope for discretionary controls in the management of the economy, thereby reducing the temptations for arbitrariness. Since discretionary controls cannot be dispensed with altogether, built-in safeguards must be provided to avoid their misuse by the authorities.

Militarization

Any consideration of the post-war experience of developing countries must also take account of the increase in expenditure on arms and armies and in the number and intensity of wars fought in the Third World. The rise in nationalism associated with the independence struggles was one contributory cause of these trends, as it was not always accompanied by a commitment to settle disputes between countries by peaceful means. Also, the breakdown of unity, and occasionally gross injustices, within heterogeneous new states frequently led to civil wars. And many of these conflicts were made more lethal and prolonged as powerful developed nations intervened on opposite sides to fight the Cold War through surrogates in Africa, Asia, and Latin America.

The arms industries of developed countries aggressively promoted the profitable sale of arms to the South; credits for arms purchases were almost the easiest to obtain–though not for liberation movements, which have generally been denied such assistance by Western sources.

By 1980 developing countries' military expenditure on average amounted to 25 per cent of the world total. Their arms imports

alone averaged $22 billion per year during the 1980s (see Fig.2.5).
It is true that arms purchases in the South tend to be highly concentrated in a few countries, notably in the Middle East, and
hence average figures of expenditure are not very meaningful. But
only a few developing countries can rightly claim that their military expenditure is proportionate either to any external threat or
to the resources at their disposal.

The direct human cost of well over one hundred cases of international and civil conflict in the South since the end of the Second
World War has been a horrific addition to the daily ravages of
poverty and deprivation. By 1980 more than ten million people
had been killed in wars fought in the Third World; many millions
more had been maimed or injured.

Not all these conflicts could have been averted by action
within the South. In Southern Africa, war has been the result of
direct and indirect attacks by the racist Pretoria regime against
neighbouring states. In the Middle East, the failure to acknowledge the right of Palestinians to a homeland is at the heart of the
South's most troubled situation. External intervention is also a
decisive element in armed conflicts in Central America. Nor can
one ignore the very real threat posed by armed insurgencies, terrorism, separatism, and fundamentalism, among other manifestations of violent conflict. Direct military threats have left no
option to some developing countries but to increase military expenditure for self-defense.

The international community has the duty to put in place a
framework that would guarantee the security of all nations
against external threats, including incursions by mercenaries.
Nevertheless, it remains an unfinished task of the countries of the
South to work out effective mechanisms for settling international
and internal conflicts through peaceful means. These mechanisms, together with the strengthening of democratic processes,
can play an important role in curbing military expenditure.

Militarization has perverse implications for development.
The diversion of resources to pay for instruments of war and re-
pression retards progress in many countries. Just as deleterious is
the growth of a military culture which is contemptuous of democracy, popular participation, human rights, or the principle of government accountability. It breeds corruption, the abuse of
power, and the consequent alienation of the people from the poli-

Figure 2.5

Arms Imports by the South, 1969-88

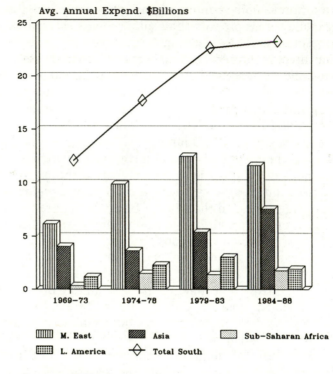

tical system. These disturbing symptoms can be seen in many countries of the South today.

It is fair to balance these strictures by a recognition of the efforts increasingly being made to avoid or bring to an end international conflict within the Third World. One of the earliest decisions of the Organization of African Unity (OAU), established in 1963, was to recognize the boundaries inherited from the colonial period so as to avoid border conflicts. Its Charter also set up mechanisms for the peaceful settlement of intra-African disputes, and although these have not been very effective, the OAU has time and again succeeded through ad hoc arrangements in dampening incipient conflicts or adding to the pressure for settlement where they have already broken out. Several Latin American countries have taken an active role, through the Contadora Group, in preventing tensions in Central America from degenerating into open war. The Non-Aligned Movement, although less well-organized for timely intervention, has, through the person of its Chairman or through other means, also tried on many occasions to preserve or re-establish peace among its members.

THE DEVELOPMENT CRISIS OF THE 1980s

It is arguable that, for all its flaws, the development experience of the South until the end of the 1970s could have provided a base for improved living standards and human development. For this potential improvement to be turned into a permanent and self-sustaining reality some corrective measures would have been necessary. These should have included institutional and structural reforms designed to ensure an appropriate balance between investment and consumption, a more equitable distribution of the benefits of growth, greater decentralization, and more active involvement of the people in the development process.

Unfortunately it will never be known whether this could have been possible. In the 1980s the international environment of the countries of the South suffered a sudden and violent deterioration, leading to a development crisis of unprecedented severity. A review of the external impulses and their effect is essential for the purpose of considering possible policy responses and future action.

The Role of the External Environment

The most prominent feature of the external environment for development in the 1970s was the large expansion of the volume of international commercial bank loans to developing countries. This occurred because the expansion of the Euro-currency markets, the recycling through the international banks of the financial surpluses of oil-exporting countries, and the economic recession in industrial countries all created excess liquidity in the international banking system and made major banks eager to lend to fast-growing developing countries.

To varying degrees and for different reasons, many of these countries were experiencing persistent trade imbalances and large fiscal deficits. The correction of these required domestic reforms which involved politically difficult choices, and also risked slowing economic growth temporarily. For the less poor of the developing countries, the abundant supply of foreign credit at low, or even negative, real interest rates therefore offered a way out which avoided the need for economic contraction and hard political choices.

But however imprudent and excessive the surge in foreign borrowing may have been in the absence of needed domestic reforms, the net transfer of resources to the South at that time was on balance very favourable for the world economy. It contributed to the maintenance of a respectable level of growth and investment in developing countries during the 1970s. This in turn helped to prevent both a worsening of the recession in the developed countries, and a further decline in the rate at which world trade was expanding.

The imbalances within and among developed countries were, however, growing, and the policies adopted to correct them caused the international trading and financial environment to deteriorate sharply in the 1980s. Having decided at the end of the 1970s that the fundamental issue was the control of inflation, governments of developed countries introduced recessionary macroeconomic policies relying primarily, though not exclusively, on monetary policy instruments. The result was, on the one hand, a substantial slow-down of economic activity in the industrialized countries of the West, which depressed international prices for commodities by reducing their demand; and, on the other, a rise of international interest rates to unprecedented levels, which not only pushed up the cost of servicing the debt but further depressed commodity prices by raising the cost of stock-holding. In effect, a large part of the cost of controlling inflation and introducing structural changes in the North was borne by the South. Developing countries had to pay out more and more to service their debt while receiving less and less for their exports. As these contrasting movements aggravated their financial difficulties, commercial banks decided to stop lending them new money, and the result was the international debt crisis of the 1980s.

The slow-down of economic activity in the industrialized countries and the corresponding fall in their demand for imports were particularly sharp in the first three years of the decade. The rate of growth of the developed market economies, which had averaged 3.1 per cent a year in the 1970s, dropped to 1.4 per cent in 1980 and 1.6 per cent in 1981, and was negative in 1982. The volume of their imports, which had grown at an annual average rate of 5.5 per cent in the 1970s, stagnated in 1980 and fell in both 1981 and 1982. To a large extent because of the fall in demand, the prices of the main commodities exported by the developing countries–other than oil–fell by 21 per cent in real terms between 1980 and 1982. At the same time there were substantial increases in international interest rates, with the six-month Eurodollar rate going up in nominal terms from an average of 8.3 per cent in 1975-79 to 14.8 per cent in 1980-82.

The developed countries began a recovery in 1983, and in 1983-88 their economies grew at an annual average rate of 3.5 per cent, with the volume of imports expanding by nearly 8 per cent a year and inflation remaining moderate on average. The recovery has been hailed in the North as the beginning of another golden era for the world economy, comparable to the decade of the 1960s. However, in the 1960s the average rate of growth of the industrialized economies had exceeded 5 per cent a year, and their imports had grown at an average rate of 9.5 per cent a year. The levels achieved since the recovery began in 1983 are therefore considerably more modest.

For the South the crucial point is that the recovery in the North was not accompanied by a significant improvement in the external economic environment for most developing countries. Nominal international interest rates did come down on average to about 11 per cent in 1983-84, and to less than 8 per cent in 1985-86, but they went up again the following year, exceeding 8 per cent in 1988. More importantly, in real terms they either remained at the same high level or rose steeply to even higher levels, depending on the deflator used (see Fig.2.6).

In addition to the impact of higher interest rates on the burden of servicing external debts, developing countries faced a sharp reduction in international commercial-bank lending. The result was

Figure 2.6

International Nominal and Real Interest Rates, 1972-88

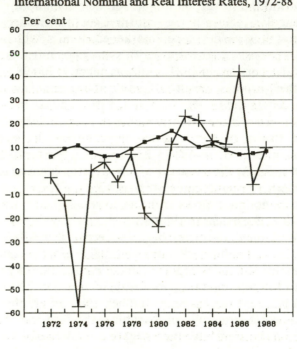

Note: The nominal rate is the six-month inter-bank Eurodollar rate. The
        real interest rate has been derived by deflating the nominal rate by
        changes in the unit value of developing countries' exports.
Source: Based on IMF and UNCTAD data.

that debt service–repayments of principal and interest
charges–exceeded loan disbursements from 1983 onwards (see
Fig.2.7). Debt-related transfers, normally from North to South,
were reversed and became a major drain on Southern economies
as from 1984. Between 1984 and 1988 the developing countries
as a group transferred to the North on this account a net amount
of $163 billion. By 1988 the only countries in the South that re-
mained net recipients of debt-related resources were those of
South Asia. However, the positive transfer to South Asia in 1988

was less than 30 per cent of that of 1982. In 1986-88, net credits from the IMF to developing countries were negative. In 1988 there was also a net transfer of resources from current borrowers to the World Bank.

Furthermore, direct foreign investment in developing countries fell by about two-thirds in real terms between 1982 and 1985, and while there was some recovery in 1986-88, it benefited mainly newly industrializing economies in Asia, while also marginally reflecting the introduction of debt-equity swap schemes in Latin America. In any case, the outflow of profits from developing countries remained consistently higher than the inflow of new investment. Export credits to developing countries declined by 70 per cent between 1982 and 1985, and became negative in 1986-87.

The reversal in the direction of debt-related transfers and the decline in other private financial flows from the North, combined with the stagnation in flows of official development finance during the 1980s, caused a sharp fall in aggregate net financial transfers to developing countries from 1982 onwards. Depending on the coverage and definitions employed, these transfers have been either positive but very small (15 per cent of the 1980-82 level for the period 1983-88, according to OECD figures) or negative, i.e. to the North, and increasingly so, from 1985 onwards. In any case for many countries in the South, notably in Latin America, net financial transfers have been negative and large for every year since 1983.

Moreover, real non-oil commodity prices, which had recovered slightly in 1983-84, fell by a further 23 per cent between 1984 and 1988. In the case of oil, the fall in that period was 65 per cent. The prices of thirty-three commodities of special interest to developing countries–excluding oil–in 1988 were 30 per cent lower in real terms than the average for 1979-81 (see Fig.2.8). In the case of food and tropical beverages, the fall was 37 per cent. In the case of oil, it was 64 per cent. As a result, by 1988 the terms of trade of developing countries had deteriorated by 29 per cent as compared to 1980, and those of oil exporters among them by 49 per cent (see Fig.2.9). The transfer of resources from the developing to the developed countries that this deterioration involved is massive: taking 1980 levels of exports and prices as a base, for the eighteen main non-oil commodities exported by developing countries it amounted to nearly $83 billion between 1981 and 1986, the

Figure 2.7

Debt Service Payments by the South less External Borrowing, 1980-88

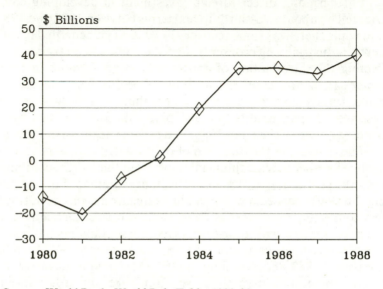

Source: World Bank, *World Debt Tables 1989-90.*

last year for which complete data are available. To put these figures in a longer perspective, the average real price of non-oil commodities for the whole of the period 1980-88 was 25 per cent below that of the previous two decades and the terms of trade of non-oil developing countries were 8 per cent below those of the 1960s and 13 per cent below those of the 1970s. Within the context of this strong downward movement, international commodity prices continued to be characterized by great instability and fluctuations.

Furthermore, there was growing protectionism in the developed countries against exports of special interest to developing countries, such as processed tropical and agricultural products, textiles, steel, petrochemicals, automotive parts, and electronics. This protectionist trend aggravated the difficulties these countries faced in dealing with their external environment. The new protectionism in the form of Voluntary Export Restraints (VERs),

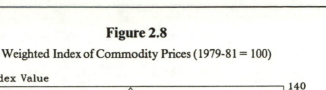

Figure 2.8

Weighted Index of Commodity Prices (1979-81 = 100)

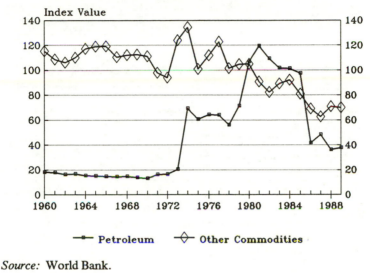

Source: World Bank.

Orderly Marketing Arrangements (OMAs), and similar measures had the invidious effect of preventing entry into the market even for the most efficient producers.

Largely as a result of these changes, most countries of the Third World experienced a profound development crisis. The deficiencies of past patterns of development may have been a contributing factor; but, by any reckoning, the sharp deterioration in the international economic environment which has been described played by far the major role. The crisis persisted even as the decade of the 1980s came to a close.

Economic, social, and political consequences of the crisis

For most countries of the South, the decade of the 1980s came to be regarded as a lost decade for development; and the expression is an understatement for a good many of them, where living standards have dropped well below their 1980 levels.

Figure 2.9

Terms of Trade for the South (1980 = 100)

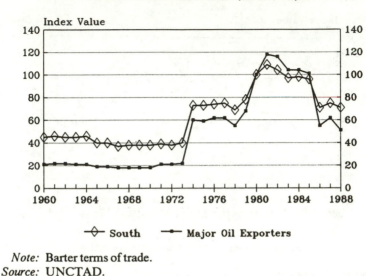

Note: Barter terms of trade.
Source: UNCTAD.

The rate of growth of GDP of the Latin American countries, which had averaged 5.4 per cent per year in the 1970s, went down to only 1.5 per cent in 1981-88; as population growth exceeded 2 per cent per year, per capita GDP declined. In Africa and West Asia, annual growth rates of 4.1 and 7.8 per cent, respectively, in the 1970s turned negative in the 1980s, and the economies of the countries in these two regions contracted by about 0.5 per cent per year in 1981-88. In both regions the annual rate of growth of population exceeded 3 per cent in the 1980s. Thus there was also a drop in per capita GDP. Figures 2.10 and 2.11 show the particularly sharp falls in per capita incomes in sub-Saharan Africa and Latin America.

The investment ratio also declined in most countries of the South; in Latin America it fell from an annual average of 24.5 per cent in the 1970s to 16.4 per cent in 1985-88. In very many countries investment in the 1980s was not high enough even to meet replacement capital demands, resulting both in the physical deterioration of basic infrastructure (including transport and com-

Figure 2.10

Gross National Income Per Capita in Sub-Saharan Africa, 1967-87

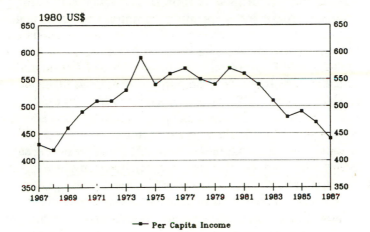

— Per Capita Income

Figure 2.11

Gross National Income Per Capita in Latin America, 1967-87

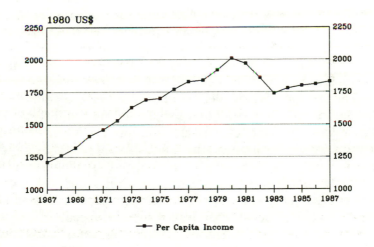

— Per Capita Income

Source: World Bank.

munications as well as schools and hospitals) and in mounting numbers of unemployed and underemployed persons.

The least developed countries, whose number increased from 31 to 42 in the 1980s, were the most severely affected. The external dependence of their economies is particularly high. They rely on exports of a few primary commodities for foreign exchange, and on imports of basic inputs and capital goods for the operation and expansion of their productive capacity. Even though the UN Substantial New Programme of Action agreed in 1981 called for official development assistance to reach 0.15 per cent of the donors GNP, the actual level in 1988 was only 0.09 per cent. In the context of steep declines in receipts from exports and sharp cuts in imports, their weak economic base had shrunk a great deal, and their external dependence was becoming steadily heavier. Many of them were also afflicted by wars, floods, drought, or famine.

The social achievements of the past decades were also brought to a halt, and in some cases reversed. Evidence of rising infant mortality has been reported from parts of sub-Saharan Africa and Latin America in the 1980s; half a million child deaths in 1988–two-thirds of them in Africa–can be related to the reversal or slowing down of economic growth. Increasing malnutrition, hitting hardest the very poorest in many countries, is still being reported from several regions. And school enrolments were falling while drop-out rates were rising in approximately one-third of the developing nations as parents could not pay fees or needed to put their children of school age to work to get whatever small contribution the children could make to the family income.

The development and debt crises of the 1980s in addition generated complex and profound social and political dislocations, whose long-term implications are still only dimly perceived. In many developing countries, the fabric of society was being torn apart, basic institutions were in turmoil, and social peace was being undermined. Governments and political systems, unable to deliver basic goods and services to their people, found themselves increasingly rejected and their legitimacy challenged.

Demographic trends aggravated the situation. In most countries of the South, children and the young account for an increasing proportion–in some cases now a majority–of the total population. At the same time, because of progress in education since the 1950s, young people had a higher level of education and higher expectations in terms of employment and upward mobility. Frustrated by the absence of economic growth and opportunity, the young tended more and more not to accept their situation passively but to rebel, in some cases turning to fundamentalist ideologies.

A similar process of disaffection also took place among older people–those who should be working and at least seeing their children enjoying higher living standards. They too had a growing awareness of how better-off people lived at home and even abroad, while the hopes they had for their own material improvement had been dashed. Accordingly, they harboured a sense of social injustice, and a feeling that they had been made to bear the brunt of economic problems which they did not understand. Social discontent mounted.

Even some sections of the middle and professional classes saw their living standards decline, and their children having less opportunity than they themselves enjoyed. If they could, they tended to migrate to developed countries, thus leaving the nations of the South still further weakened and disadvantaged.

In the face of all these social factors, recourse to oppression and military force was in some cases seen by governments as the only way to keep the situation under some degree of control. Where this happened, the foundations of democratic society were still further eroded, and a denial of basic human rights was added to the suffering–and the frustrations–of the people. Even though there has recently been a decline in the number of authoritarian regimes in the South, the governments replacing them are often insecure and fragile. The problems facing them are so serious that they find it difficult to maintain or consolidate their authority by democratic means.

There was in effect a general erosion of the political and economic effectiveness of State and government in the countries of the South; those in power were overwhelmed by the combination of internal and external pressures, these often being in competition with one another. The enforced cuts in public expenditure further undermined the governments' capacity for action, while the deteriorating conditions of service of government employees sapped the latter's morale and integrity. This state of affairs made government policies even more ineffective, and added to the loss of governmental legitimacy and support.

The economic crisis and, in particular, the debt problem and the manner in which it was handled by the creditors thus contributed to social and political destabilization in the Third World. The resulting volatile mix of tensions and contradictions, and often national dependency, threatened the reality of independence of many nations of the South and their peace and security; world peace and security were also jeopardized.

The exceptions to this picture of retrogression and decline in the 1980s were China, whose economy grew at a rate of 9.4 per cent per year, and the South and East Asian economies (including India and the newly industrializing economies of East Asia), which grew at a rate of 5.5 per cent per year. In the two most populous countries of the South, India and China, the adverse and unstable international environment had negligible effects, because these countries were to a considerable extent self-sufficient in capital goods and food and had small foreign debts at the beginning of the 1980s. Their previous achievements in raising domestic savings and investment rates, in agricultural and industrial modernization, and in the development of human resources also made them less vulnerable to external shocks. In addition, their efforts to achieve fast economic growth were supported by successful reforms in their systems of development planning. However, the considerable increase in their external debt in the 1980s may significantly affect their future development.

The newly industrializing economies of East Asia were also rapidly able to overcome the impact of the slow-down in international trade because their export sector was highly diversified and exports of primary commodities did not feature, or were not a major element; their import structures were flexible. Moreover, thanks to their concentration on exports of manufactures they benefited from improved terms of trade in the 1980s. These economies have therefore not had to make painful structural adjustments, but have been able to continue their successful industrialization policies as well as to maintain their investment levels. On the other hand, some of the negative features of these development experiences–sacrifices in popular consumption and suppression of workers' rights–are now beginning to surface in the form of growing social and political unrest. In any case, the unique features of these experiences must be kept in mind if useful policy lessons are to be learned from them.

Shortcomings in the adjustment process

The setbacks of the 1980s exposed the structural weaknesses of developing countries and showed that appropriate macroeconomic policies are indispensable to provide a stable basis for day-to-day decision-making. The crisis has made it even more urgent to undertake structural reforms in order to strengthen the performance of the public sector and its resource-generating capacity, improve tax systems, and create a stable environment in which the private sector can play its role in line with national priorities. Also it is now very clear that reforms are required to promote exports, the earnings from which could be used to pay for imports and thus to contribute to the efficient management of the balance of payments.

However, in the adjustment process of the 1980s, these needed reforms were frustrated by an unbalanced international approach towards structural adjustment and by the conditionality prescribed by the international financial institutions. The macroeconomic policies–in particular fiscal and exchange rate policies–virtually forced upon developing countries as part of programmes for stabilization and structural adjustment were geared to achieving a quick, short-term improvement in the balance of payments. Safeguarding the interests of international commercial banks even at the cost of a severe economic contraction thus became the primary concern of international strategy on debt management.

Further, the programmes for stabilization and adjustment pressed upon developing countries did not provide for sufficient external financial support to permit adjustment to occur and endure without choking their growth. The programmes were based on unduly optimistic assumptions about the speed at which structural maladies could be corrected. In addition, they were generally shaped by a doctrinaire belief in the efficacy of market forces and monetarist policies. This combination of priorities and policies aggravated the developing countries' economic woes and social distress in a number of ways.

In particular, the complete disregard of equity in prescriptions for structural adjustment consisting of cuts in public spending and changes in relative prices had devastating effects on vital public services like health and education, with especially harmful consequences for the most vulnerable social groups.

In the 1980s, the proportion of government expenditure devoted to health fell in most countries of sub-Saharan Africa, in more than half those of Latin America, and in one-third of the nations of Asia. According to the United Nations Children's Fund (UNICEF), in the thirty-seven poorest nations of the world, spending per head on health care was cut by nearly 50 per cent, and on education by nearly 25 per cent in that decade. And at a time when the poor were suffering an already substantial drop in income, governments scrapped or sharply reduced, in the name of resource efficiency, food subsidies and other selective redistributional measures. The application of such policies accentuated the maldistribution of income within developing countries, while in many cases their beneficial impact on public finances was negligible–and is certainly outweighed by their long-term economically detrimental effects.

Nor did fiscal retrenchment lead to enhanced efficiency in the public sector, or to its replacement by efficient private activities. On the contrary, in many cases fiscal contraction was responsible for a waste of resources in the form of increased unemployment and underuse of productive capacity. Coupled with excessive emphasis on curbing the expansion of domestic credit, it was usually designed to generate surpluses on external trade so as to provide foreign exchange for servicing debt. Because the ability to earn more through exports was severely constrained, trade surpluses were achieved largely by restricting imports, even the most essential ones. As already indicated, under these conditions many developing countries became net exporters of capital to the industrial countries of the North, a perverse outcome by any reckoning, made worse by additional transfers occasioned by the adverse turn of the terms of trade.

Thus, after several years of 'adjustment' many countries found themselves in the position of having unwillingly or unwittingly caused large and irrecoverable losses to their economy and undermined their growth prospects; their levels of public savings remained inadequate for financing vital investments that would allow the economy to make a sustainable recovery. For despite continual international talk about 'growth-oriented adjustment', the possibility of raising domestic savings and investment in order to resume growth had been compromised by the policies employed to achieve fiscal adjustment. Consequently, even if there should be significant debt relief, the resources released through reduction in debt-service payments might in many countries be insufficient to bring investments to the level required after the prolonged period of retrenchment.

In the area of trade and industrial policies, although there is undoubtedly a need for structural reforms, the approach in the typical adjustment package was likewise marked by excessive dogmatism and a lack of common sense. At a time when the scarcity of foreign exchange had become the major obstacle to economic growth, countries were pressed into undertaking maximum liberalization of imports very quickly. The result was that goods offering high profits to the importer were imported in preference to goods essential for the smooth running of the economy. Often in such cases the external accounts could be brought into balance only through a larger devaluation than would have been necessary if the imports had been restricted to the spares or inputs necessary for the local productive sector and to other essential goods.

In the more diversified semi-industrial economies, insistence on free trade policies irrespective of national conditions led to many conflicts with development priorities. The combination of depreciated exchange rates, depressed real wages, and economic contraction certainly generated 'recession-led exports', i.e. exports made possible by diverting economic resources away from needed internal consumption or investment. However, as the resulting export revenue was not available for paying for additional imports but had to be mostly used for servicing the debt, the export drive did not provide the means of realizing broad-based and sustainable export-led growth.

The indiscriminate insistence on the simultaneous expansion of commodity production in many countries led to more than proportionate declines in the value of primary exports of developing countries as a group; for some of those dependent almost entirely on one or two primary products it even caused a net worsening of their foreign exchange position. The oversupply of world commodities was thus aggravated, contributing to the prolonged depression of commodity prices and to a further worsening of the earning capacity of the developing countries.

By the standards of the policies forced upon developing countries by the multilateral financial institutions, many countries had 'adjusted' and others were persisting in the effort. But the result for a large number of them was a decade of development in reverse–neither redistribution nor growth– and a worsening of the prospects for future development. The policies of developed countries and of the international financial institutions they control must bear a heavy responsibility for forcing developing countries on to a path of prolonged stagnation and retrenchment.

The crisis and South-South co-operation

The 1970s witnessed a considerable expansion in the flow of trade, technology, and capital among developing countries. Indeed, for the first time in the post-war years, trade among developing countries expanded faster than world trade. The rising demand for imports of the members of the Organization of Petroleum Exporting Countries (OPEC) and their large balance-of-payments surpluses provided a significant stimulus to co-operation among developing countries. The experience of the 1970s generated hopes that at long last the South might have acquired an impressive combination of capital, technology, and markets to support a diversified programme of South-South co-operation.

In the event, these hopes were not fulfilled. Not surprisingly, the development crisis in the 1980s seriously disrupted and undermined South-South co-operation. Regional and subregional programmes came under serious strain; many became de facto inoperative. The fall in foreign exchange resources has added new barriers to South-South trade as few countries in the South are in a position to give credit, and lack of information often inhibits alternatives such as countertrade arrangements. In general, the shortage of resources has weakened the developing countries' ability to provide institutional support for South-South co-operation, even when the political commitment remains strong. The management of the domestic crisis becomes the priority in the allocation of resources, action to build up South-South co-operation being postponed until more favourable times.

For the same reasons, South-South solidarity also suffered. This partly explains why the developing countries had difficulty in agreeing upon, and collectively putting forward, a common platform for negotiations with the North, for example in the Uruguay Round. Paradoxically, this loss of solidarity took place at the very time when the South needed it most in order to make its voice heard in a consistent and decisive manner.

The debt crisis so far provides an example of a missed opportunity for collective action. Had the debtor nations, or even the major ones among them, stood together in negotiations with the North, and insisted on what are essentially just changes in the terms and conditions for debt-service payments, their own peoples might have suffered less in the process of honouring national commitments, and some improvement might have been achieved in the workings of the international financial system.

The crisis and North-South relations

Internationally, the massive development crisis of the 1980s and the suffering it inflicted on the South did not become an occasion for systematic action to deal with the underlying causes of the crisis or to counteract its effects. The developed countries refused to acknowledge that there was any need for intervention to make the international economic environment more favourable to development. The worst slump in international commodity prices since the 1930s was accompanied by a total absence of any counter-cyclical measures to stabilize and support the commodity economy. Any proposals for a negotiated global approach to the debt issue were dismissed by the governments of developed countries, which regarded debt as a matter to be dealt with by creditors and individual debtors on a case-by-case basis. In general, these governments denied that there was anything fundamentally wrong with the world economic system or with North-South relations. This complacent view of things reflected the rigidly ideological position prevalent among decision-makers in many developed countries who saw the unfettered operation of market forces as always best, whether at the national or at the international level.

Especially serious was the sustained attack on multilateralism, and in particular on the more democratic institutions of the United Nations system, which took place during the 1980s. This attack was prompted largely by changes in political direction in some powerful countries of the North and the reassertion of the philosophy that 'might is right'. In this view there was little sympathy or patience with the position and needs of other, weaker countries. As a result, decision-making power at the global level became increasingly concentrated in a small number of developed countries, which de facto act as a self-appointed directorate for managing the world economy.

Forced by the increasing complexity and interdependence of their national economies, the major industrialized countries of the North accepted the need for a degree of institutionalized co-ordination of their separate policies–hence the annual Group of Seven meetings. The evolution of this summit Group and its supporting structures further encouraged these countries to see themselves as the custodians of the world economy and to disregard the basic principles of multilateral discourse and decision-making embodied in the United Nations Charter. Because the combined economic weight and power of the countries that make up the Group of Seven is so great, its decisions have enormous impact on the rest of the world, which has no opportunity to influence the content or timing of those decisions.

It is from this group of developed countries that stemmed the notion that the development crisis was attributable to misguided domestic policies followed by the developing countries. Those developed countries were able to use the international financial institutions to impose their view on Third World countries and at the same time to demand that the latter should 'adjust' their economies through contractionary policies. The policies prescribed by the World Bank and the IMF were thus inevitably unbalanced; they did not seek any adjustment by the developed countries to take into account their own heavy contribution to the troubles of the South.

This was a form of neo-colonialism: the world's economic metropolises were forcing on the South the whole burden of adjustment to an impaired world economy, while themselves continuing to grow. What is more, the weakening of Third World countries due to the debt crisis and depressed commodity prices was also used by the North as an opportunity to influence their domestic choices and to impose on them externally determined values, policies, concessions, and patterns of development. The social and political costs of inappropriate measures were then paid by the victim countries and their peoples–and any resulting instability was used by the North as a further opportunity for external intervention. Indeed, given these trends, it may not be an exaggeration to suggest that the establishment of a system of international economic relations in which the South's second-class status would be institutionalized is an imminent danger.

THE BASES FOR RENEWED HOPE: HUMAN RESOURCES AND SCIENTIFIC AND TECHNOLOGICAL DEVELOPMENT

And yet, despite this gloomy picture, and the widening gap in income per person between the developing and the industrialized countries which is a symptom of the disparity between North and South, there is still reason for hope. The post-war achievements of the South provide a base upon which it can still build.

Paramount among them are the cumulative gains since 1950 in developing the human resources and laying the technological foundations for sustained growth and development. We have pointed to some shortcomings in the science and technology policies of the countries of the South. But the achievements must not be forgotten, and it is fitting that we should close this discussion by recalling them.

Progress in these areas ran, in general, on parallel lines. However, the advance in the formation of human and social capital was greater and more widely spread. All countries–large and small, high-income and low-income, early starters and late-comers– shared in it in different degrees. The levels achieved varied, but that was as often the result of initial conditions as of efforts made. On the other hand, the success in the production of capital goods embodying physical technology was spotty, being limited to a few countries which started with more favourable conditions and devoted special efforts to it.

The success of the South in using scientific advance for human and social betterment was impressive. Death rates dropped from 25-30 per thousand in the 1950s to 10-15 per thousand in the 1980s. Infant mortality fell from near 180 per thousand to around 70. Life expectancy rose from about 40 to over 60 years. Within a few decades, much of the South had started to narrow the social distance that separated it from the North (see Figs.2.12 and 2.13 for a breakdown by regions).

Equally important was educational progress, particularly in the numbers involved. There were widespread increases in literacy rates. Enrolment in primary education increased sixfold, in secondary education eighteenfold, and in higher education twenty-fivefold (see Figs.2.14 and 2.15). Although still much needs to be done to improve the quality of the educational services provided, the South has set in motion the building-up of a stock of skills which, under improved economic conditions, can begin to bear fruit.

Some economies, mainly in Asia but also in other regions, were successful in the technological modernization of their production systems. They were able to meet the basic needs of their people, raise their rates of savings and investment, and expand the stock of physical and human capital.

The economies that made the greatest headway in transforming their production systems had several features in common. They had high rates of capital formation, ranging from 25 to 30 per cent of GNP. Their governments actively promoted the build-up of national capabilities to import, adapt, and diffuse technologies. In particular, they had altered their intellectual property laws and systems to serve national objectives; they did not automatically grant import monopolies to foreign transnationals. These governments increased the human and financial resources devoted to research and development; encouraged the growth of design and engineering capabilities; and offered general as well as special incentives. They established domestic intermediate and capital goods industries, while importing some of the most advanced technologies.

In addition these economies achieved remarkable success in creating social capital and using it effectively. For example, several of them rapidly improved the technological basis of their agriculture, thereby achieving a measure of food security. For this purpose they set clear priorities, and concentrated their research and development resources on fixed targets in the absorption and mastering of imported technologies and their diffusion in the production process.

Figure 2.12

Infant Mortality in the South and the North, 1965 and 1986

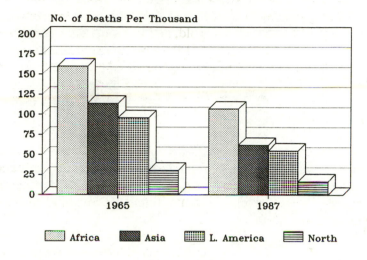

No. of Deaths Per Thousand

Figure 2.13

Life Expectancy in the South and the North, 1965 and 1986

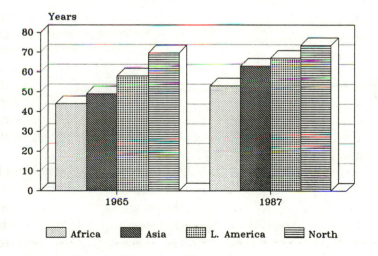

Source: World Bank, *Social Indicators of Development, 1989.*

Figure 2.14

Gross Primary School Enrolment in the South,
1965 and 1986

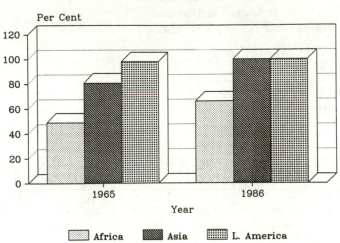

Figure 2.15

Gross Secondary School Enrolment in the South,
1965 and 1986

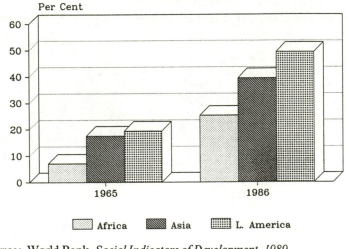

Source: World Bank, *Social Indicators of Development, 1989.*

In doing all this, their governments played central roles. They set the agenda: to move quickly along the line from import substitution in light manufacturing, to basic intermediate goods, to capital equipment and engineering, and to heavy chemicals and electronics industries. They gave the broad directive signals and, in the most successful cases, also ensured that these were rigorously followed.

Sometimes even the frontier technologies employed in nuclear energy, space, electronics, and, in some instances, in defence industries, were mastered. Whatever may be said about the merit of some of these achievements, one lesson stands out: countries that succeeded in upgrading their domestic technological capability had thereby also acquired the ability to jump from the very conventional to the frontier technologies. The time-lags involved were significantly cut down.

Thus, there is a brighter side to the past development experience of the South than that usually associated with it. And this experience offers grounds for a more hopeful outlook than is sometimes recognized. It can also contribute significantly to collective efforts at self-reliant development on the part of the South as a whole. For the way forward passes through the mobilization, by all countries of the South, acting individually as well as collectively, of their very considerable human and material resources towards the attainment of the goal of a people-centred development.

Self-Reliant and People-Centred Development: The National Dimension

3

THE NEED TO REORIENT DEVELOPMENT STRATEGIES

In most regions of the South there is a deep awareness of the limitations of past development strategies and a growing conviction that the way out of the present crisis does not lie in returning to those strategies. At the same time, there is profound disillusionment with the policies that a large number of developing countries are now being obliged to follow under the dictates of the international financial institutions. The need is therefore increasingly felt for finding a path of development that will lead the countries of the South out of the current crisis, into a future of equitable and sustained development.

The South cannot count on a significant improvement in the international economic environment for its development in the 1990s. The development of the South will therefore need to be fuelled by its own resources to a much greater degree than in the past. The countries of the South will have to rely increasingly on their own exertions, both individual and collective, and to reorient their development strategies, which must benefit from the lessons of past experience.

The balance between the different elements of a development strategy must necessarily be country-specific. But a self-reliant and people-centred development path will need to be guided by certain basic principles and objectives.

Priority must be given to meeting the basic needs of the people. Hence there should be a strong emphasis on food security, health, education, and employment, all of which are essential for enhancing human capacities to meet the challenge of sustained development.

The experience since the 1950s has clearly shown that basic needs can be satisfied only within a rapidly expanding economy. It is therefore crucial to revive economic growth, reorient its content, and sustain it at an acceptable pace. The growth strategy should include among its main objectives the broad-based modernization of peasant agriculture and the strengthening of the pace of industrialization while also improving its employment-creating effects, competitiveness, and trade performance.

Concern for social justice has to be an integral part of genuine development. A fairer distribution of income and productive assets like land is essential as a means of speeding up development and making it sustainable. The development of human resources should similarly be an important concern, as it can simultaneously bring equity and efficiency into the economy. In their measures to enrich the capabilities of their people, the countries of the South should seek to achieve, by the year 2000, universal primary health care, literacy, and elementary education; a substantial increase in secondary and higher education and in vocational and technical training; and a slowing-down of population growth.

People-centred strategies of development should be consistent with the evolving culture of the people. While development will necessarily entail changes in cultural norms, values, and beliefs, modernization should not be antithetical to the culture of a people and should contribute to its internal evolution.

A development strategy designed to imitate the life-styles and consumption patterns of affluent industrial societies is clearly inconsistent with our vision of development for the South. It would accentuate inequalities, for it would be possible to secure such high consumption levels for only a small minority of the population in each country. Because it leads to a high level of imports and energy use, it would also cripple the growth process and intensify economic and environmental strains.

The democratization of political structures and the modernization of the State should also have a high priority. A democratic environment which guarantees fundamental human rights is an essential goal of development centred on the people as well as a crucial means of accelerating development. Not only should democratic institutions be created and strengthened, but there should be encouragement of the formation of non-governmental and voluntary organizations that would be capable of assuming increased responsibility for economic and social advances. By mobilizing local human and financial resources, such grass-roots organizations not only help to meet the felt needs of their members, but may in time become important pillars of the democratic system.

For the foreseeable future, most countries of the South will have mixed economies in which the State and market mechanisms will have to complement each other in a creative way if their development potential is to be realized. For this to happen, reforms are required in the machinery of government in addition to the reorientation of policies. The aim should be to modernize the State apparatus, as well as to create a stable and development-oriented macroeconomic framework, encourage entrepreneurship, initiative, and innovation, and make the public sector more efficient.

A people-oriented development strategy will have to take much greater note of the role of women; a nation cannot genuinely develop so long as half its population is marginalized and suffers discrimination. Women, who invariably bear a disproportionate share of poverty, also had to bear the major burden of adjustment to the crisis of the 1980s. Yet, in almost all the countries of the South, they play a vital role in productive activities and in maintaining their families and households. Thus, on the grounds of both equity and growth, development programmes must give due prominence to the specific concerns of women and ensure that ample resources are marshalled to satisfy their needs and aspirations.

The creation, mastery, and utilization of modern science and technology are basic achievements that distinguish the advanced from the backward world, the North from the South. The widening gap in overall development and wealth between the nations of the South and those of the North is to a large extent the science and technology gap. Thus future development policies will need to address with greater vigour the closing of the knowledge gap with the North. Knowledge is vital to the future of the South, for development will depend more and more on the benefits derived from the advances of science and technology. Progress in this field calls for the overhaul of educational systems, in order that more attention may be given to education in science and to training in engineering and technical skills. It will also require science and technology policies which lay down clear sectoral priorities, integrate science and technology in national plans, and provide adequate resources for strengthening scientific and technological capability.

While the nations of the South undoubtedly suffer from the deterioration of the biosphere caused largely by the production and consumption patterns of the North, they are also increasingly facing environmental damage associated with their own development. This includes the degradation of natural resources due to population growth and economic pressures, the contamination of air and water associated with rapid industrialization, and urban pollution due to the unchecked growth of cities. There is therefore a need to take full cognizance of these hazards to ensure that development is indeed sustainable. The utilization of natural resources must be rational and consistent with their preservation, and the use of technologies that are environmentally sound must be promoted in the industries of the South. Developing countries will also have to check rapid and uncontrolled urbanization.

Many of the goals and policies advocated in this chapter can complement each other over time, and our discussion will often stress their mutually reinforcing links. But we recognize that in the design of development policies and the allocation of public investments, many trade-offs, often sharp ones, will arise between the different national objectives—as, for instance, between the creation of social and physical infrastructure, between industrial and agricultural priorities, or between the expansion of exports and domestic demand. Inevitably, difficult choices will have to be made on the range of objectives to be achieved and the balance between them. These choices will necessarily differ from one country to another.

THE DEVELOPMENT IMPERATIVE

Fast and sustained economic growth is an inescapable imperative for the South. A rapidly expanding production of goods and services is the only material basis for improving the well-being of its people. It is estimated that 360 million persons will be added to the labour force of developing countries in the 1990s. Only rapid economic growth can ensure that they will have the chance of earning a decent livelihood. A slow rate of growth will condemn developing countries to increasing poverty and underemployment. The importance of high rates of investment and savings and of utmost efficiency in the use of resources is therefore self-evident.

Growth, essential as it is for creating the resources that can provide people with a better life, is not an assurance by itself of people-centred development. The process of growth has to be oriented so as to raise the income and productivity of the poor and to promote a sustainable use of the scarce natural resources and the environment. All this requires a careful examination and modification of the development strategies of the past.

Development patterns and priorities will, however, vary among countries according to their stage of development, size, resources, and many other factors, including their cultural heritage. In predominantly agrarian societies, institutional reforms and policies to make smallholder farming more productive assume special significance. In many semi-industrial developing countries, the orientation of industrial strategies to create mutually reinforcing links with the agricultural sector becomes important. In all cases, measures have to be taken to develop an industrial base well adapted to national requirements and potential, and to improve its ability to keep abreast of technical progress and to seize opportunities in international markets.

The size of a country, as measured by its area and population, materially influences its development pattern. A large domestic market permits economies of scale to be exploited in a wide range of industries. In contrast, smaller countries, without the benefit of a large domestic market, have to rely more on specialization and exports. Typically, the now prosperous small economies–in both North and South–advanced by exploiting niches in export markets they could efficiently supply. Thus foreign trade is of particular significance to the small countries.

Agricultural Development and Food Security

The South has recorded some impressive advances in food and agricultural production since the 1950s. India has ended famines since independence and is now self-sufficient in food grains. China's success in ensuring food for a billion people scattered over a huge territory poorly served by transport has been spectacular.

Hunger and malnutrition nevertheless continue to be widespread in the developing world. According to the World Bank's latest estimate, close to a billion people in the developing countries are too poor to buy enough food to sustain their energy. Over 50 per cent of them live in South Asia and East Asia. Nearly a third are in sub-Saharan Africa, and about a tenth in Latin America and the Caribbean. Projections by the Food and Agriculture Organization (FAO) for the year 2000 indicate a further rise in the number of people without enough food in the South. The situation is particularly serious in sub-Saharan Africa where wars, drought, environmental damage, and inadequate policies have caused food output to fall, leading to a sharp rise in dependence on food imports.

Chronic food insecurity is the result of a persistent lack of economic capacity to grow or buy the minimum essential amount of food. The causes are many, varying from country to country and from region to region. Among these are: inequalities in land ownership and distribution, particularly in some Latin American and Asian countries, resulting in landlessness or a lack of sufficient land of reasonable quality for smallholder farmers; limited employment and income opportunities for both the rural and the urban poor; underinvestment in basic rural infrastructure; lack of capital and credit for smallholders; government policies that tend to discriminate against the agricultural sector, particularly food production; inadequacy of basic social and extension services in rural areas, including poor dissemination of technical knowledge; and deficient systems for food distribution and marketing. In many countries, these conditions are perpetuated as the rural poor have little weight in political structures and therefore limited influence on national policies.

Broad-based agricultural progress and sustained improvement in the productivity and income of the rural poor are central to achieving food security in predominantly agrarian economies. A strategy based on modernizing the small- and middle-peasant sector and geared to achieving food security is also the best means by which the agricultural sector can fully contribute to equitable and sustainable development. Experience shows that treating peasant agriculture merely as a source of 'surplus extraction' or 'primitive accumulation', through manipulation of the agricultural terms of trade, forced sales of farm products at low prices to the State, or agricultural taxation, can in the end be highly coun-ter-productive. Such treatment of the agricultural sector amounts to an unfair distribution of the gains of economic growth between urban and rural areas. The consequential stagnation in rural in-come in turn impedes efforts to speed up industrialization, whose success depends on an expansion of the markets for what industry produces. The end result is the retardation of the growth process as a whole, while food insecurity persists or becomes worse.

The harmful results of agricultural neglect can also be seen in the gradual conversion of many developing countries, parti-cularly in Africa and Latin America, from food exporters into net food importers. This shift has also in part been hastened by the policies of developed countries, whose heavy subsidies to their own farmers have depressed world food prices, thereby hamper-ing the drive to expand food output in many developing countries. High rates of population growth and rapid drift to cities have also accentuated the disparity between production and consumption trends. This situation has been aggravated by changing patterns of food consumption. Imports of cheap food and discriminatory government policies often encourage the consumption of foods that are not produced domestically. The South's development ex-perience, as well as that of today's industrially advanced nations, clearly indicate that a diversified economy with a large industrial sector can hardly be achieved unless a modern, broad-based, and highly productive agricultural sector is built up.

Future agricultural development will also have to place greater emphasis on environmental sustainability. Lately, fears have been expressed about the possibility of a global food short-age due to increasing environmental stress. In many parts of the world, the degradation of natural resources such as the deteri-oration of soils, falling water-tables, desertification, and defores-tation are contributing to lower yields and a decline in cultivated areas. Climatic changes that might be caused by the greenhouse effect could also accentuate the threat to global food security.

Reforms in systems of land tenure

Gross inequalities in land ownership have always been obstacles to widespread agricultural progress and to the achievement of food security. The intense concentration of land ownership often results in a slow expansion of cultivated land, hinders the growth of agricultural productivity, and distorts the pattern of technical progress, leading to inefficient use of the resources of rural areas. When agricultural modernization occurs in these conditions, it fails to upgrade the economic and technological capabilities of small farmers and agricultural workers. The result is a shrinking peasant-economy and an increase in technological dualism, rural underemployment, and demographic pressure on land. Agricultural modernization needs to be broad-based if it is to make its full contribution to achieving people-centred development goals.

Land reforms leading to more equitable patterns of ownership and more efficient land use are indispensable for increasing agricultural production and food security. The experience of many developing countries bears ample testimony to this. The patterns of land ownership and land use vary widely in the South; it is not possible, therefore, to generalize about the ideal institutional conditions for agricultural growth without taking into account the specific characteristics of the country concerned.

There are, however, certain distinct regional requirements. In sub-Saharan Africa, the aim should be to ensure that the inevitable changes in the egalitarian traditional systems of land tenure do not lead to high concentration in ownership or to systems of 'open access'. In many Latin American countries, there is a clear case for land redistribution in favour of the poor and for policies to prevent concentration of land in the hands of a few large owners. And in Asia, along with land reform, legislation to improve protection of the interests of share-croppers and agricultural workers is required.

There can be many benefits from land reforms. They facilitate the redirection of investment, credit supplies, and other services towards small and middle peasants. As each rural family is made responsible for its own land, production, and livelihood, the need for expensive and administratively demanding food subsidies, rationing programmes, food-for-work projects and the like is minimized. The State can then deploy its limited administrative resources to greater effect on the provision of technical assistance, extension services, credit, and marketing support; the delivery of these services is in fact likely to become more complicated as a result of the need to serve many smallholders instead of a small number of large landowners. Moreover, the exodus of landless and workless rural people to the cities can be slowed down, reducing the burden on the State to provide urban social infra-structure and other social services. To make land reform efficient it is necessary to adopt a wide range of support measures designed to improve productivity, modernize peasant agriculture, and expand and regenerate farm land.

Infrastructure, land development, research and extension, storage, and credit

For food security to become a reality, the State's investment and promotional policies will also need to be reoriented in favour of small peasants and co-operatives. This will require enlarged expenditure on infrastructure and technological improvements. Irrigation and transport have to be rapidly expanded. Research and development has to be directed to the generation and dissemination of agricultural technologies that serve the needs of smallholder farmers. Efforts will need to be made to provide institutional credit to the vast majority of smallholders, who do not have access to such credit. No less important will be action to improve human capabilities through investments in education and training and in basic social services.

The preparation of land for cultivation through levelling, irrigation, and drainage, and such supporting infrastructure as roads, electricity, and marketing facilities, are critical in promoting agricultural production. In many African countries, measures that would make it possible to begin farming on large areas of potentially rich land could greatly stimulate agricultural growth. In the land-scarce countries of Asia, irrigation and drainage, which can increase yields as well as allow multiple cropping, seem the most effective way to step up output. There is substantial scope for such development through small, labour-intensive projects, which can often be carried out on a co-operative basis.

The contribution that agricultural research and extension can make to technological transformation in agriculture is evident from the experience of several countries of the South in the last few decades. The success achieved by the Green Revolution in Asia has lessons for countries with sluggish agricultural growth. Yet it is also clear that Green Revolution technologies cannot simply be transferred from one region or country to another. By and large, as evolved so far, they are better suited to stable, uniform, resource-rich conditions with good water supplies and soils, as in the alluvial plains and deltas in much of Asia, parts of Latin America, and small areas of Africa. Those technologies are not equally productive in the ecologically complex and fragile environments of the interior areas of the three continents, especially areas with dry-land and rainfed agriculture, uneven topography, and poor or eroded soils.

Green Revolution technologies have created problems in some countries. Sustained increases in output have become dependent on the continual release of new varieties of seed as earlier high-yielding ones lose their resistance to diseases and pests. The wide-spread use of a few varieties has tended to accentuate the problems of crop disease as biological diversity is reduced. The improper use of fertilizers and chemicals has caused health problems and has also contributed to the contamination of supplies of drinking water. The new technologies have also increased farmer dependence on agricultural research centres and, in some cases, on Northern transnational firms.

To effectively serve the needs of farmers, research has to be more localized and sensitive to farmers' conditions and requirements in different areas. In this respect, a 'farming systems' approach to agricultural research, which takes the farm as an integrated production unit, has proved effective in many countries of the South, as it gives greater attention to an efficient use of all the resources available to poor farmers, to the constraints they face, and to their own felt needs.

Africa, in particular, needs a strong system of agricultural research to carry out location-specific research in conditions of fragile soils, scarcity of irrigation water, diversity of crops, and vagaries of climate. Most of the countries in the region cannot afford such a system on their own, and its introduction therefore requires much greater co-operation among them. Such co-operation may also make it possible to establish strong links with the international agricultural research centres affiliated to the CGIAR and to develop and test technologies. Special attention should be given to women as major food producers in terms of training, extension, access to inputs and credit.

Sound management of the environment is a condition for sustainable agricultural development. In the past, the technologies used in some areas to secure rapid increases in output and profits have been highly destructive of soil, water, and forests. Accordingly, agricultural research should give priority instead to identifying techniques that are likely to enhance yield, that are compatible with local farming conditions, and that can be applied over long periods, especially in tropical and sub-tropical regions, without damage to the environment.

In this regard, it is worth noting the increased interest in organic farming, spurred by growing concern about the environment, in many countries of the North. Recent research points to its competitiveness vis-à-vis chemical-based agriculture and its ability to meet food requirements in an environmentally sustainable manner. The traditional expertise of the South can thus become a great asset as organic farming becomes part of the mainstream of world agricultural techniques.

As important as the strengthening of research to benefit smallholders is the building-up of effective agricultural extension systems that encourage the adoption of new technologies and that provide a mechanism for monitoring their effectiveness in actual use. Extension techniques suited to smallholder conditions are required to overcome the natural caution of poor farmers who can ill afford to take risks with new farming practices. To promote the wide use of new technologies, risk-sharing schemes, credit support, and an assured supply of such inputs as high-yielding seeds, fertilizers, and pesticides are also needed.

Farmers suffer heavy crop losses due to inadequate and inefficient systems of storage. In some countries, particularly in sub-Saharan Africa, crop losses, including the damage caused by pests, are estimated to be as high as 40 per cent of the total harvest. The introduction of improved post-harvest technologies, including simple but effective methods of pest control, and better on-farm and off-farm storage facilities, could thus substantially increase the supply of food. As women have the principal responsibility for the storage of crops in many countries, special efforts will have to be made to ensure that women benefit from support measures, especially training and investment.

Smallholders' limited access to institutional credit has been a principal barrier to their adoption of new technologies. It has been estimated that in the mid-1980s only 5 per cent of farmers in Africa and 15-20 per cent in Asia and Latin America had access to formal credit. Credit in rural areas is in many countries still provided by money-lenders and traders, often at usurious interest rates. Such sources may be useful in an emergency but are hardly suitable for financing agricultural development. There is thus a clear need to expand the availability of credit at reasonable rates. Such credit facilities can be provided in a variety of ways: encouraging banks to expand their operations in rural areas and establishing specialized institutions for rural credit; helping rural communities, and within them especially women, to transform their traditional savings and loan institutions into more formal financial organizations; relaxing the stringent eligibility criteria applied by most lending institutions and introducing forms of collateral that are not property-based (e.g. group guarantees); simplifying lending procedures in order to reduce transaction costs; and the promotion of grass-roots institutions to help in the administration of credit and improve the viability of rural credit schemes.

Price incentives

The agricultural terms of trade are an important determinant of the distribution of income between rural and urban areas; there is also considerable evidence that small-peasant agriculture responds to price incentives within the limits of its technological capacity. In the past, policies on tariffs, exchange rates, and domestic prices have often discriminated against agricultural producers, including peasant farmers. Effective protection for agriculture has been low or negative in many developing countries because of high protection for industries; overvalued exchange rates and domestic-price policies have reinforced this bias against farming and discouraged the cultivation of food and other crops. A policy framework that offers farmers adequate incentives to increase production is essential for agricultural progress and moving towards food security.

Off-farm employment

In a number of developing countries where a large proportion of the rural poor have no land, the scope for land redistribution is limited by its scarcity and the already small size of holdings. Therefore, the provision of off-farm employment, both in productive public works and in rural industries, must figure prominently in any strategy for promoting food security in countries with a large mass of landless people who cannot be given land or employment in the modern sectors of the economy. We shall come back to this issue in the discussion on industrial policy.

Food subsidies

Food subsidies and food rationing have been widely used as a means of making food readily available to the poor. In China in the 1950s, rationing was vital in ensuring adequate food supplies for large masses of people. Cuba used food rationing to attain what are among the highest levels of nutrition and health in all Latin America. However, their experiences also confirm that, in achieving sustained improvements in food security, a crucial role was played by structural and policy reforms to enhance human capabilities and enable the rural poor to increase their output of food and other basic goods.

The experience with food subsidies has in fact been a mixed one. Their successful use is circumscribed by administrative weakness. They place a heavy burden on public finances, and there have been instances where the combination of growing budget deficits, rapid increases in demand for food, and inelastic supplies has eventually led to the breakdown of the food distribution system. The high cost of subsidies also reduces the resources that can be spent on the infrastructure and services needed to enable the rural poor to increase food production and the urban poor to raise their nutritional standards.

In addition, the benefits of subsidies may easily 'trickle up' to the upper-income sections of the population unless they are effectively targeted to low-income groups. One way of avoiding this risk is to subsidize nutritious but so-called low-prestige foods, such as cassava, beans, and coarse grains, which are consumed mostly by the poor. Food subsidies must be closely integrated with nutritional programmes, priority being given to the special needs of women and children, who, both in numbers and in severity, suffer the most from malnutrition and poverty.

Strengthening a Broad-Based Industrialization

The need to promote industrialization in the developing countries remains as strong as ever. Only rapid industrial development can create the resources to satisfy the basic requirements of their populations for food, health, education, and shelter, and to provide jobs for their growing labour force. Along with the development of a mass internal market for basic goods and the strengthening of forward and backward linkages within the national economy, these countries will also need to rapidly expand manufactured exports in order to strengthen their balance of payments and make their economies less vulnerable. In today's highly competitive international economy, success in this task will be vitally linked to the modernization of their industrial and technological base, and thus to their efficiency in using, absorbing, and diffusing knowledge-intensive methods and processes of production within industry.

To achieve these objectives, developing countries need to improve on their previous industrialization strategies, which have often been inappropriate to their own needs and resources. Sometimes, the industries established were not well-adapted to local conditions and skills, made little or inefficient use of domestic resources, and required a high level of imports and energy inputs. Appropriate links with agriculture and regional balance in industrial development were, in particular, neglected. Further, industries often relied too heavily on a sheltered domestic market and failed to seize opportunities in international markets, with negative consequences in terms of economies of scale, technical change, and learning processes. Inadequate attention was paid to the possibility of setting up multinational enterprises of the South to serve regional markets.

In many cases, protection by high trade barriers was given to local enterprises, often linked with, or owned by, transnational corporations, producing for a small domestic market constituted by a minority of the population, and making little contribution to exports. Even though this pattern of industrial growth temporarily boosted production and employment, its potential was soon exhausted. Because the industries in question made heavy demands on energy supplies and on the urban infrastructure and relied largely on imported inputs and capital goods as well as on high protective tariffs—with the consequence that production and modernization proceeded at a slow pace—this pattern of industrialization became unsustainable.

Particular importance needs to be attached to industry's links with agriculture. The rapid expansion of the cultivation of food crops can be facilitated by industrialization. Expanding agricultural activity generates increasing demands on the industrial sector, especially in large agrarian economies. It requires a growing supply of tools and implements, consumer goods, and services, from the manufacturing and other sectors of the economy to the farmers. To eradicate rural poverty in countries with high population density or rapid population growth, it is also necessary to create employment on a large scale not only in agriculture but also in other activities, particularly manufacturing and construction of infrastructure.

An important part of such new industry need not be capital-intensive and could be located in rural areas, as was done, for example, in China and other East Asian economies. Rural industries can be highly efficient in promoting labour-intensive processes and the processing of local resources. More generally, the spread of small industries throughout the countryside and the improvement of infrastructure in rural areas are key elements of efforts to reduce disparities of income and wealth and to create a better balance of economic opportunities between urban and rural areas. At the same time, rural industries should give greater emphasis to the production of consumer articles and agricultural inputs adapted to local conditions. A mechanization of agriculture phased in more rationally than in past attempts would not only contribute to broad-based improvement of agricultural productivity but also to industrial development. The production of simpler, modern agricultural tools and implements would be an activity suitable for small-scale industries, which as they expanded would in turn add to the reservoir of industrial skills and create employment opportunities.

Economic efficiency and technological dynamism have remained relatively neglected goals of industrial policy in all but a few developing countries. Overcentralized and bureaucratic planning mechanisms, lack of consistency between sectoral and macroeconomic policies, and disregard of recognized economic principles often provided inadequate incentives to reduce costs and improve quality. They also led to inefficient use of capital and energy and a slow rate of technical advance. An important objective of policy reforms should be to correct these distortions.

The State's promotional policies in the industrial field have often relied too heavily on indiscriminate tax incentives, subsidized credit, or protection against imports. In many cases these concessions have been granted as giveaways and not made conditional on satisfactory performance; the results have been to bestow unfair benefits on a favoured few at the taxpayer's expense, to place an additional burden on public finances, and to retard advances in technology and learning processes within the private sector. In a number of cases, incentives like tax holidays have been given to benefit special interests and have not been governed by objective economic considerations. These approaches have also made it difficult for governments to adapt policies to changed conditions and priorities. The end result has been misallocation of resources, inadequate creation of employment, and the waste associated with the failure fully to exploit economies of scale, defeating the whole purpose of the government's industrial policy. An end to this system of indiscriminate protection and subsidization must be high on the agenda for reform in economic policy.

The poor record as regards the creation of employment has been a particularly serious shortcoming of past development processes, and it is closely related to the neglect of economic efficiency. Generating sustainable employment for the massive and ever-increasing underemployed and unemployed labour force is fundamental to a people-centred development approach. This requires the promotion of innovative mechanisms to fulfil the people's right to a livelihood.

Even though it will be necessary to introduce capital intensity in many parts of the industrial structure, future policies need to promote the adoption of labour-intensive methods more purposefully so as to enhance the employment benefits of industrial growth and its multiplier effects on the rest of the economy. A shift in industrial output towards mass consumption goods can by itself increase labour intensity and employment in industry as well as reduce its foreign exchange requirements. A reform of industrial incentives to favour small-scale and labour-intensive enterprises, together with research aimed at reducing dependence on capital-intensive technology, is also an important ingredient of strategies designed to increase employment in the industrial sector.

Another defect of past approaches was that industrial development was often unevenly distributed within countries, causing regional imbalances which tended to accentuate the adverse social and environmental effects associated with industrialization. An industrialization process that takes advantage of opportunities for creating rural industries and small and medium-sized enterprises can help to achieve a better balance in industrial development. Specific measures are also needed to avoid the concentration of economic activity in large urban centres and to promote its dispersal to small and medium-sized cities.

Development of Service Industries

Developing countries should seek to make use of the expanding opportunities in the service industries. These constitute, as in developed countries, a large sector in the South. They are important not only in the informal sector but also in such areas as tourism, finance, construction, and communications. The contribution that efficient service industries can make to economic growth by providing a wide range of services at low cost to the productive sectors–agriculture and industry–is now fully recognized.

Recent progress in science and technology has also opened up new areas in the service sector that developing countries should fully exploit. Advances in telecommunications and informatics not only contribute to making production processes more efficient, but also represent new poles for rapid growth. The mastery and widespread use of these technologies is essential for maintaining the South's competitiveness in the world market. Opportunities are also expanding for international trade in services, and a few developing countries have achieved some success in exporting services related to construction and other contractual services and even in such high technology areas as computer software and data processing.

Trade Strategies for Development

Export growth and diversification

In many developing countries it has become imperative to diversify exports and to accelerate the rate of growth of manufactured

exports. The importance of export performance to economic recovery and industrialization has become more visible as the scarcity of foreign exchange has become the major obstacle to
economic growth. Imports have already been so compressed as to
leave little scope, in the short term, for foreign exchange savings
through additional reductions in imports.

Current world economic conditions are aggravating the unequal relations between North and South and are less favourable
to the expansion of manufactured exports from the South than in
the 1960s or 1970s. However, even in the depressed and adverse
international environment of the 1980s, the developing countries
were able to expand exports of manufactures–and to increase
their market share in these exports. Part of this increase was
forced by the contraction of the domestic market in semi-industrial countries such as Brazil and Mexico, but the experience nevertheless indicates that there are still considerable opportunities
for manufactured exports in international markets. Export opportunities can grow further as economic recovery in the South
widens and advances are made in South-South co-operation.

Past experience suggests that success in exporting depends on
a range of internally consistent policies. A stable and predictable
macroeconomic framework and, in particular, a realistic exchange rate are vital to the promotion of manufactured exports.
The experience with trade policies, even though it continues to be
a controversial subject, provides at least two major lessons. First,
as the experiences of rapid growth in industry and exports in East
Asia show, protection of the domestic market is not inconsistent
with export success. In these economies, because industrial protection was flexible and frequently adjusted to changing conditions and priorities, it became, in a dynamic setting, an important
component of the industrialization and export strategy. These export-led growth experiences of the post-war period are in fact best
described as processes of 'circular and cumulative causation' between export, productivity, and output growth, in which import
substitution, growth of the domestic market, and export dynamism all reinforce each other through the interplay of increasing returns, domestic and foreign competition, and rising managerial
and technical skills.

The second lesson is provided in particular by the less successful export record of several Latin American countries.   Where

they are sheltered by heavy and indiscriminate protection, industries have no incentive to look for export markets. Protection, in fact, works as an implicit tax on exports, which, unless compensated by equally costly export subsidies, can seriously impede the growth of manufactured and other exports. In such circumstances, there is certainly need to reduce gradually the levels of protection, to rationalize protection in line with the perceived long-term comparative advantage in the economy, and to ensure that the tariff and exchange rates do not discriminate against exports.

Where strategies of export promotion have been successful, their successes have been considerably facilitated by the creative involvement of the public sector, reflected in the establishment or encouragement of export promotion institutions, the opening-up of marketing channels, as well as a supportive framework of industrial policy and public investments. Indeed, industrial policy often played an active role in promoting domestic competition, offering incentives to technical advance and export expansion, and in periodically varying the pattern of investment in line with the changes in long-term comparative advantage. In addition, such successes as have been achieved through export-based industrialization have often been closely linked to the evolution of an institutional structure, including facilities for scientific, technological, and industrial research, as well as the expansion of vocational training and university education to meet the rising demand for skilled workers, technicians, and engineers.

Trade policy in small economies

The development of exports is especially important in small countries, which, owing to their limited domestic markets, must necessarily rely on trade and specialization in order to achieve economic development. They are also less likely than large countries to face demand constraints on the expansion of their exports, given their small size within the world economy. Some of these countries possess a great potential for export industries based on the processing of agricultural products or other natural resources. The export earnings of such industries initially help to make up for the lack of a domestic sector producing capital and intermediate goods by providing the foreign exchange with which to pay for imported technology and other inputs. The same applies to exports of labour-intensive products which, as shown by the experience of several developing countries, can lead the growth of industry and employment in countries with larger populations but less well endowed with natural resources.

The development experience of very small states in the South illustrates particular and persistent handicaps which require special attention. Preferential economic arrangements, favourable location, or the potential for such activities as mining, tourism, and fisheries, combined with sound economic management and open economic systems, have enabled some small states to overcome constraints imposed by their limited domestic markets, the high per capita costs of installing and maintaining infrastructure, and of providing specialized services.

However, in general, small developing countries have experienced difficulty in diversifying their economic structures to the point where they could lay the foundations for self-sustaining and stable development. Thus, not unusually, even relatively high levels of per capita income coexist with dependence on a few industries. Specially in countries with a population of around a million or less, this leads to the persistence of instability and vulnerability. In such circumstances, there is a strong case for economic integration with other small states in the same region which should then jointly seek to enter into stable trading arrangements with major trading partners.

Import substitution

A stronger emphasis on export promotion should not, however, lead to the neglect of the scope for industrialization through import substitution.   Agricultural progress and the expansion of manufactured exports will generate, over time, a greater demand for industrial products. In the initial stages of economic expansion, this growing demand will be filled or partly filled by imports, but in time it becomes difficult to sustain an adequate flow of imports, especially in the less industrialized countries with large needs and limited capacity to step up exports.   Simultaneous efforts to establish or enlarge domestic industries capable of satisfying the growing demand for industrial products assume greater importance. Moreover, in the longer term, success in fostering a dynamic manufacturing export sector and in diversifying the pattern of exports is crucially linked to diversification in the internal economic and industrial structures, and to changes in the size and composition of local resources, including technological capabilities. Import substitution is part of this process of transformation. A country cannot export manufactures without building the capacity to produce them, and for this purpose import substitution can provide the necessary impulse. It would be naive to expect developing countries, in particular those which are struggling with basic production problems, to become fully-grown exporters of manufactures unless they first set up industries to manufacture goods to replace imports.

Past experience shows, however, that import substitution policies have to be improved. Industries to be promoted need to be carefully assessed to determine their suitability in the current state of the country's development and the prospects of securing a comparative advantage in international trade over a reasonable time. Permanent and indiscriminate protection should be avoided, for it might aggravate income disparities, discriminate against agriculture and exports, or create monopolies. Moreover, a greater emphasis has to be placed on forward-looking policies relating to the development of human resources and to science and technology, rather than on mere trade protection.

Accordingly, the reform of industrial and trade policies should be tailored to the need both to develop a dynamic manufacturing export sector and to make sustained efforts at efficient import substitution. The pace and timing of reforms should, of course, take into account the economic situation and industrial strength of the country concerned, both of which vary greatly from one country to another.

THE DEVELOPMENT OF HUMAN RESOURCES

Social deprivation remains widespread in the developing world, in spite of substantial improvements during the post-war period in health care, literacy, and education. Almost half of the developing world's children are still not protected by immunization against communicable diseases. In the rural areas of the developing world, nearly two-thirds of families are still without safe drinking water and an even higher proportion is without adequate sanitation. The proportions in urban areas are of the order of one-quarter and two-fifths. With present trends in enrolment and drop-out rates in primary schools, the children–especially girls–of the poorest 15-20 per cent of families in the South are not likely to become literate.

This state of affairs can and should be remedied. The obstacles to remedial action derive from social and cultural as well as economic factors. There are, however, three aspects in the design of policies to which attention needs to be drawn. First, there is the absence of delivery systems to reach the very poorest, particularly in regions that are remote and badly served by roads. In these cases access to health care and education, as well as to water supplies and sanitation, is often sadly deficient. Second, in most developing countries there is a skewed distribution of the benefits of social expenditures. The pyramid of access to social services is such that the people in the upper-and middle-income groups in the urban areas benefit most from public social spending. Third, in the pursuit of modernization there is a tendency to neglect traditional systems of knowledge and indigenous practices which could be cost-effective in providing some basic social services.

These shortcomings are interconnected and reflect the low social and political weight of the rural poor. Often the establishment of a modern hospital or technical college in an urban centre takes priority over the provision of health and educational services to a remote rural region. Especially in low-income countries, the scarce resources devoted to social services tend to be concentrated on urban areas. However, if this tendency is unchecked, the result can be a vicious circle. The lack of services in rural areas accelerates the drift to the cities, as the rural poor migrate not only to look for employment but also to secure access to education and health services and a better life for their children. This influx adds to the pressure on schools, clinics, and other social services–and to overcrowding–in the towns. The end result can be seen in many semi-industrial countries in the South: chaos and squalor in the towns while rural areas remain severely deprived of social services.

Breaking this vicious circle requires a committed effort to improve education, health services, water supplies, and sanitation in the rural areas. In middle-income countries, what is called for is a more balanced distribution of public expenditure on social services so that cities are not favoured at the expense of the villages. In low-income countries, with fewer resources, the establishment of efficient delivery systems becomes crucial. Changes in this sphere should, however, be only one element in the redirection of development policies towards the rural poor; their impact would be small if other development policies had a contrary thrust.

Besides their major role as a vehicle of social progress, the development of human resources and the provision of basic public goods invariably broaden an economy's resource base and strengthen its capacity to achieve economic growth. It is true that not all the great advances in the satisfaction of basic needs in the past led to an outstanding pace of economic growth. But there is evidence that the fastest-growing countries in a given period and within a given per capita income group typically had higher than average levels in the development of human resources (especially in education) at the beginning of the period. Large investments on human resources also tended typically to speed up growth performance in comparison with periods preceding such investment.

Universalization of Primary Health Services

The provision of primary health services available to all requires a comprehensive set of measures. Delivery systems to reach more of the rural and low-income urban population are of special importance, as is the education of the community in nutrition and in the prevention and control of common diseases. Other requirements include the availability of community health workers; immunization against the main communicable diseases; control of locally endemic diseases; the provision of essential drugs and basic complementary services such as safe water, sanitation, and maternal and child health services.

Some of these objectives can be achieved without very heavy expenditure. Diarrhoea and a few diseases preventable by vaccines–measles, neonatal tetanus and whooping cough–cause almost half the child deaths in the world and are probably responsible for half of all cases of malnutrition of children. There are cheap vaccines that provide immunity against these diseases, and oral rehydration is a low-cost remedy for diarrhoea. The supply of clean drinking water can also greatly contribute to the improvement of health.

While some items in the package may be relatively inexpensive, the provision of universal primary health services on a permanent basis will involve large outlays of financial resources. According to the World Health Organization (WHO), primary health could be provided at an annual cost of $10 to $15 per person. This is more than the average now spent on health care in the developing world, especially in the low-income countries of Africa and Asia. The severe scarcity of resources makes it all the more obligatory that there should be tighter priorities in health planning and greater attention to cost-effective delivery. In several countries, efforts to copy systems of developed countries centred on hospitals and curative services, with inadequate emphasis on primary care and preventive medicine, accentuate the consequences of resource constraints and reduce the impact of the actual expenditure. The capacity to provide universal primary health care will be enhanced if, along with wider delivery systems, there is a graded and more equitable pattern of charges for health services.

In the provision of health care, countries of the South should consider making greater use of systems of traditional medicine, especially those based on medicinal plants. These systems are widespread in the South but need encouragement if they are to develop further. In particular attention must be given to placing traditional medicine on a scientific basis, and measures should be taken to protect the plant wealth of developing countries.

Expanding Educational Opportunities

Primary schooling has made striking progress in the South. Since 1950, gross enrolments at the primary-school level have increased sharply in all developing regions. The goal of universal primary education remains, however, unattained. On present trends, according to United Nations projections, not all children of primary school age–and this applies particularly to girls–will be in school by the year 2000 in a large number of countries in Africa and South Asia, and in several countries in other developing regions.

The progress already achieved strongly suggests, however, that the objective of universal primary education is fully attainable within a decade. Its achievement will require giving it top priority in public expenditure; it is also vitally linked to advances in the social status of women. But in the 1980s school enrolment rates fell and the number of children dropping out of school rose because of increasing poverty; this reverse makes it all the more urgent to take action in support of a sustainable recovery of growth. In addition, such action should be accompanied by measures to make curricula more relevant to the basic economic, social, and cultural needs of society.

High rates of illiteracy in many countries reflect not only inadequate school enrolments but also the persistence of adult illiteracy. Nevertheless, experience suggests that it is realistic to aim at universal literacy. Through large-scale literacy programmes several developing countries have greatly reduced illiteracy among adults; parental literacy has in turn helped to raise school enrolments. Tanzania, for example, has lifted the literacy rate from 30 per cent in 1971 to 90 per cent today through adult literacy programmes using retired teachers, primary school teachers, specially trained primary-school leavers, and students finishing secondary school.

The expansion of secondary and higher education has also been rapid, and most countries have significantly narrowed the educational gap with the North. Secondary-level enrolment rates comparable to those of developed regions (and close to 100 per cent) have, in fact, been reached by a few countries, notably Cuba, Yugoslavia, and the newly industrializing economies of East Asia. The enrolment rate in tertiary education for males in these Asian economies is even significantly above the average in the developed countries (38 versus 33 per cent). Overall, however, the educational gap between North and South remains large. A target of at least 75 per cent for the gross enrolment rate in secondary schools by the year 2000 appears attainable for many developing countries, especially in Latin America and Asia.

Besides improving enrolments, most developing countries need to raise the quality of secondary and higher education and to adapt it to development needs. Insufficient attention has been given to the importance of fostering a science and technology culture through the educational system. Education has too often continued on the lines set in the past, and has been too academic and unsuited to the scientific, vocational, and other needs of societies in the process of modernization. This is not a call for inculcating purely materialistic values; education should aim at producing young people who are not alienated from their own culture and community but are equipped to contribute to, and benefit from, the progress of their societies.

University education of a high standard is an important instrument of modernization and development. However, under pressure to accommodate more students, universities have tended to neglect quality. A further point to be taken into account is that, as costs per student rise substantially at higher educational levels, the educational budget comes under strain. The pace of expansion and the improvement in quality of advanced education may therefore be limited by the shortage of resources, especially in countries with severe budgetary constraints and rapid population growth. Hence university expansion will have to be carefully planned and linked to development needs and priorities. Distance education could be a cost-effective way of satisfying some of the demand for higher education.

The strengthening of educational systems–essential for narrowing the knowledge gap with the North–will thus require giving high priority to a number of tasks. Progress in literacy and primary education needs to be accelerated, ensuring especially the full incorporation of girls into the school system. The reform of curricula, particularly to foster technical and scientific skills at all educational levels, will be needed to adapt education to society's economic and cultural requirements. More generally, a committed effort must be undertaken to raise educational standards, especially at secondary and higher levels, where the distance from the developed world is most evident and growing. Only then will there be a sound basis for accelerated development and sustained social progress in the South.

Implementing Population Policies

Rapid population growth presents a formidable challenge for most developing countries. The developing countries as a group have the most dynamic demography in the world and, by the end of the century, will have four-fifths of the total world population. However, demographic trends vary greatly in the developing world. In Asia as a whole, population growth has declined to below 2 per cent a year; it is expected to proceed in the 1990s at rates of around 1.2 per cent a year in China, 1.7 per cent in South Asia and the rest of East Asia, and 2.9 per cent in West Asia. In most of Latin America too, rates of population growth are on the decline and are expected to average around 1.9 per cent a year in the 1990s. The trend in most of Africa, in contrast, is still upward, with rates of over 3 per cent a year forecast for the 1990s in sub-Saharan Africa.

Past trends in population will be mirrored in the evolution of the size of the labour force and in the changing structure of the population. The South's labour force is expected to continue growing at the high annual rate of about 2.3 per cent up to the year 2000, subject, however, to great regional diversity. While in China the labour force will grow at about 1.2 per cent a year, it will grow at around 2 per cent in South Asia and the rest of East Asia, 2.4 per cent in Latin America, and at a rate reaching or exceeding 3 per cent in West Asia, North Africa, and sub-Saharan Africa. The age structure of the population by the year 2000 will also show wide differences. The child-dependency ratio (children up to 14 years in relation to the population of working age, i.e. 15-64 years) is expected by then to range from over 70 per cent in sub-Saharan Africa and West Asia, 50 to 60 per cent in Latin America, South Asia, and North Africa, to a low 40 per cent or less in East Asia and the developing countries of Europe. In developed countries, the ratio is expected to drop to nearly 30 per cent.

Demographic trends are responses to economic, social, and cultural factors. The vibrant demography of the South is the outcome of its achievements in raising life expectancy and reducing mortality, in particular infant mortality, combined with persistently high fertility. The wide interregional variations in population growth are also in a way consistent with the great differences in population size and density. With its area and natural resources, Africa has the potential to accommodate a much larger population than at present, in contrast, for example, to most of Asia and several Latin American countries. However, in view of the limited availability of financial resources, and of good quality land in several of its countries, action to moderate population growth is a compelling need even in Africa.

A rapidly increasing population strains the capacity of the economy to provide enough and adequate jobs. For as the number of job-seekers swells, the resources available for creating more jobs shrink. Through its effects on the age distribution within the population, fast demographic growth leads to the situation in which each working person bears a much higher burden of dependency (in terms of demand for food, health care, housing, and schooling) than in countries where the population is growing less fast.

In addition, even though population growth may not be an ultimate cause of poverty, it can drastically impair a country's ability to develop its human capital. Advances in the development of human resources–education, training, health–are of a cumulative nature; past investments create better conditions for later improvements and, vice versa, past neglect compounds the difficulties for the future. Accordingly, where population growth outstrips a country's capacity to develop its human resources, the consequence can be a vicious circle of stagnation and underdevelopment.

The rate of population growth tends to decline as a country becomes more prosperous. But some recent experience in the developing world suggests that a steep decline in fertility can occur in countries at different levels of economic development. The observed decline is attributable to a combination of greatly improved rates of child survival, expanded family planning services, rising educational levels among young girls and, more generally, to advances in the social and economic status of women. Higher rates of child survival improve the predictability of the family's life cycle and encourage parents to adopt family planning practices. Access to family planning services also has a strong effect in the transition to lower fertility rates, as is shown by the high levels of contraceptive use achieved in some poor countries. Educated women and women with their own income and assets tend to delay having children, reducing their child- bearing span. Educated mothers are also better able to care for their children's health and to use contraceptive methods. Changes in male attitudes are, however, also important, and efforts to encourage population planning need to be directed to men as well as women.

The emphasis on checking excessive population growth should be accompanied by attention to the distribution of the population, often concentrated in areas ill-equipped in terms of natural resources or public services. The problem of population pressure in urban areas is acquiring very serious proportions in the South. Ceaseless migration to the cities–the result of both greater economic opportunities in urban areas and poor living conditions in the countryside–has strained the life-supporting capabilities of urban centres. This has happened at a time when public finance to expand public utilities and social services is becoming increasingly limited. Policies offering effective incentives and disincentives to encourage a balanced distribution of population should be vigorously pursued as a matter of priority.

In sum, a strong commitment to slowing down population growth through integrated population and human resource planning can bring large personal and social benefits in most developing countries. High priority for the improvement of child survival rates, expansion of female education, improvement in the economic and social position of women, and the rapid extension of family planning services are the key strategic elements. Their results would be of immediate and direct benefit to couples who, by exercising their preferences, are able to gain greater control over their own lives. But indirect major benefits would also accrue to society as a whole. As population pressure eases, social services, investments in human resources, and employment opportunities can all be increased.

Social Indicators

A strong commitment to improving human resources implies that government policies should be designed and systematically assessed in terms of social goals and achievements. Rather than focusing on increases in the gross domestic product as the central objective and using it as the main measure of development, such a commitment requires the formulation and evaluation of development policies to be guided by a wide array of social and economic indicators which adequately encompass social welfare and human development in their widest sense.

The impact of the crisis of the 1980s in many developing countries has made the need for more effective development indicators and their use in policy design and evaluation increasingly felt and accepted. In some countries, many statistics of social indicators are compiled and analysed, and various indicators of welfare, quality of life, human and community development, environmental quality, etc. are being proposed. Valuable work has been carried out in several United Nations agencies which have issued guidelines and handbooks on social indicators. A useful contribution to the definition of social indicators has also been made by a meeting of experts convened in Caracas in 1989 by the government of Venezuela and the South Commission.

The basic concerns of the Caracas meeting in outlining an alternative set of development indicators were:

- To facilitate the social mobilization of the poor so as to increase their own participation in the management of basic services.

- To provide timely feedback and tools of assessment to countries so that they could make their socio-economic and environmental policies more effective.

- To challenge the traditional terms and definitions still being used in global discussions on development.

- To examine new options for development paths, since it is widely agreed that those followed by the countries of the North cannot be replicated in the South.

- To increase the bargaining power of the South over adjustment policies so that their harmful effects could be mitigated.

For development performance to be effectively assessed in relation to the wider goals of development, priority should be given to the gathering, on a regular and timely basis, of the minimum information needed to identify geographic areas and social groups at high risk. Such basic indicators as infant mortality, weight at birth, and ratios of weight and height to age, for which the data are relatively easy to compile, are capable of being broken down by sex, geographic area, and economic and social group. They have proved extremely useful to several countries in taking action to protect vulnerable sections of the population.

Countries with the ability to establish larger databases can go beyond this basic information to compile other indicators, including composite indicators. These may cover such determinants of the social situation as nutrition and health, education, water and sanitation, housing, status of women, child development, employment and income, and public safety. At the same time, efforts should be made to improve or complement GDP indicators with a view to assessing structural trends in the incidence of poverty, income distribution, depletion of non-renewable resources, and environmental degradation.

STRATEGIES FOR SCIENCE AND TECHNOLOGY

The profound impact of the recent advances in science and technology in the North has created a more difficult setting for devising policies for science and technology in the South. It is incumbent on all countries in the South to make and sustain efforts over the longer term to improve their own capabilities in this field. The appropriate thrust and priorities may well vary from country to country, but a common, fundamental objective must be to enlarge the pool of scientifically qualified personnel without whom efforts at modernizing the societies of the South will be hobbled.

The efficient use of scientific and technological advances is essential for the economic development and social progress of the South. The absorption of knowledge-intensive techniques and the more efficient use of raw materials, energy, and labour are indispensable for increasing productivity and international competitiveness, and thus for the success of economic adjustment and restructuring in the South. A shift in the pattern of production and exports from raw materials to manufactures and, within the latter, to products with high and medium R&D intensity, is required to counteract the adverse consequences of the decline in the prices of the South's commodities, including oil.

In the near future, the South's own capacity to achieve breakthroughs in science can be expected to remain modest. Even in those developing countries which possess a substantial scientific and technological base, their ability to make a major contribution to world science will depend on their having the rare scientist of genius backed by advanced research facilities. The South will have to rely to a large extent on imported technologies for the purpose of modernizing and developing its economies for some time to come. Countries must be able to pick the technologies most appropriate to their circumstances and, in many cases, to adapt them to make them appropriate. The demands of economic growth are such that the South has to accelerate the pace of acquiring, adapting, and using the stock of technological knowledge built up in the North. But in the longer run, the South must also acquire an ability to develop by itself technologies suited to its need and factor endowment.

Science and technology need to be integrated effectively into national development plans and policies. The contribution that science and technology can make to development and the broad national priorities should be clearly spelled out. It must also be recognized that a nation cannot develop capabilities in science and technology without spending an irreducible minimum of resources. Very few countries of the South devote more than a meagre 0.5 per cent of their national income to research and development; by contrast developed countries allocate 2 to 3 per cent. The yawning gap in knowledge between the North and the South will get even wider unless the South greatly expands its allocations for research and development.

As already argued, the meaningful extension and use of R&D requires a critical minimum of investment. The experience of the developed world and needs of the South suggest that at least a doubling of the existing allocations for R&D in developing coun- ‧tries, is required. This would bring their level close to the 1 per cent of GNP recommended by UNESCO. This proposal does not imply a transfer of funds from the education budget; it rather envisages use of additional resources which could come from savings in defence spending and from external financing.

In regard to human capabilities, the goal should be at least to triple the number of scientists and engineers. This will require strengthening the educational system and, especially, raising the status of scientists in society. The existence of a scientific infrastructure, the availability of equipment, access to foreign literature, international contacts, and adequate remuneration and incentives are prerequisites for creative work and productive research, and for the development and application of science and technology. A sense of responsibility towards society on the part of the scientists and technologists is also needed. They should be committed to making efficient use of the available, limited resources, and to the efforts to solve crucial problems facing the countries of the South. Changes on these lines can reduce and perhaps even reverse the brain-drain from the South to the North.

A strong foundation in basic sciences is vital for the growth of applied science and technology. It has not been adequately appreciated in the South that a meaningful transfer of technology cannot take place unless the recipient countries develop their own capabilities in basic sciences. Thus an adequate stress on education in basic sciences, backed by an effective system of research, is an essential component of any genuine national policy for the development of science and technology. It is only through a sound system of education and research in basic sciences that countries can provide a secure foundation for training the scientists, engineers, technologists, and technicians whom the South will need in increasing numbers. Producing trained personnel on whose advice they can rely is also necessary if they are to be able to make the right choice of imported technologies, to adapt, absorb, and diffuse them in the production system, to ensure their efficient use, and in due course to develop a national capability to generate new technologies.

In order to achieve the necessary scientific and technical knowledge in any society, science teaching has to be given emphasis throughout the educational system. At primary level an understanding of what science is, deals with, and can achieve needs to be promoted; at secondary level much greater emphasis needs to be given to teaching mathematics and the basic elements of the core sciences. It is often weaknesses in these sectors which lead to the present situation in the South where–in comparison with the developed countries–a much higher proportion of students in higher education follow courses in the liberal arts and humanities than in science subjects.

There is an urgent need to reform the present systems of incentives and rewards so as to ensure that both at the secondary and university level an increasing proportion of students will opt for technical and professional courses. A larger percentage of students in the science and engineering disciplines would not only strengthen the scientific and economic basis of developing countries but also contribute to the decline of the high rate of unemployment among university graduates.

There is at present almost everywhere in the South a big gap between personnel having received middle-level technical and vocational training and highly trained professionals. Upgrading the required technological skills is usually specific to particular tasks and firms. Enterprises, both public and private, should therefore be encouraged through incentives to expand in-house and on-the-job training.

The experience of developing countries that have achieved rapid technological transformation underlines the strategic role played by a demand-specific concentration of domestic research and development closely interlinked with production units. Enlarged effort in this area will not yield commensurate results, however, unless it is integrated into national development planning, and inputs and outputs are carefully monitored. It will be particularly important to establish sectoral priorities. Also, financial institutions will need to provide special facilities for entrepreneurs seeking to harness new technologies for development. In some countries venture-capital funds can make an important contribution in this regard.

The priorities should reflect the level of development, resource endowment, and the thrust of future growth. There can be no single model for all countries. None the less, the first area to be developed will usually be classical low technology, followed by applied sciences provided that some expertise in basic sciences is already available. The last area to be developed will generally be science-based high technology. Yet, typically, large and medium-sized developing countries seeking to compete in the world market will have no option but to make simultaneous advances in all four areas of science and technology.

Sectoral priorities will also differ among countries. Large countries that are semi-industrialized and have medium level of income could aim at rapidly raising the research and development capacities in, say, chemicals and engineering and then move on to the production and application of new science-based technologies. Medium-sized countries with similar characteristics could start with technologies for producing consumer and intermediate goods before embarking on a few areas requiring high technology, e.g. electronics, pharmaceuticals, and transport equipment. Low-income countries, ranging from very small to large, for the most part do not have a significant industrial and technological base. They should give attention to the technology for modernizing and diversifying agriculture, processing agricultural or mineral products through medium and small industries, and for manufacturing farm implements, construction equipment, some chemicals including pharmaceuticals, and simple machine tools.

Thus in the design and implementation of science and technology policies, each country will have to prepare its own blueprints within the framework of a longer-term strategy. But whatever its size or characteristics, each country will need very rapidly to raise its ability to make the right technological decisions, for these decisions will shape its future. Critical factors for success are the recognition of the close interconnections among the different areas of science and technology–basic and applied science, low and high technologies–and the realization of advances in all of them.

Recent developments in high technologies have complicated the South's tasks by affecting production methods and processes even in conventional primary industries such as textiles, cement, iron and steel, petrochemicals, automobiles, and power generation. In importing capital goods, equipment, and technologies for these industries, developing countries need, to a greater extent than before, to guard against the danger of being burdened with obsolete, inefficient equipment. In future the choice of technologies will be even more difficult because even where the basic knowledge about these technologies is in the public domain, production processes can be outdated by the rapid incorporation of high technologies.

Since there are so many demands on scarce resources, both financial and human, the choices for most countries in the South are severely constrained. For the small low-income countries, the options are plainly limited; even the initial steps may prove very difficult. As discussed in the next chapter, these constraints can be eased if South-South co-operation is vigorously promoted. These countries can also benefit from the experience of other countries in the South that have achieved a measure of success in incorporating technological advances in their production systems.

THE STATE, PLANNING, AND THE MARKET

Achieving people-centred and self-reliant development depends on a nation's ability to harness and utilize the energies of its people. Development can be achieved only if a nation's people–its farmers, workers, artisans, traders, businessmen, entrepreneurs, and public officials–are able to use their energies creatively and discharge their functions effectively. This in turn is critically dependent on the establishment of efficient institutional mechanisms–both private and public–that enable all economic actors to play their roles. An important issue of policy that all nations need to address is what economic activities are best undertaken by the State and what are best left to the private sector.

In this context, it is necessary to make a distinction between three economic roles of the State:

- its responsibility for macroeconomic management
- its planning and regulatory role, through which it influences the allocation of resources in the public and private sectors
- its role as an entrepreneur

In all countries, the State alone can assume the responsibility for macroeconomic management. It has to apply fiscal, monetary, and trade policies designed to create a favourable environment for growth, while avoiding inflation and excessive external deficits. In most developing countries, it is a condition of consistent macroeconomic management that the State must be actively involved in certain strategic decisions of long-term importance, such as those influencing or determining the overall rate of investment and savings in the economy, the pace and direction of technical change, the expansion of basic social services, and balanced regional development.

In its planning and regulatory roles, the State may be able to achieve its objectives, in some cases, by using taxes or subsidies to influence market forces. In some other cases, it may have to use physical controls to achieve broad national objectives, such as preventing a concentration of industries in overcrowded urban areas, or it may have to invest directly in areas or activities where private enterprises are unable or cannot be relied upon to achieve the desired results.

There has hardly been a historical case of sustained economic growth and development without the active participation of the State as a regulator and promoter. By their very nature unregulated market systems pay little or no heed to such strategic areas as basic industries, health and education services, scientific and technological research, and the preservation of the environment and natural resources. It is particularly unlikely that the free play of market forces would result in the growth with equity that a people-centred development strategy seeks to achieve. Excessive reliance on market forces can lead to concentration of economic power and wider disparities in income and wealth, to the underutilization of resources, to unemployment and to the wastage of the savings potential, with the result that the pace of development and technical progress is retarded.

The extent to which the State engages directly in productive enterprises will depend upon the basic social philosophy, the capacity of the private sector, and the State's management capabilities. However, in many developing countries, the record of direct State management of enterprises in the productive sector has not been good. Whatever may have been the compulsions at an earlier stage in nation building, and whatever the social and political philosophies that bear on development strategies in the future, we believe that the role of the State as entrepreneur should now, for most developing countries, be more selective and discriminating as well as more efficient. These two objectives converge, for if the State's role becomes selective it has a better chance of becoming more efficient. Finally, it is in the interest of sustained economic growth that government intervention should not prevent enterprises from operating on the basis of normal economic principles conducive to their efficient functioning.

The roles of the State and the market will necessarily vary, and depend on the country's developmental stage and experience as well as its inherited set of social institutions. In countries that have yet to industrialize, or where the private sector is weak, the State's role may have to go beyond macroeconomic policy to launching and managing productive enterprises. In countries that have advanced in industrialization and have a dynamic private sector, the State, besides setting broad economic policies, may confine itself to charting the path of development, identifying and promoting sectors for new investment, encouraging entrepreneurship, and preventing unacceptable inequalities in economic power and in income.

There are, however, some common tasks that governments in all developing countries will have to undertake in pursuing the goal of people-centred development. Besides the creation of a stable, growth-oriented macroeconomic framework, these tasks include the promotion of economic efficiency and technical advance through improved planning mechanisms; the reform of the management of public systems; and the pursuit of policies for mobilizing resources and strengthening the performance of public-sector enterprises. For the State to undertake its varied development functions, a prior condition is, however, its own modernization.

The Modernization of the State

In many parts of the South the precursor to the modern State was the colonial State, which essentially served the interests of the metropolitan power. It needed to be thoroughly recast in order to serve the needs of newly independent nations. Some countries have succeeded in this task. They have built up the machinery of a modern State adapted to the needs of their particular society and culture, enabling them to pursue their developmental goals effectively.

Other countries have been less successful. Often the State has become an arena for social conflict, and therefore powerless to discharge its developmental function. In many cases the State has failed to build up a cadre of civil servants, with sufficient training and skills and imbued with a spirit of public service, for the complex tasks of administration. In the 1980s, the budget cuts that were part of structural adjustment programmes further weakened the State's management capacities.

The modernization of the State will require a number of political and institutional reforms. The State is best able to perform its demanding functions when there is a national consensus on the goals and purposes of development, and on the apportionment of the costs as well as the benefits of development. Democratic institutions, which allow full participation and through which such a consensus can be reached, are therefore not only an objective of people-centred development, but its very means as well.

Participation in the political process means much more than the opportunity to exercise the vote. It means as well having a political climate that not merely tolerates dissent but welcomes it. Dissent is at their heart of participation, for participation must imply the right to say to the establishment in all spheres–'yes' or 'no' or 'but'.

There is a need to recognize to a greater extent than at present not only the right of the formal, political opposition to hold, and to advocate, another view, but also the right of all others in the society to do so. The system of political participation we envisage is one that is underpinned by an ethic that allows all ideas to contend. Of course, all democratic rights carry concomitant responsibilities. But the primary need is to keep the processes of political participation open at all levels. The South does not need help to do this, certainly not from the North where the record is not everywhere unblemished. The South has to act responding not to new fashions, but in its own self-interest in the cause of real development.

Accountability to the public, transparency of government activities, and an independent and honest judiciary are essential attributes of a democratic system. Accountability not only requires enforcement of the rule of law but the existence of independent systems for public evaluation of government conduct. It is important that the public should have access to information on the activities of the government. In this respect, the role of the media becomes vital.

Institutional reforms must include the drawing-up and enforcement of rules and regulations that unambiguously delineate the responsibilities and functions of government bodies. Civil service codes and regulations not only ensure that public servants are aware of their duties and rights, but also help greatly to foster an ethic emphasizing service to the citizenry and respect for the rule of law.

For the State to function effectively, government institutions must have resources adequate for their assigned activities. In the past, there have been many instances of the use of government funds for private ends. There have also been severe misallocations, with outlays on arms and on defence and security establishments outstripping expenditure on development.

There is a clear need in most countries of the South to realign national budgets so that the bulk of public expenditure is devoted to social and economic activities, without being wasted on the military and security services. Such a redistribution could enable State agencies to carry out their developmental functions more effectively. It could also release resources for training civil servants and for giving them incentives to upgrade their professionalism and capabilities.

There is also a need, we believe, for more open discussion of the extent of corruption and its detrimental effects on development and on society. This must be the basis for vigorous efforts to curb this growing evil. Measures that would greatly help these ef-

forts include the restoration of democratic processes and press
freedom where they have been impaired, avoidance of bureau-
cratization and over-regulation, firm action on narcotics traffic-
king, curbing militarism, and improving accountability and
control in areas such as public employment and private and public finance.

The Reform of Macroeconomic Policy

No country can make economic progress without reasonably stable macroeconomic conditions. Fiscal, monetary, and exchange
rate policies must be used to achieve a high level of savings and
investment while avoiding excessive balance-of-payments deficits
and controlling inflationary pressures. Such a macroeconomic
setting is essential to provide a reasonably predictable basis for
making economic decisions, particularly those relating to investments in new industrial and commercial undertakings, and therefore for continuing economic growth.

Past economic management in many developing countries often failed to reconcile these objectives, and this failure had highly
adverse consequences for their development. As a result of competing demands on public funds and the influence of various
pressure groups, budget deficits and credit creation have been allowed to grow in place of genuine redistributive policies and tax
changes to increase government revenues. This has proved to be
destabilizing. The resulting strains on the balance of payments
and the exchange rate and the consequent inflationary pressures
have not only distorted resource allocation and growth, fuelling
speculation in financial and other asset markets, but have also
had adverse effects on income distribution and the living standards of the poor. In short, sacrificing fiscal and monetary discipline has not served the cause of long-term development.

While the basic tasks of macroeconomic management are
fairly obvious, the maintenance of a sustainable external balance
together with reasonably stable prices and growth of aggregate
demand is subject to particular difficulties in developing countries. Fluctuations of aggregate demand in many countries, especially those with small and open economies, are often externally
generated through export and terms-of-trade shocks on their balance of payments. The scope for demand management through

fiscal and monetary policy is thus severely limited by balance-of-payments constraints; these can only be dealt with by an active and responsive management of exchange rates and trade policy. The postponement of action in these areas has in the past often created conditions calling for more abrupt and disruptive changes in policy later on.

The appropriate mix of exchange rate policy and trade restrictions depends on the particular country's circumstances and economic structures and the degree of openess of the economy. In the face of irreversible changes in external conditions, exclusive recourse to trade restrictions can be counter-productive as it delays the ultimately inevitable correction of the exchange rate and the transformation of internal economic structures.

In some cases, however, exclusive or even heavy reliance on adjustments in exchange rates may not be the most effective course of action. In particular, in the face of severe balance-of-payments shocks, there may be no level of the exchange rate which, in combination with fiscal and monetary policies, is able to reconcile the internal and external balance under a socially acceptable pattern of income distribution. In these circumstances, the use of trade restrictions is essential to moderate the negative effects of import reduction and prevent the further contraction of economic activity that would otherwise take place.

In addition, fiscal and exchange rate management needs to take into account the fact that the short-term consequences of currency devaluation in developing countries can be far from smooth. In some countries, depending on the nature of their exports and imports as well as the network of their financial relations with the rest of the world, sharp devaluations can have very severe effects on living standards, cause inflation, and lead to excessive idle capacity and rising unemployment. Moreover, the frequent devaluation of the currencies of commodity-producing developing countries can contribute to the persistence of excess supplies and depressed prices in commodity markets.

The procyclical pattern of capital inflows, whereby, for example, credit rationing in international financial markets becomes more acute at times of balance-of-payments difficulties, introduces an element of additional instability. This was exemplified in an extreme and crude form by the international debt crisis of the 1980s. The experience of this decade indicates that countries with capital controls are better equipped to face the growing instability of the international financial system. This recent experience also shows that the effectiveness of capital controls is linked, among other factors, to the effective eradication of macroeconomic imbalances.

Progress towards stabilizing the domestic macroeconomic framework encounters special difficulties in countries with entrenched high inflation, where inflation itself has become a determinant of the state of their public finances. In these cases restoring a stable macroeconomic framework may require an adjustment approach not based exclusively on fiscal and monetary measures. In particular, efforts at achieving broad agreement on incomes policies may be needed; but these in turn can only be effective if the costs and benefits of stabilization and adjustment are equitably shared among the different social groups. Without such precautions, as recent experience has shown, the pursuit of stability through fiscal and monetary discipline can lead to very considerable idle capacity and to rising unemployment, and still not contain inflation. In some cases, the establishment of pre-conditions for effective economic management may even involve–after years of successive failures to curb high inflation and cure stagnation–a broad-based social contract and the rebuilding of a rudely shaken national consensus about the goals and instruments of social and economic policies.

Reform of the Planning Process

An improved use of national resources, which is clearly essential for achieving development objectives in the South, is dependent on reforms in systems of development planning. A planning system needs to recognize the appropriate arenas for State intervention, the limits to the State's capacity to intervene effectively, and the contribution that a reformed price system can make to the realization of development goals. It must provide both a guide for direct State interventions and the mechanisms for steering private enterprise into selected areas of productive activity through various incentives and a judicious use of market signals.

In many countries, the planning processes so far used will have to be reformed in several ways if national planning is to become efficient. A primary aim in the reform of planning processes should be to achieve an appropriate balance between centralization and decentralization as well as between public control and private initiative. Centralization and discipline in macroeconomic management are essential to create a policy environment that is balanced, stable, and development-oriented. Similarly, public control at strategic points is necessary to ensure that scarce resources are not used wastefully. At the same time, there is great scope for changes in planning and regulatory mechanisms in order to enhance economic efficiency; to promote domestic competition, innovation, and technical progress; and to strengthen the ability of the various sectors of the economy to compete and seize opportunities in both domestic and international markets.

On the other hand, a measure of decentralization in economic management is needed to promote self-reliant and people-centred development. In the past a paternalistic approach to planning has inhibited participation at the grass-roots level, in both the design and the execution of development programmes. As the State, rather than society as a whole, is seen as the main agent of development, the result has been widespread apathy. Participation by the people can help to ensure that development activities, and the technologies, services, and inputs involved, are appropriate to the resources, skills, or environmental situation in the areas and communities they are meant to benefit. Without popular involvement, the absorption of new processes or the use of new facilities is likely to take longer, even where these are appropriate.

It is also evident from past experience that a 'top down' approach to planning and modernization can meet with resistance if it neglects to take account of local and traditional knowledge. Most countries possess time-tested reserves of indigenous knowledge and practices whose continued application, where necessary with adaptation, can enrich development and secure wider popular mobilization in support of development efforts. Through devolution and decentralization, development planning should build upon the reserves of knowledge and experience at the grass-roots level.

The Role of the Business Sector

Sustained growth and development require, moreover, the full and efficient participation of the business sector, including public enterprises, private firms, co-operatives, other socially-owned enterprises, and micro-businesses. The relative importance of these elements will vary from country to country. In those countries following a socialist development strategy, the role of the private sector may be less relevant. However, the successful examples of development in the South clearly show that economic growth is vigorous only in a climate in which the business sector, as defined above, can thrive.

The strengthening of an entrepreneurial business sector is linked to a number of factors. In the first place, the importance of the entrepreneurial function has to be recognized, and entrepreneurship has to be actively encouraged by the State. The State can give this encouragement through a variety of measures: training for aspiring entrepreneurs; promoting contacts and interaction between business leaders, politicians and public officials; attracting new industries by providing basic services–buildings, power supplies, technical and business advice–in e.g. industrial zones; the provision of venture capital on favourable terms; offer of tariff and other protection where appropriate; and information on market prospects for promising new areas for investment.

Secondly, the long-term success of the business sector is tied to stability and predictability in the environment in which it operates. In order that the environment should be conducive to the growth of entrepreneurship, there must be an assurance that laws and regulations will be consistently applied, and, as noted earlier, there must be a macroeconomic framework which allows economic calculations to be made with a high degree of certainty.

Thirdly, governments should take a hard look at the various promotional and regulatory laws governing activities, for it has been found that some regulations inhibit the efficient performance of business enterprises. Such laws and regulations should be simplified or modified and made transparent; equally, the conditions for providing incentives (or imposing sanctions) should be clearly laid down and tied to performance criteria. Successful industrial policies in the developing world clearly suggest that achievement should be rewarded with incentives carefully assessed and granted when specific targets, for instance in technical improvement or export expansion, are met.

The object in revising regulations should be to foster competition and technical modernization. Creativity and innovation require a careful balance of promotion and competition. Bureaucratic impediments can discourage productive investments and technical efficiency; they tend to create monopolistic situations even when that is not the intention, and so stifle entrepreneurial initiative, the lack of which is characteristic of underdevelopment.

In carrying out a people-oriented development strategy, governments should ensure that their policies towards the business sector do not ignore the part played in the South's economic life by micro-businesses—small household enterprises, non-household enterprises employing a few people, self-employed producer-vendors and traders. They produce, distribute, and sell a great variety of consumer articles, and provide a range of services, catering to the needs of the mass of the people. If policy-makers neglect the role of micro- businesses in economic activity—and their place in people-centred development—the economy and the community are deprived of the further benefits the informal sector can bring, and the informal sector itself becomes vulnerable to exploitation by the more powerful formal private sector through unregulated sub-contracting arrangements.

Strengthening Tax Systems and Public-Sector Enterprises

Sustained development in the future will require more determined action to mobilize domestic savings, particularly in the public sector. The modernization of peasant agriculture, for example, will necessitate a sharp increase in the share of investment allocated to agriculture in many countries. Large-scale investments will have to be made in rural infrastructure—irrigation, transport, credit, technical assistance, storage, research on technologies and farming systems—and in basic and technical education.

Similarly, since most basic social services, chiefly health care and education, are paid for out of public funds, progress in this area is also inextricably linked to the resources generated by the public sector. Based on the experience of low-income countries, recent World Bank estimates suggest that sub-Saharan Africa will need to double social expenditures from 4-5 per cent to 8-10 per cent of GNP in order to provide universal primary education, primary health care and family planning, food security, and nutrition by the year 2000.

Thus, in order to perform its central role in promoting development and, in particular, to achieve food security and offer basic social services to the entire population, the State must strengthen its capacity to mobilize the requisite resources. Institutional reforms and policies to make tax systems more efficient and public enterprises profitable are indispensable for this purpose.

Tax reform

The amount of tax revenue a government can raise is clearly dependent on the productivity of the economy and is also influenced by its own administrative capabilities. However, there is scope in many countries for the tax system to be reformed in ways that would produce higher responsiveness in tax revenues so that they grow faster than national income. In many developing countries systems of direct taxation, although seemingly progressive, with the rate of tax rising with income levels, are riddled with exceptions; they are also unduly complicated, seeking to promote too many objectives, and hence often beyond the capabilities of tax authorities to administer. Simpler systems may produce better results and also make tax systems fairer and more efficient even if they are nominally less progressive. It is also often possible to broaden the tax base, i.e. to enlarge the sources from which tax is collected. This will be the first step in some countries, especially in those where exports of primary products are a source of the bulk of tax revenue and where personal income tax is not levied or yields very little. The use of taxes on land, both as a source of revenue and as a lever for inducing owners to make more productive use of land, is another possible avenue for reform.

At the present stage in many developing countries indirect taxes will probably remain a principal source of public revenue. Any reform should aim for a system of indirect taxation that is both elastic and progressive, restrains conspicuous consumption, and does not discriminate against exports. The differentiation and reform of export taxes in order to encourage the local processing of raw materials and export of processed products assumes special significance in commodity-exporting countries. Promoting the economical use of exhaustible natural resources and the preservation of the environment should also be made important criteria in policy both on pricing and on taxation.

Public-sector enterprises

In most developing countries, the public sector has played a pioneering role in many basic and strategic industries. While examples abound of countries where the performance of State-run industries has been decisive in achieving rapid national development, there are others in which public enterprises have functioned well below their potential and been a drag on development. In the latter the failure of State undertakings to generate adequate internal resources has reduced the State's capacity to finance the expansion of social services or agricultural infrastructure or to launch new industries.

It is not the size of the public sector that accounts for these differences in performance. There are countries with large public sectors functioning efficiently and generating sizeable surpluses; there are others where much smaller public sectors have been much less successful. Experience points to the influence of market structures, organizational factors, and the relationships between the State and public enterprises as largely accounting for these differences.

Where public enterprises fail to make a profit, pricing policies or operational inefficiencies are generally to blame. In practice, the two are related, for defective pricing-policies affect efficiency, and poor efficiency affects prices. Enterprises in the public sector are generally not free to set their own prices. Government policies curbing the freedom of an enterprise to charge realistic prices for its products limit its earnings and therefore its ability to improve its productivity through further investment; this results in lower efficiency and keeps costs high.

In many countries the practice of keeping the prices charged by public-sector enterprises unduly low has in many cases amounted to subsidizing goods or services mainly consumed by people in the higher- and middle-income groups in the cities. Subsidized fuel for car owners and subsidized electricity for residential buildings for upper-income groups are examples. So is the plentiful supply of water to the richer quarters of a city, in contrast to a neighbouring slum where water is not readily available.

Many of the subsidies perform no distributive role in terms of improving equity and, as the examples cited show, in fact have the reverse effect by benefiting those who are well off. And they lead to public-sector losses which drain resources that could be used to meet more pressing social needs. Sometimes public-sector prices are misused in the often futile attempt to achieve short-term macroeconomic objectives like curbing inflationary tendencies. The obstacles to the overhaul of pricing policies are often political, and where this is the case, the need for political reform is all the more pressing.

In the sectors where major public enterprises usually operate, e.g. public utilities like energy supplies, operational inefficiency is often linked to their monopolistic status, for they are immune to competitive pressure to keep costs low. Where entry into the market by potential competitors is barred by licensing regulations or legal restrictions, however, there is scope for encouraging competition by changing the legislation or regulations.

Organizational factors also play a prominent part in influencing efficiency in the public sector. Where State-owned enterprises have been successful, they have generally had a high degree of managerial and financial autonomy, a manageable number of clear commercial and social objectives, and transparent accountancy, government control being exercised only in such strategic areas as the setting of economic and financial targets.

Conversely, the overlap of public-enterprise finances with the national budget, including a lack of transparency in cases where State-owned undertakings are made to sell goods or services at subsidized prices, has often led to unclear relationships and confusion of responsibilities. Similar effects result from the multiplicity of sometimes divergent objectives that public enterprises are called upon to achieve. Their lack of operational independence, due to political constraints on management and pricing decisions or to excessive, day-to-day control over input, employment, and investment decisions, aggravates problems of accountability and can, in the end, lead to a lack of concern with the efficiency of the enterprise as a whole.

Privatization

Developing countries have recently been under strong pressure to privatize State-owned enterprises as a means of curing inefficiency, and several countries have gone some way in this direction. The issue needs to be addressed without ideological bias. Rather, there needs to be in each case a careful consideration both of the costs and of the benefits of alternative policies, the social role that a public enterprise is discharging, and the capabilities of private enterprise within the country.

In some countries, the public sector has acquired a number of private enterprises that were facing bankruptcy, purely to avoid the laying-off of workers. There are, however, better ways of providing alternative employment and reducing the costs of a closure to the poor; in any case, the State cannot buy all private enterprises that are in trouble. Where an enterprise has been nationalized for such reasons, and is losing money and not performing any major social role, the State would, by returning it to private ownership, vesting it in a co-operative, or closing it down, give a clear signal that it would no longer subsidize inefficient undertakings.

In other cases, public enterprises were created to serve an important social objective, such as the development of a disadvantaged region, or to initiate the local development of a new economic activity. In the course of time, this pioneering function may have been fulfilled, and, depending on the state of local entrepreneurial capabilities, the enterprise may be sold to the private sector. In some circumstances, however, privatization may not be feasible; for example, if the public enterprise is the only major undertaking in a region and, on a private cost-benefit evaluation, no private enterprise would take its place. In these cases, the lack of infrastructure and other facilities is often the source of low operational efficiency.

There are also public enterprises that perform a crucial function in strategic industries. In some cases, public ownership may respond to the need to exercise national control over a critical natural resource, e.g. oil. In others, the private sector may lack the financial resources and organizational capability to take over responsibility from the public sector. In many cases, privatization would turn a public monopoly into a private one, and the need to avoid a private monopoly may have been the reason why a public enterprise was set up in the first place.

Privatization does not, therefore, offer an across-the-board solution. In some cases, privatization may lead to greater efficiency, particularly if the State's management capacities are severely limited. Yet it may be impractical or undesirable in some sectors, particularly those of strategic importance for the development process. In addition, past experience suggests that the efficiency of public and private enterprises is correlated. Both are greatly influenced by such factors as the dynamism of entrepreneurship, the institutional mechanisms for the use and allocation of resources, and the nature of the State itself.

THE GENDER DIMENSIONS OF DEVELOPMENT

Women account for more than half the South's population. They participate in the development process in a myriad ways, but their contribution to economic and social change continues to be inadequately recognized and greatly undervalued, because male-dominated cultures have given them an inferior position in society, and custom, taboo, and the sexual division of labour keep them subordinate to men.

Throughout the South, women's labour is vital to the production of goods and services. Now increasingly active in industry, women have throughout been widely involved in agriculture, particularly in the crucial area of food production, providing over half the agricultural labour force in the South. In Africa, for example, most adult women are engaged in agricultural activity, growing and processing the bulk of the food consumed, and marketing the surplus. In Asia and the Pacific, women's labour is important in occupations allied to agriculture and food production, such as fisheries and food processing, as well as in rural household industry. Throughout the developing world, rural women's activities in agro-forestry and soil-conservation schemes not only provide major support to food production, but also add to the environmental balance in ecosystems.

Likewise, in Latin America and the Caribbean, and to a lesser extent in other regions of the South, more and more women are entering the industrial and services sectors, besides becoming prominent in informal economic activities as traders and home-based workers. The majority of women, in both rural and urban areas of the South, combine these economic pursuits with their vital social role as home managers and mothers, bringing up the young and caring for their families.

The majority of women in developing countries carry the double burden of poverty and of discrimination. They are almost invariably paid less than men for the same work, and their entry into better-paid jobs is often blocked. In some countries they do not have the right to own land. They have less access than men to credit, and limited access to such productive resources as irrigation water, fertilizers, and technologies. It is also evident that health services and educational facilities are not equally available to them. For these and other reasons women suffer disproportionately from poverty, illiteracy, and malnutrition. Those who are heads of households are almost always among the poorest 10 per cent of the population.

Economic, social, and cultural factors have combined to produce a situation in which most development efforts have tended to discount the potential social and economic contribution of women, and so fail to mobilize and benefit from this vital human resource. There is a persistent misconception that the value of women's contribution to the economy and to society is adequately recognized and their needs and interests are satisfied if they are made the beneficiaries of certain welfare programmes.

The adjustment programmes of the 1980s have made the position of women worse. Many have lost jobs in the formal sector. While some have been able to start certain new activities in the more flexible informal sector, the lack of credit and appropriate training limits the income they can derive from them. Increases in food prices and cuts in educational and health services have meanwhile made it more difficult for women, as home managers, to meet family requirements. In urban areas, increasing economic difficulties have forced women to take to badly paid domestic work and in some cases even to prostitution. In rural areas, non-agricultural activities have become more and more necessary. The result has been to intensify the already severe pressure on women's time, leading in some cases to reduced attention to child care.

The mobilization of women as equal partners in all developmental processes therefore needs the priority attention of policy-makers. The means by which this could be achieved have been outlined in recommendations adopted at United Nations conferences held in 1976, 1980, and 1985 in Mexico City, Copenhagen, and Nairobi, where specific measures were proposed by international consensus, particularly in the Forward-looking Strategy adopted at the Nairobi Conference in 1985, as well as in many national documents. There is now, however, a compelling need to convert this consensus into action.

It needs to be recognized that development policies designed to ensure equity and full participation in society should give priority to raising the social and economic status of women. For example, an agricultural strategy that aims at self-reliance as regards food and nutritional security must give prominence to the role of women as food producers and as providers of health care. An industrial strategy focusing on the cost-efficient provision of consumption goods by using available skills needs to take account of women as major producers and consumers of most essential items of daily life. Women's participation in the fast-growing services sector should be properly reflected as an integral part of national plans to develop this sector.

It is essential, therefore, that the concerns of women should be incorporated within the framework of national development policies in a comprehensive manner. Adequate resources should be made available to meet their needs. The allocation of resources and technological choice in the main sectors, such as agriculture (including irrigation) and industry, need to be examined to determine their likely impact on women's productive activities. Policies to protect and enhance women's income-earning capacity and an upward assessment of their contribution in all economic sectors would lead towards greater equity among all social groups, and promote self-reliance, popular participation, and environmental protection.

The evidence of earlier attempts at integrating women into development planning indicates that it is not enough merely to provide resources or formulate programme objectives. There is a need as well for instruments and mechanisms which are responsive to the gender dimension in developmental activity. The design of strategies, training of development agents, and restructuring of legal and administrative systems should reflect the important role of women in the economy and society. What is no less important is that these changes should be accompanied and supported by deliberate endeavours to foster a gender-sensitive culture.

Where necessary, existing legal systems should be modified so as to facilitate the integration of women in the mainstream of the economy. Legal mechanisms may need to be created or strengthened in order to promote women's right to social justice and equity. Concerted efforts must be made to eliminate obstacles women face in such crucial areas as land tenure, to give them equal access to credit, and to grant them legal rights, especially in land ownership.

A gender-sensitive approach to development is not just a political imperative, but a basic condition for sustained economic and social progress. It requires changes in all societies, but it calls for radical changes particularly in societies in which traditional perceptions of women as inferior to men continue to prevail and in which the preservation of their culture continues to be invoked to justify the subordination of women. A commitment to people-centred development requires purposeful efforts to weaken the hold of such perceptions and to bring about more enlightened social attitudes to women. Changes will be hastened to the extent that women themselves become actively conscious of their rights, and work to safeguard them. They need to create strong organizations, solidarity networks, and special channels and mechanisms to advance their interests. Aware of their role in the transformation of the nations of the South, they must also mobilize themselves to work in partnership with men to meet the challenges their societies face.

CULTURE AND DEVELOPMENT

We refer here to culture in its widest sense, including:

- The values, attitudes, beliefs, and customs of a society. Paramount among these are religious beliefs and ethnic and national symbols and traditions, but they also include secular views about the human condition and human relations, individual and social priorities, morality, and rights and obligations, all of which may be institutionalized in various degrees.
- The activities in the society which express and enrich, while at the same time transforming, those values, attitudes, beliefs, and customs. The activities range from grass-roots endeavours and undertakings (e.g. the production of folk art and handicrafts, the creation and performance of folk music and dance, popular festivities and other forms of collective entertainment) to specialized cultural forms (literature, music, painting, theatre, dance, film-making, including television,

etc.). The products they generate become, in their turn, part of the culture of the society.

Culture must be a central component of development strategies in a double sense: on the one hand, the strategies must be sensitive to the cultural roots of the society, to the basic shared values, attitudes, beliefs, and customs; on the other, they must include as a goal the development of the culture itself, the creative expansion, deepening, and change of the society's cultural stock.

Lack of concern with cultural values in development strategies can produce social reactions, from apathy to hostility, that hinder efforts to implement them. Economistic approaches to development, insensitive to the dominant cultural and social mores of a society, can even evoke fundamentalist and obscurantist responses which are inimical to development and may even set it back.

In order to involve the people as active participants, development must be consistent with their fundamental socio-cultural traits; only then can the enthusiasm and creative potential of the people be mobilized. A culture-sensitive process of development will be able to draw on the large reserves of creativity and traditional knowledge and skills that are to be found throughout the developing world. Such enrichment will give development firmer roots in the society and make it easier to sustain development.

But culture is not only an inheritance of the past. In order to survive, a culture needs to renew itself so as to cope with present-day issues. Indeed some traditional cultural traits are inimical to development, and even to human dignity. People in the South should face the challenge of cultural renewal. A good starting-point would be the objective study of their own history. This would help them to reassess traditional values with a view to emphasizing those conducive to renewal and progress.

Further, concern with cultural identity does not imply rejection of outside influences. Rather, it should be a part of efforts to strengthen the capacity for autonomous decision-making, blending indigenous and universal elements in the service of a people-centred policy. Predominant among the latter are the values of democracy and social justice, and the scientific temper.

It is now widely appreciated that the application of technologies has clear social implications. The need for a culturally sensitive approach to the increasingly important function of science and technology in modernization has to be recognized. This will not only further a more harmonious transition to modernization, but could also reinforce the cultural base of the society.

The governments of the South should adopt clear policies and priorities to foster cultural development. In some cases these may take the form of Cultural Development Charters setting out the basic rights of the people in the field of culture, the essential conditions to attain them, and the role of the State in the process. The policies should pay due attention to the following aspects:

- *The right to culture* This includes both the possibility for the citizen of enjoying the products of culture and of taking part in the creative activities that express and enhance culture. In the modern world, formal education is a principal channel for the transmission and perpetuation of culture. Access to education is therefore a crucial component of the right to culture. At the same time, to serve the goals of development, the education system must be informed by the country's cultural ethos.

- *Cultural diversity* Because most nations in the South have a mixture of cultures, there should be respect for cultural diversity and concern for the rights of cultural minorities. The decentralization of cultural policy, particularly in the larger developing countries, is an essential means of ensuring that the interests of all cultural groups are advanced.

- *Cultural role of the State* The State is responsible for preserving and enriching the cultural heritage of the society, creating the conditions for the flourishing of cultural activities, and guaranteeing access to them for the population as a whole. The State must exercise these functions with due regard to the freedom of cultural and artistic creation, limited only by genuinely superior societal concerns. However, it is crucial that the State should be active in the cultural field. Adequate resources should be devoted to promoting cultural activities at the grass-roots level and to encouraging the growth of professional work in the cultural field.

Attention should also be paid to the scope for developing cultural industries—handicrafts, folk arts, book publishing, the music industry, film-making, cultural tourism. This would be a means of blending the preservation and enhancement of the cultural heritage of the countries of the South with productive activities and income generation.

DEVELOPMENT AND THE ENVIRONMENT

Over the last two decades, concern has deepened about the many
adverse environmental consequences of world economic growth.
Much apprehension has been expressed about such dangers as
global warming and damage to the ozone layer that certain production and consumption patterns have created for the global environment. Increasingly, other types of environmental damage,
such as the denudation of important watersheds, desertification,
and the destruction of tropical forests–concerns usually specific
to a nation or a region– have also received considerable international attention. Calls have been voiced for 'sustainable development' and for establishing environmental standards in industry,
and important international and regional protocols have been
drawn up to control the emission of certain dangerous gases.

The global and North-South aspects of environmental issues
are discussed in Chapter 5. We deal here with the challenges these
issues pose for domestic development in the South.

The Environmental Challenges to the South

The direct environmental hazards faced by the nations of the
South are many and varied. They include the continuous degradation of land under cultivation; desertification in the arid and
semi-arid zones of the South; degradation of water resources; deforestation in tropical areas; threats to fish resources, both sea
and freshwater, from pollution through the dumping of chemical
and other waste, or overfishing; the release of noxious gases and
the discharge of untreated industrial effluents; and severe pollution and squalor in many of the large cities of South.

The factors behind the increasing environmental stress in
many of the countries of the South can be grouped into the following basic categories: increasing pressure on natural resources
due to high rates of population growth; systems of property rights
and land tenure that accentuate this pressure; the dynamics of
agricultural development that result in a bimodal agricultural
production system; economic pressure, mainly from the North,
leading to overexploitation of natural resources; the imperative of
industrialization and economic growth; the adoption of energy-
intensive patterns of consumption modelled on those of the
North; and unplanned and uncontrolled rural-urban migration.

The South's rapid demographic growth, largely the result of improved nutrition and health services, has put increasing pressure on natural resources, its extent varying according to the availability of cultivable land and the system of land tenure. As land is scarce in many regions of the South, it is cultivated without respite, often resulting in the mining of nutrients and in their depletion. Traditional systems of crop rotation, which usually left some land fallow for regeneration, are increasingly being abandoned owing to the need to grow more food for an expanding population.

A similar phenomenon may also be observed within the system of shifting cultivation found in many parts of tropical Africa and Asia. Here, again because of population pressure, the fallow periods in which the land regains its nutrients, and which in certain cases used to exceed 20-25 years, are becoming progressively shorter. This leads to increasingly poorer harvests, causing a downward spiral in productivity and leading eventually to the degradation of the land. Population pressure has also resulted in cultivation being extended to unsuitable or marginal lands. Because of the fragility of their soil and also because of exposure to severe water or wind erosion, such areas quickly become unproductive.

Another consequence of population pressure on natural resources is the deforestation taking place in many countries of the South, as farmers seek new lands on which to grow food and raise cattle. Commercial ventures seeking new sources of timber aggravate the problem. FAO estimates that up to 11 million hectares of tropical forests are cut down each year. This over-exploitation has a number of adverse environmental impacts. The soil covered by natural forests is usually fragile, and its use for crop or livestock farming therefore soon degrades it, even making it unsuitable for the replanting of trees. The destruction of the natural plant-cover quickly results in severe erosion and in water run-offs which damage the natural water-regimes. In addition, the clearing of forest on steep watersheds heightens the risk and volume of floods and landslides. A further damaging consequence is the extinction of plant and animal species unique to tropical forests. These are believed to contain about half of the world's known plant and animal species; their loss would not only cause ecological imbalances and diminish biological diversity, but also affect the production of valuable industrial and pharmaceutical substances.

Similar to the impact of increasing human pressure on natural resources is that of expanding animal populations on grazing lands in semi-arid and arid zones. Rapid growth in animal herds is partly a result of better veterinary services but is sometimes the result of ill-designed rangeland development schemes. The uncontrolled growth in the animal populations in rangelands has led to overgrazing and the loss of the natural plant-cover. This makes these lands susceptible to wind and water erosion, and to their conversion into deserts. As much as 80 per cent of the rangelands in Africa and the Near East are thought to face a moderate-to-severe risk of desertification.

In addition to these pressures on the land, the economic pressure on countries in the South to earn foreign exchange also accentuates the tendency to overexploit natural resources, particularly forests. Some countries, for example, have allowed private firms (mainly transnational corporations) to carry on an unregulated exploitation of natural forests, often as a way of compensating for falls in export earnings due to a decline in commodity prices.

Further, in many countries, changing systems of land tenure and property have had a negative effect on the way in which natural resources are exploited. In regions where communal property systems used to prevail, as in much of sub-Saharan Africa, external pressure for change has weakened customary rules on the allocation and use of land. While traditional rules limited land access to clan or tribal members and also set conditions on the use of the land, external pressure has made countries open the land to overuse, in disregard of traditional restrictions. Lands under transitory systems of land tenure (i.e. those between customary communal property and freehold) and lands under unstable systems of tenure are perhaps among the most vulnerable to environmental degradation, for in such situations customary protective rules do not apply, nor is there an individual freeholder to take care of his property.

Other forms of tenure that have permitted, or even encouraged, excessive use of land and other natural resources are systems allowing free and unconditional access to all users. Whether these resources are grazing lands, mangrove swamps, or coastal fishing waters, they are invariably overexploited in such circum-stances, resulting in their degradation or depletion. For while such areas are generally under the State's nominal ownership or protection, the State is often unable to monitor or regulate their use effectively.

Regimes of property rights and agricultural policies that have allowed dualist or bimodal systems of agricultural production to be applied have also contributed to environmental stress. Where this is the case, while traditional cultivation systems prevail in much of the country, large tracts of land (usually the most pro-ductive and irrigable land) are brought under commercial culti-vation using modern, capital-intensive technology. This is usually accompanied by the displacement of smallholders or tenant farmers, who are either bought out or evicted, leaving them no option but to encroach on marginal lands. While the pressure on land may not appear to be high when considered nationally, the marginal lands cultivated by the displaced farmers are often un-der extreme stress and rapidly become degraded.

As in the North, though still to a very much smaller extent, industrialization–which must be a necessary part of economic growth–is responsible for certain environmental dangers. In a number of countries of the South, air pollution by the release of gases and substances from the burning of fossil fuels has begun to be a growing hazard. So has the uncontrolled and unregulated disposal of industrial waste, which contaminates rivers, lakes, and underground water resources.

Severe income inequalities, resulting in particular patterns of demand for industrial goods, also contribute to environmental stress in many countries of the South. Such income maldistribu-tion is invariably accompanied by the adoption by the rich of the consumption patterns of the North, leading to increasing demand for products whose manufacture or use are highly energy-inten-sive and have an impact on the levels of atmospheric pollution.

Economic growth and industrialization in the South have en-couraged rural-urban migration, which in turn has contributed to the now familiar overcrowding and congestion of urban centres and to the consequential severe environmental damage. Because the growth is unplanned and unregulated, a large proportion of the poor inhabitants of these crowded cities–mainly migrants from the rural areas–usually lacks such basic services and amenities as safe drinking water, waste disposal and drainage, and adequate housing and space. The consequent unsanitary conditions produce serious health hazards, and occasionally the risk of epidemics.

Domestic Policies for a Better Environment

The countries of the South will need to make a concerted effort to counteract environmental stress, as sustained development will require the preservation and development of natural resources, as well as their rational exploitation. The South has no alternative but to pursue a path of rapid economic growth, and hence to industrialize; it must therefore take action to control the environmental hazards that accompany such growth.

Given the complexity of the environment, it is necessary for countries to adopt an integrated approach. The protection of the environment should not be the sole responsibility of one department or ministry but should be taken into account by all government and non-governmental bodies concerned, and should be reflected in their plans for new economic activities. Further, all appraisals of new development projects should take their environmental costs into account. The environmental impact of various human activities should also be reflected systematically in the national accounts.

Legal provisions on environmental matters will be required in all countries. Environmental improvement cannot, however, simply be decreed; it requires the concerned involvement of all citizens. It is therefore essential to create a broad awareness of the actual or potential hazards threatening the country's environment and of what the people themselves can do to reduce them. If grass-roots institutions are associated with the drawing-up of codes for environmental protection, there is a greater chance that they will be implemented.

Perhaps, in the long term, what could be most crucial in many countries would be policies directed at slowing down population growth and thus reducing the pressure on natural resources. In addition to these broad measures, the countries of the South will need to take specific steps to guard against environmental degradation, while continuing to pursue rapid economic growth.

The reorientation of development strategies to give high priority to smallholder agriculture can assist efforts to prevent the depletion of natural resources. Integrated rural development programmes to improve the productivity of land already being cultivated will reduce the pressure on smallholders to bring marginal lands under cultivation. In many cases, land reforms that ensure equitable access to land and water resources will relieve the pressure on marginal and poor lands, which is often intensified by skewed land distribution. Strategies that tend to secure a reasonable balance in the level of regional development can make an important contribution to checking the concentration of population and thus reducing environmental stress in densely populated regions. Governments will, in addition, need to devise systems to regulate open access to natural resources. Such regulation is essential in order to halt the environmental degradation that results from excessive use, and to ensure the economical exploitation of these resources. Also, the expansion of rural industry will reduce dependence on agriculture for income generation and, correspondingly, the pressure on natural resources.

The expansion of rural industry will, moreover, help to reduce the high rates of rural-urban migration now found in many countries, and to prevent the further deterioration of the environment in their cities. National urban development plans, aimed at reducing the environmental pressures faced by their fast-growing urban centres, must be part of comprehensive action to save the environment.

Another direction in which action should be taken is in encouraging the rational use and management of rangelands that are threatened with desertification. This would involve stabilizing the animal population at levels within the carrying capacities of these lands. In some cases, such action may have to be complemented by measures to protect the livelihoods of nomadic and semi-nomadic herdsmen using these areas.

Environmentally conscious rural development programmes must make provision for the sound management of water resources. This will require the protection of river and lake catchment-areas; the more efficient use of water in irrigation schemes; the encouragement of small, community-managed irrigation schemes co-ordinated with larger schemes of irrigation, provided that the latter are efficiently controlled; the protection of surface and underground water from industrial or chemical pollution; and the pricing of water supplies in urban areas to reflect the actual costs of supply and to encourage its more economical use.

The rational exploitation of forests, the encouragement of programmes of afforestation, and the search for sources of fuel to replace firewood should also be part of efforts to relieve rural environmental stress. Successful techniques, such as agro-forestry, which allow the use of forest areas for the production of crops and for raising livestock as well as for the rational exploitation of timber and other forest resources, have been evolved in a number of developing countries. These should be applied in countries where there is a risk of forests being destroyed owing to population pressure.

In attempting to build an environmentally sustainable economic and social order, the South should seek to develop and make use of its indigenous systems of agriculture and industry. Such ecologically-sound systems have been virtually lost in the North but form the basis of everyday life in large parts of the South. These systems can be usefully adapted and made part of the South's development efforts. Given the substantial contribution they can make, they should not be discarded in the quest for modernization.

In addition to these measures to protect their natural resources, developing countries will need to take action to prevent air and water pollution caused by industrial activities. Regulations to control the emission of gases and the disposal of industrial waste need to be enacted where they do not now exist and existing regulations need to be strictly enforced. The acquisition and development of technologies that are both energy efficient and environmentally safe are also necessary. All these steps are required to safeguard the global commons shared by the South and the North.

But many of the measures the South can take to curb industrial pollution, particularly the emission of dangerous gases, will depend in large part on co-operation by the North in the transfer of energy-efficient and environmentally safe technologies. Without such co-operation, the South will find it very difficult to reduce industrial pollution, given the necessity to achieve high rates of economic growth. Even with it, however, continued economic growth in the South will in all likelihood necessitate the increased use of fossil fuels. The stabilization or reduction of air pollution throughout the world will thus require the North to reduce its own emissions radically. This is just, as well as necessary, given the enormous disparity in the levels of energy consumption between North and South, and the indisputable right of the South to develop rapidly to improve the well-being of its people.

* * *

This chapter has discussed some of the principal development goals that, in our view, countries of the South should seek to achieve over the next decade and beyond. We have suggested the main elements that any long-term, people-centred strategy would have to include, and drawn attention to the broad issues which may arise in the process of its implementation. We have laid emphasis on national self-reliance, the mobilization of domestic resources, and far-reaching policy reforms as critical factors for the success of the South's development efforts. It is clear, however, that the achievement of its objectives would be greatly assisted by enlarged co-operation within the South and by a restructuring of North-South relations.

Mobilizing the South: Towards Greater Co-operation among Developing Countries

4

THE STATE AND PROSPECTS OF SOUTH-SOUTH CO-OPERATION

The crucial challenge that the developing countries face collectively is how to strengthen and diversify South-South co-operation.

South-South co-operation has been a goal of developing countries' foreign policy for close to four decades. It has evolved in response to changes within the South, as well as in the world economy and in the South's relations with the North. A great deal of intellectual, political, and organizational energy has been invested in South-South co-operation, much has been learned but so far not much has been achieved. More pragmatic approaches are now being followed to overcome difficulties in building bridges within the South.

A Brief Overview

The idea of collective self-reliance had its origins in the liberation and anti-colonial movements after the Second World War. Lasting bonds between peoples and nations of the South were forged as the basic principles of collective action and self-reliance were crystallized through the common struggle against imperialism and hegemony. The process of decolonization was accelerated because anti-colonial movements supported each other, and also because of collective political action taken at the United Nations by developing countries.

Developing countries, including those on the verge of independence, were soon questioning the very basis of the management of international economic relations and the global division of labour, which were an outgrowth of the colonial era. They began to advance jointly a number of proposals on how the international economic system–its structures and the way it was managed–should be changed and how multilateral institutions and the industrial countries of the North should assist them to overcome poverty and make economic progress.

The Afro-Asian Conference at Bandung in 1955 was the first indication of the entry of a self-aware South into the world arena. The founding of the Non-Aligned Movement in 1961, and of the Group of 77 in 1964, marked the start of collective action by the South to advance its common interests.

South-South economic links also came to be established–at bilateral, subregional and regional levels–as developing countries turned to each other for mutual support in a bid to end their exclusive orientation towards the North.

In the early 1960s Latin America and the Caribbean led the way in putting in place a number of regional and subregional institutions designed to expand their development opportunities. The Latin American Free Trade Association (LAFTA) was established in 1960 by Argentina, Brazil, Mexico, Paraguay, Peru, and Uruguay and joined later by Ecuador, Colombia, Venezuela, and Bolivia; LAFTA was replaced in 1981 by the Latin American Integration Association (*Asociación Latinoamericana de Integración*–ALADI). The subregional organizations included the Central American Common Market (CACM), the Caribbean Free Trade Association (which led to the Caribbean Community–CARICOM), the Andean Group, and the East Caribbean Common Market.

In Africa, the East African Economic Community, the Maghreb Permanent Consultative Committee, and the Central African Customs and Economic Union (*Union douanière et économique d'Afrique centrale*–UDEAC) came into existence during the 1960s. At the same time, the first steps were being taken towards setting up the Association of South East Asian Nations (ASEAN). The League of Arab States, a political forum expressing the urge of these states for unity and liberation from external domination, was making preliminary moves at that time to develop economic programmes. Its initiatives led to the establishment of several institutions for economic and social co-operation within the region.

Regional institutions for political co-operation were also created, as exemplified by the Organization of African Unity (OAU). Formed in 1963 by the continent's then independent states to support the struggle for its total liberation and to defend their sovereignty, the OAU has ever since sought to project a collective vision for strengthening Africa's new nations and their position in the global economy.

There was also an early awareness of the need for co-operation between countries of different regions within the South. The Tripartite Trade Expansion and Economic Co-operation Agreement linking Egypt, India, and Yugoslavia was followed by several bilateral arrangements between countries from different regions. China, Cuba, and India launched substantial programmes of technical assistance and financial co-operation benefiting a large number of developing countries in different regions.

The efforts to widen South-South links–both global and regional–inevitably encountered the rigidities of a world economy organized along a North-South axis. Most countries of the South had little to sell other than primary products; their trade consisted largely of exchanging these for manufactures from the North.

Some countries had, however, begun to process their raw materials before export. A few others had also made progress in setting up industries to manufacture articles they had previously imported. In a number of cases, this process of industrialization began to run into difficulties due to the narrowness of domestic markets. While some sought to exploit opportunities in the Northern economies by undertaking the production of labour-intensive manufactures for export, many were also seeking to expand subregional and regional trade.

There was considerable optimism about South-South co-operation in the 1970s. This period was marked by the thrust of OPEC on the world scene, and by the increased activism of the Non-Aligned Movement and the Group of 77–which led to the adoption by the United Nations General Assembly of the resolutions on the New International Economic Order and of the Charter of Economic Rights and Duties of States. There were also numerous attempts to energize the various schemes established for economic integration and co-operation and to set up new ones.

The intervention in the world oil market by petroleum-exporting developing countries, acting as a group through OPEC, in order to achieve remunerative returns, was a landmark in collective self-reliance in the South. For the first time, through united action, a group of developing countries wrested control of the production and pricing of a vital commodity from the North. It demonstrated to the rest of the South not just the political and strategic value of collective action, but also its economic benefits. This combined intervention created vast new resources, some of which were used for providing significant flows of development assistance and investment within the South.

The 1970s were a period of self-confidence and hope for the South. The decade saw improving commodity prices, low real interest rates, OPEC surpluses, and buoyant growth in many developing countries. Starting from low levels, South-South trade grew dynamically, nearly doubling its share in total world trade (excluding fuels) between 1970 and 1981. Financial flows among developing countries, including investment, increased. Several new regional financial institutions were established.

The widening opportunities of the 1970s gave rise to a spate of initiatives to enlarge South-South co-operation. In Africa, four important subregional organizations were established during this period: the West African Economic Community (*Communauté économique de l'Afrique occidentale*–CEAO), the Mano River Union, the Economic Community of West African States (ECOWAS), and the Economic Community of Central African States (*Communauté économique des états d'Afrique centrale*–CEEAC). In Asia, the Bangkok Agreement of 1975 created a preferential-trading area covering a number of countries. In Latin America, the formation of the Latin American Economic System (*Sistema Económico Latinoamericano*–SELA) introduced an innovative mechanism–the ad hoc action committees–for promoting joint development activities. It also served as an agency for co-ordinating action by Latin American countries as a group and their position in multilateral development forums. In the Arab region, arrangements were made to set up the Co-operation Council for the Arab States of the Gulf (Gulf Co-operation Council–GCC).

For a while, OPEC's success had raised the prospect that collective action by the South would have an impact on the restructuring of international economic relationships. But this opportunity was not fully utilized. The changes introduced in the system of world economic decision-making were marginal and did not alter the fundamental patterns of the North-South relationship. The OPEC members with surplus capital demonstrated generosity in expanding development aid to much higher levels as a proportion of their GDP than those reached by any developed country, before then or since. The investment of a part of their financial surpluses in some countries of the South was on a substantial scale. In addition a number of OPEC countries offered employment opportunities for large numbers of workers from other developing countries, and markets for commodity and technology exports from the South. None the less, the bulk of their imports of goods and services continued to come from the North, and it was in the North that they invested most of their surplus funds.

In spite of the opportunities forgone during the 1970s, the expectations engendered by the initiatives in South-South co-operation remained high. The beginning of the 1980s was marked by the ambitious Caracas Programme of Action on Economic Cooperation among Developing Countries, adopted by the Group of 77 in 1981.

The many plans and programmes for stepping up South-South collaboration could not, however, be effectively implemented. There were several unfavourable factors, including inadequate and ineffective institutions; lack of resources; and insufficient political commitment on the part of governments, who were preoccupied with other developmental matters. These weaknesses were to show themselves—and to grow—as the development crisis of the 1980s unfolded.

The crisis forced the governments of most developing countries to concentrate on domestic economic management, short-term objectives, and their relations with the developed countries. South-South co-operation was downgraded in their priorities.

As part of their adjustment programmes, the developing countries, except a few in Asia, sharply cut their total imports in the first half of the 1980s. This curtailment had a negative impact on South-South trade. In addition, worsening balance-of-payments difficulties affected the earlier schemes for liberalizing South-South trade and made the arrangements for financing, payments, and clearing much less effective. The resulting drop in intra-group trade was notable in a number of regional and subregional groupings. This decline affected in particular arrangements to which heavily indebted middle-income developing countries–chiefly in Latin America–and the sub-Saharan African countries were parties. A large fall in inter-Arab trade was also registered during this period.

Furthermore, owing to the reduced emphasis on development planning, the growing privatization of State-owned enterprises, and the diminished role of governments in economic activity–another consequence of adjustment policies–some of the basic premises of the accepted model of co-operation among developing countries were no longer applicable. Government co-operation in the integration of production and investment activities, uneven as its progress had been, suffered a set-back, as national policies curtailed demand, investment, and growth. Financial flows among developing countries became much smaller, as the price of petroleum declined and OPEC surpluses dwindled.

These conditions of crisis inevitably reduced the capacity of developing countries to act collectively. This loss of momentum was reflected in the activities of the Non-Aligned Movement and the Group of 77. The South became weakened on the global scene. The developing countries were unable to resist the moves by the developed countries to change the global development agenda, to downgrade discussions and negotiations in those United Nations bodies where the Group of 77 and members of the Non-Aligned Movement had previously deployed their collective strength most effectively, and to move many of the key development issues into the ambit of the Bretton Woods institutions and GATT, where the North was–and is–in full control.

Most significantly, the vulnerability of individual developing countries vis-à-vis the North made it impossible for them to make an effective collective stand on the debt issue and to go beyond broad statements of policy. Short-term considerations and the concerns of individual countries took priority over issues of common interest to the South as a whole. Differences surfaced among debtor countries and also between regions, as they struggled against threatening economic and social collapse.

During the same period several regional conflicts and wars further sapped the South's ability to recover its strength, and limited the activities of important organizations of the South, including the OAU and the Non-Aligned Movement. In some instances, political change in particular countries, or disagreements and rivalries among countries, diminished their commitment to already frail schemes of co-operation and caused them to terminate some co-operative arrangements.

On the whole, therefore, while moves to promote South-South co-operation have involved much effort and produced many initiatives and schemes, the practical results have been rather limited. In most cases, idealism has not been tempered by a degree of practicality or matched by commitment to action. A tendency to underestimate obstacles and the effort and time needed to get tangible benefits has often left expectations unfulfilled and thus led to frustration and even cynicism. It has generally proved easier to co-operate in the political sphere, where important joint initiatives continued to be mounted and sustained. On economic issues there has been a wide gap between, on the one hand, the rhetoric of solidarity, the ambitious objectives in international resolutions, and the many programmes set out in intergovernmental agreements, and, on the other, the action that has ensued.

Lessons of Experience

One of the chief shortcomings of South-South co-operation has been weak organization and lack of institutionalized technical support, both at the international level and within most countries. The intergovernmental institutions set up to advance co-operation have, in many cases, lacked professional support and financial resources. Collective action and negotiations at the global level have been hampered by the lack of a facility capable of providing continuing technical and intellectual support—as the secretariat of the Organisation for Economic Co-operation and Development (OECD) provides for the developed market economies—or even mechanisms for regular consultation, co-ordination of action, and settlement of differences. Equally harmful has been the common failure to reflect the objectives of co-operation in national plans and policies, or to incorporate the goals of South-South co-operation in the mandate of public agencies and institutions.

In most developing countries, there has been meagre public support for co-operation with other developing countries because little systematic effort has been made to explain to the people why

South-South links are needed and how these links would benefit them. In the absence of such efforts, they have tended to continue to look to relationships with the North as the vehicle for economic progress and have failed to appreciate the value of links within the South.

Insufficient attention has been given to the need to improve information flows within the South in order to enlighten public opinion about conditions in the South. Information flows tend to be largely between the North and the South; intra-South information channels are few and weak. In very few developing countries is adequate information available about other developing countries –their institutions, cultures, products, and capabilities.

These weaknesses are particularly serious because attempts to create relationships among developing countries have to contend with the habit of using familiar links with the North. These links have the support of powerful domestic and foreign interests, including transnational companies. It is not uncommon for them to try to block new South-South economic connections by planting doubts about the capacity or intentions of prospective partners in the South.

The political factor, while not sufficient by itself, is of immense importance to the fortunes of most regional groupings and other programmes of co-operation, particularly during their take-off phase. The experience of the last two decades has demonstrated that it is the vision, will, and commitment of those directly involved, and especially of the top political leaders of the South, that have proved to be crucial factors in the success or failure of initiatives in co-operation.

A Strengthened Rationale

While the set-backs of the 1980s may have dampened morale and lowered expectations, they have dramatized the importance of South-South co-operation for development and the role it could play in supporting developing countries in their efforts to counter forces and processes eroding their economic independence. It is clear that, had they been well-established and diversified, links among developing countries could have eased their difficulties during this period. Moreover, changes in the South, in the North, and on the world scene are increasing the need and enlarging the opportunities for South-South collaboration.

The changing South Progress within the South can give new substance to the process of co-operation among developing countries. Many of them have greatly diversified their economies in the last three decades. High levels of industrialization have been achieved, giving rise to new complementarities among developing countries, both within regions and interregionally. These broaden the potential scope for flows of trade, technology, and capital between developing countries on mutually beneficial terms.

The newly industrializing economies of the South have now established their competitive credentials in a broad range of manufactured products, and in some cases are outselling the North in world markets. The increasing sophistication of the South's exports, as measured by research and development (R&D) intensity, is illustrated in Fig.4.1. Thanks to the high quality of its exports, the traditional prejudice against products from the South in the world at large, including the South itself, is breaking down.

An important task in the 1990s is to improve communications within the South, in order that buyers may become more familiar with the productive capacities and competitiveness of Southern suppliers. In support of these interchanges, more attention should be paid to issues of trade finance, for such financial facilities can lubricate both the trading process and market expansion in the less developed areas of the South.

Balance-of-payments surpluses in the South are now concentrated in a very small number of economies. At the same time, however, the South's investments in the capital and money markets of the North add up to a substantial total. Even if the bulk of these are held as reserves on short-term account and have to be offset against debt liabilities, the resources at the disposal of the South are considerable. It must be the South's objective, therefore, to create conditions in which an increasing proportion of these assets could be mobilized for investment in the South's development.

Many situations call strongly for co-operation among the developing countries, e.g. in the management of shared natural resources, in dealing with common environmental problems, and in harnessing science and technology to the specific needs and con-

Figure 4.1

Shares of the South in Imports of Manufactures by
Developed Market Economies, by R & D Intensity

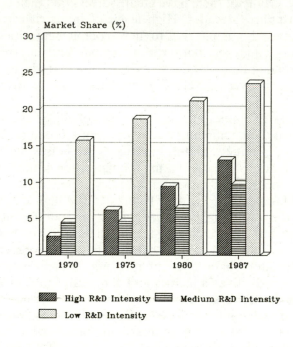

Note: Excluding China.
Source: UNCTAD.

ditions in the South, particularly for the purpose of expanding
food output to keep pace with population growth. In such areas
as communications, air transport, and other services, where large
and powerful enterprises of the North are vying for control of the
global market, the developing countries will need to collaborate
with one another in order to secure and maintain a role for themselves.

In sum, the South is today better equipped than a decade ago
to advance co-operation; it is also in greater need of co-operation
in a number of areas.

The changing North The rationale for South-South co-operation has also been reinforced by changes taking place in the North and by trends in the world economy and world trade during the 1980s, and the prospects for these during the 1990s.

It has become apparent that the dynamic of economic growth in the North is no longer a reliable or sufficient motor for generating sustained growth in the South. The growth of world trade slowed down in the early 1980s, and it is unlikely to return to the high rates of the 1960s. The share of the South in world exports also declined in the 1980s after reaching a peak in the 1978-80 period (see Fig.4.2). Neither can the South rely on the North to provide it with technology on terms and conditions that suit the South or to help it to generate its own technology. In the area of finance, while every effort should be made to promote the Southward flow of surplus savings from developed countries, there is no assurance that this will take place in adequate volume. On the contrary, all the signs point to continuing stagnancy in capital flows from North to South in the years to come.

Revolutionary advances in science and technology and economic changes are giving new capabilities to industrial countries, which are becoming less dependent on raw materials produced in the South. Moreover, in a number of cases, some of the developing countries' earlier advantages, such as cheap labour, are being eroded.

It is quite likely that the changes in East-West relations and within the countries of Eastern Europe (which are discussed in the next chapter) may cause the North to divert attention and resources away from the South, at least in the short and medium term. In the period immediately ahead, the South may well have to face a more homogeneous and confident North preoccupied with its own problems and opportunities.

These changes and trends in the North make it essential for the South to look to its own collective resources. The South will have to compensate by its own exertions for this unfavourable international environment. It will need outlets for its manufactured exports other than in the North, where rising protectionism could in any case be a major obstacle, especially if a large number of developing countries attempt to expand their exports at the same time. It will have to rely increasingly on its own financial resources to

Figure 4.2

Shares of the North and the South in World Exports,
1970-87

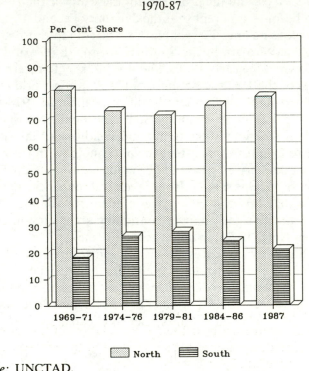

Per Cent Share

| | 1969–71 | 1974–76 | 1979–81 | 1984–86 | 1987 |

North   South

Source: UNCTAD.

support a large part of its development. And it will need to build
or expand its own scientific and technological base.

None of this can be achieved by individual countries acting
alone. South-South co-operation will be increasingly necessary
to provide an additional engine for powering the South's economic expansion and to supply the financial lubricant for its
smooth operation.

The changing world scene As outlined in Chapter 1, there are
global developments that point to the need for more vigorous
co-operation within the South. So far as environmental issues are
concerned, it is clear that the developing countries should work
together to safeguard their interests in responding to the North's

concern about global environmental risks. Similarly, the illicit traffic in narcotic drugs calls for co-operation among developing countries that are affected, both in curbing the traffic and in agreeing with consuming countries in the North on a durable global solution.

Likewise, the South must close ranks in order to meet the challenges posed by the large existing, and possibly future, economic groupings of the North, or to deal with the efforts by powerful developed countries to strengthen their spheres of influence in the South. The growth of regional co-operation in the North–the extension and intensification of integration in Europe and the formation of the Canada/US Free Trade Area–reinforces the case for co-operation among the countries of the South, especially on a regional basis. However, it must be recognized that some of these regional movements in the North–as well as proposed arrangements for economic co-operation among Pacific-rim countries–already contemplate closer ties with some developing countries. Since the latter are likely to be major economies of the South, these developments have the potential of weakening South-South co-operation as a whole. All the more reason to ensure a context in which South-South co-operation is actively pursued by all countries of the South.

Moreover, developing countries will have to respond collectively to new alignments in East-West relations if they are to be able to protect their interests as a group and to exert some influence on the course of this historic process. They must also act as a group in order to participate in the shaping of future global relationships, whether these concern trade negotiations, the reform of the United Nations system, the exploitation of the global commons, or the uses of outer space.

In facing these issues and trends, no developing country, or even group of developing countries, can–on its own–expect to wield significant influence in determining the final outcome. To be able to play an influential role and to negotiate from a position of strength on such important issues, the developing countries will need to act together.

South-South Co-operation Reaffirmed

In line with this rationale for South-South co-operation, there has been a growing reassertion of interest in and support for inter-regional, regional, and subregional economic and political co- operation among developing countries. In South Asia, the creation of SAARC–the South Asian Association for Regional Co-operation–has brought together several countries that had not previously been part of any subregional group. In 1988, Egypt, Iraq, Jordan, and the Republic of Yemen established the Arab Co-operation Council. In addition, five North African countries–Algeria, Libya, Mauritania, Morocco, and Tunisia–agreed to form the Arab Maghreb Union. In Latin America, the Rio Group of Eight, composed of Argentina, Brazil, Colombia, Mexico, Panama, Peru, Uruguay, and Venezuela, was set up in 1987. A number of regional and subregional groups have drawn up plans to expand their activities, among them: CEAO, CEEAC, ECOWAS, Preferential Trade Area for Eastern and Southern African States (PTA), Southern African Development Co-ordination Conference (SADCC), UDEAC in Africa, ASEAN in Asia, ALADI, the Andean Group, CACM, and SELA in Latin America, and CARICOM in the Caribbean.

The existing multilateral financial institutions of the South, primarily based in West Asia, have continued to demonstrate the vital role of finance in sponsoring and sustaining South-South co-operation in key economic areas, not least in the creation of infrastructure.

The renegotiation of the Lomé Convention once more brought together a group of African, Caribbean, and Pacific (ACP) developing countries in a common negotiating posture vis-à-vis the European Community; one of the issues concerned the scope and nature of financial support for their own co-operation and integration schemes.

The establishment of the Global System of Trade Preferences among Developing Countries (GSTP), the efforts to revitalize both the Non-Aligned Movement and the Group of 77, and the creation of the Summit Level Group for South-South Consultations and Co-operation are among other manifestations of the

South's new dynamism and the desire to strengthen links and improve co-operation among the countries concerned.

It is relevant to note in this context an increasing number of contacts, networks, and initiatives at the non-governmental level in many areas of economic, social, and cultural activity and of research. They have generated information and experiences, which provide alternative possibilities for horizontal co-operation and partnership. Among many such important initiatives are the Third World Academy of Sciences, the Third World Network of Scientific Organizations, and Development Alternatives with Women in a New Era (DAWN).

There have also been political and diplomatic initiatives in Latin America, Africa, and Asia that show a new willingness by countries of the South to settle political disputes and even military conflicts through regional and subregional efforts and mechanisms.

ADVANCING SOUTH-SOUTH CO-OPERATION: STRATEGY AND PROGRAMMES

Clearly, the developing countries will need to agree on a global strategy for South-South co-operation. Such a strategy should serve as a basis for elaborating more specific regional, sub-regional, and national programmes of co-operation.

The political sphere remains an area of major South-South initiatives. In fact, many of the South's present co-operative undertakings in the economic field have originated in political groupings, as can be seen from the experience of the NAM. A typical recent example is provided by the Contadora Group of Latin American countries, which was formed for the purpose of averting war in Central America; having contributed to this objective, it led to the creation of the Rio Group, which is active in the economic field. Another notable case is SADCC, an economic arrangement which stemmed from the concern of a group of African countries to strengthen their solidarity in the struggle against the apartheid regime in South Africa. The prevention of military conflicts and the negotiation of agreements on disarmament are objectives which obviously call for co-operation in the political field. Such co-operation should be broadened to include exchanges between political parties and parliamentary bodies in the South.

By its very nature, the process of South-South co-operation is bound to develop its own momentum and diversify in scope in time. The strategy, however, should identify the broad fields in which co-operation should be pursued, indicating the long-term goals to be achieved. It should propose a set of activities to be undertaken in each area in the short and medium term. These should address critical issues and needs, hold promise of success, and have a potential for further widening and deepening South-South co-operation. The strategy should also set out the main steps to be taken in implementing both the short- and medium-term programme and in reaching the long-term goals. As a contribution to the formulation of such a strategy, the Commission has attempted, in the pages that follow, to outline a set of objectives and activities which it considers important for advancing the process of South-South co-operation.

The Foundations

To begin with, we wish to emphasize two broad areas which are of special significance in any move to advance South-South co-operation and strengthen the foundations on which it is to be based. The first has to do with building South consciousness at the national level, while the second concerns the development of human resources.

Building South consciousness

Acceptance of South-South co-operation as a strategic objective should be promoted actively among the political leaders, civil servants, businessmen, academics, and other professional groups in all developing countries. It should also be promoted more broadly, to reach all levels and sections of society. The people's support and participation are an essential part of the foundation on which South-South co-operation can be built.

Thus, strong emphasis should be placed on the need to promote 'South consciousness' among the people in developing countries, and to strengthen their belief in the South, their mutual trust, and their commitment to South-South co-operation.

South consciousness should be developed to become a part of the ethos of all developing countries. The study of the South's history and values–and contemporary processes and events affecting the South–should figure prominently in the educational programmes of secondary schools and universities in the Third World.

Beyond this, there is a need to create a constituency of active supporters of South-South solidarity in each developing country. Clearly identified groups, ranging from political parties to professional and business associations and grass-roots non-governmental organizations, can make specific contributions to the process of South-South co-operation. They should be kept regularly informed, and also encouraged and assisted to relate directly to their counterparts in other developing countries.

One important measure to promote people-to-people contacts would be to ease travel restrictions for tourist and business travel between developing countries. It is a paradox that people from the North cross the frontiers of developing countries with much greater ease than people from the South. Developing countries should therefore negotiate the elimination of visa requirements on a reciprocal basis. Insofar as the shortage of hard currency limits South-South travel, they should consider setting up special clearing accounts to facilitate tourist movements within the South or in their particular regions.

In every developing country a national committee for South-South co-operation should be established, whose members would be prominent citizens from different walks of life, to advise the government, to lead civic action, and to link the various groups that foster South-South co-operation. It should design programmes for mobilizing public opinion and bringing the concept of solidarity and co-operation closer to the people and their daily lives.

Ministries, departments, and other government agencies should internalize the objectives of South-South co-operation and become more South-oriented. Each country should put in place arrangements to facilitate administrative, educational, and other contacts with developing countries, and in general to create an environment that would encourage collaboration with them. All governments should consider the designation of a ministry or department to be responsible for promoting South-South co-operation, which would include regional and subregional co-operation, as is already the case in some developing countries. It is desirable that a cabinet-level minister should have responsibility for South-South matters. Career incentives should be offered to public servants to attract them to serve in institutions established under co-operation arrangements.

Each country in the South should formally set out, in its statements of national policy or its development plan, explicit objectives relating to South-South co-operation. A country adopting a five-year indicative plan could, for example, outline its strategy for South-South co-operation, laying down specific targets and highlighting the links between such co-operation and national objectives. In addition, there should be regular procedures, including the use of statistical and other indicators, for reviewing performance in meeting goals of co-operation with other developing countries. Were the results of such reviews to be reported to a joint body of developing countries, their analysis would yield valuable information about the global status of South-South co-operation.

Unlocking the human-resource potential

Knowledge and skills are critical ingredients of economic development. If the young people of the South could be educated to a higher level and their skills developed, the productive potential of the South—and its strength in the world economy—would be vastly increased. Though many countries have acquired impressive educational capabilities, serious deficiencies in education and training exist in practically all developing countries, especially in science and technology.

Co-operation among developing countries can go a long way towards remedying these deficiencies. Yet, the movement of students between countries of the South remains small, especially between regions, though a few countries have undertaken impressive programmes of student exchange. At the same time, hundreds of thousands of students from developing countries study in the North at great expense.

As development proceeds, the demand for higher education and training in the South will rapidly increase and diversify. Developing countries will find it difficult to pay for increasingly large numbers of students wishing to study in the North; many countries will also not be able to offer all the necessary specialized courses in their own institutions. The inability to satisfy the rising demand for higher education may well have a harmful impact on development in a number of developing countries.

South-South co-operation could ease this constraint through greater use of educational facilities within the South. Higher education in the South would cost much less than in the North, need be in no way inferior, and would also be more appropriate for the conditions of the South. Those completing their courses would also be likely to return to their own countries. Over a period of time, those who study in other countries of the South will become valuable assets to their countries and part of the constituency for building up South-South co-operation.

South-South educational co-operation can greatly help in upgrading the human resources of the South. A programme should be drawn up to enlarge educational links and to provide for a much greater flow of students within the South. Countries should be free to participate in any part or parts of the programme.

The following should be among the areas covered by the programme:

- education in the basic sciences, engineering, medicine, and public health
- technical and vocational training, including industrial apprenticeships
- distance-education programmes, especially at regional and subregional levels
- the development of entrepreneurship and management skills.

Basic sciences and engineering The objective should be to address current weaknesses in the teaching of mathematics and sciences at the primary and secondary levels through co-operation in the preparation of a programme for improving the skills of teachers. Lead institutions should be identified for different linguistic communities of the South, and the possibilities for co-operation among all of them explored.

At the tertiary level, the programme should be concerned with expanding access to, and improving the quality of, establishments of higher education. Gross tertiary enrolment-ratios in the South rarely exceed 15 to 20 per cent, and are well below that percentage in many countries, notably in Africa and the Caribbean. The ratios in Europe and Japan are 30 per cent or higher, and in North America about 55 per cent. Given the constraints, the countries of the South have to rely on mutual help in raising the enrolment rate. At the undergraduate level, this help could be in the form of arrangements among universities in each continent for exchanges of staff, teaching materials, and students. In some newer areas of teaching–for example, molecular biology, genetic engineering, or computer science–exchanges between continents should be encouraged.

At the graduate level, there are already several centres of scientific education and research in the three continents, which should be invited to take the lead in building up a network for graduate studies in particular specializations. The selected institutions should be designated as part of a South Network of Centres of Excellence to provide advanced training for students from other developing countries. Special efforts should be made to secure adequate financing for these centres, so that they can build up their capacity to serve the South.

As a complementary measure, a Foundation of the South should be established to award at least ten thousand 'South Fellowships' each year to outstanding students from developing countries for study within the South. The Foundation should draw its financial support from both governmental and non-governmental sources. A proportion of the scholarships should be reserved for students from the least developed countries.

Health The South can draw on a considerable fund of its own experience of measures taken for reducing infant mortality, controlling disease, extending life expectancy, spreading birth control, providing primary health care, and formulating policies for the import, production, and distribution of pharmaceuticals. Yet, in the health sphere links with the North continue to be very much stronger than those with other developing countries. This imbalance needs to be corrected. In so far as developing countries can provide the requisites of health care, every effort should be made to reduce their heavy reliance on the North in this field. One way would be to develop co-operative arrangements for postgraduate training in medicine and public health within the South.

An area offering considerable scope for co-operation, with the prospect of promoting scientific advances in the South, is that of indigenous medicine. Interest in the South's system of traditional medicine has existed for some time in the medical and public-health communities in the developed countries. The South itself should now undertake efforts to tap this source of knowledge and skills so that the benefits may be shared widely. Governments should sponsor programmes through which the results of research on indigenous systems of medicine would be disseminated among other countries in the South, and also offer training in these systems to students from other developing countries.

Technical and vocational training In the vast majority of developing countries, opportunities for acquiring or upgrading technical or industrial skills are very limited. The large number of persons who are reported as unemployed or underemployed have had little, if any, formal training. Technical and vocational schools are only able to accommodate a very small proportion of the young people.

National, regional, and subregional internship and technical assistance programmes should be set up to promote flows of educational, medical, and technical personnel among developing countries. They should work in the field, share experiences, and provide technical support throughout the South, particularly in the least developed countries.

The newly industrializing countries are well-placed to offer training in these fields. South-South mechanisms of co-operation could play an important role in organizing technical assistance schemes for making available teachers in technical and vocational subjects from these countries to other developing countries as well as offering apprenticeships for training supervisory personnel. These schemes should be organized with appropriate assistance from the private sector.

Distance education Modern communications technology is reducing training costs at all levels, including the costs of programmes for raising adult literacy. The use of radio and satellite and cable television enlarges the possibilities for regional co-operation in distance education. Some regional educational institutions have already established distance-education programmes, and there is much scope for further developments of this kind. Such expansion would facilitate interregional co-operation in the South in the sharing of experiences and distance-education materials, which could include materials that promote South-South co-operation.

Entrepreneurship and management skills Although the development of entrepreneurship and of managerial skills should reflect a country's own historical, cultural, economic, and social background, considerable opportunities exist none the less for co-operation among countries in these areas, especially at the regional and subregional levels, but also between regions.

Despite their differences, the countries of the South face the common task of encouraging their people to value hard work, discipline, and achievement. It is within an environment in which these are respected that high levels of productivity, savings, and investment—as well as innovation and enterprise—can be realized. The educational system must be the principal conveyor of these values. Educational exchanges between countries inevitably entail exposure to the work habits and styles as well as to the value systems of the host countries. Through co-operation in the field of education, countries of the South can help one another to create a climate conducive to achievement and entrepreneurship.

Follow-up For a South-South programme of co-operation in the development of human resources to be launched and built up, institutional support will be required. The South Secretariat, proposed later in this chapter, should, as one of its initial responsibilities, prepare detailed schemes for each of the components mentioned above and make proposals for mobilizing human and financial resources to put the schemes into effect.

As part of this programme—and in order to assist exchanges—arrangements should be made for circulating within the South information about the courses offered by educational institutions, fees, and availability of scholarships, etc. The proposed South Foundation should be a focal point responsible for administering fellowship programmes, reviewing exchange experiences, making recommendations to governments for further action, maintaining statistics, and publishing an annual report on South-South co-operation in the development of human resources. Similar bodies could be designated regionally.

Through the pooling of resources, experiences, and skills, South-South co-operation in the field of human resources can help countries along the path to development. This is also a way of increasing understanding and solidarity within the South, and therefore of helping push forward South-South co-operation itself.

The Functional Areas

The building blocks for South-South co-operation are many and varied. The following functional areas deserve priority and sustained attention:

- Finance
- Trade
- Industry and business
- Services
- Transport and infrastructure
- Food security
- Science and technology
- Environment
- Information and communication
- People-to-people contacts

Finance

Finance has proved to be the critical missing link in the entire range of South-South activities. Schemes of co-operation, whether in trade, production and investment, education, or science and technology, need adequate financial resources to be viable.

We have selected several areas in which co-operation in financial matters or the financing of co-operation in economic matters is greatly needed. These forms of co-operation involve institutions and mechanisms already in existence, i.e. regional financing mechanisms, regional development banks, multilateral institutions, and South-South development assistance. In the longer run, we envisage new institutions, notably a South Bank which would initially finance trade and ultimately provide development finance. In the following paragraphs we identify the central issues arising in connection with these institutions and mechanisms, and indicate the principal areas for policy intervention.

Multilateral clearing and payment arrangements Effective clearing and payments arrangements continue to be of prime importance to the functioning of regional trade groupings. There are currently five such arrangements operating in the South: the Credits and Payments Agreement of ALADI (formerly LAFTA, 1965), the Asian Clearing Union (1974), the West African

Clearing House (1975), the Central African Clearing House (1979), and the Preferential Trade Area Clearing House of Eastern and Southern African States (1981). Two other arrangements, the Caribbean Multilateral Clearing Facility and the Central American Clearing House, suspended operations in the mid-1980s because of the accumulation of unsettled balances.

Clearing and payments arrangements can be more effective in promoting the expansion of trade if a credit element is built into them. The absence of credit support for financing the swings in the balance of payments inevitably leads to tighter rules for settlement, reduced willingness of members to expand trade, or the accumulation of arrears.

Several facilities providing lines of credit for regional trade are in operation in the South. These include the Central American Stabilization Fund (1969), the Latin American Reserve Fund (1988) which replaced the Santo Domingo Agreement of LAFTA (1969), the Andean Reserve Fund (1976) established under the Cartagena Agreement, the Arab Monetary Fund (1976), and the ASEAN Swap Arrangement (1978). Shortage of funds has, however, reduced the effectiveness of these arrangements, which in 1987 together provided less than $700 million in credits. The balance-of-payments difficulties of the 1980s have greatly impaired the ability and willingness of surplus countries to extend credit. As a result, the potential for trade liberalization of most of these arrangements is not being realized.

There is thus a need for the creation of an adequate resource base that would enable clearing and payments arrangements to overcome their difficulties and fulfil their mandate more effectively. Shortages of foreign exchange admittedly set limits to the expansion of credit arrangements. Yet even within these limitations, a stronger political commitment would make it possible to mobilize additional resources in support of viable arrangements. This issue deserves the priority attention of the countries that are members of the various trade and payments arrangements.

The objective of trade expansion among developing countries has the broad approval of the international community. Financial support to subregional, regional, and interregional trade and payments arrangements should therefore be a legitimate function of international financial institutions like the IMF, the World Bank, and the regional development banks. The developing countries should raise this matter in these institutions and urge them to set up special facilities for providing financial support to viable trade and payments arrangements in the South. In the longer term, it should be the South's goal to support such facilities from its own resources.

Export-credit financing facilities Export credits have a major influence on the growth of trade, particularly trade in non-traditional and capital goods. Several developing countries have set up institutions to provide export credits, backed up by credit insurance and guarantee facilities. However, the capacity of most developing countries, particularly the smaller ones, to extend such credits or to set up financially viable institutions for that purpose is limited. Therefore, high priority attaches to the establishment of subregional, regional, and interregional arrangements for financing the expansion of export-credit facilities that could contribute to the growth of trade among developing countries.

At present, there are five regional or subregional financial institutions in the South providing short- and medium-term credits for financing trade within their own regions as well as exports to developed countries. They are: the Latin American Export Bank (*Banco Latinoamericano de Exportación*–BLADEX), a private multinational bank; the Andean Trade Financing System (*Sistema Andino de Financiamiento del Comercio*–SAFICO), operated by the Andean Development Corporation to finance trade in non-traditional exports among the countries of the subregion; the Inter-American Development Bank Trade Financing Facility; the Islamic Development Bank; and the Inter-Arab Trade Finance Facility set up by the Arab Monetary Fund and the Arab Fund for Economic and Social Development for the purpose of financing and promoting inter-Arab trade. These facilities, however, cover only a limited number of developing countries, and some of them are used to finance exports to countries outside their regions, including exports to developed countries.

There is a clear gap in developing countries' arrangements for export-credit financing. It is essential that subregional and regional groups should establish effective export-credit facilities where they do not now exist. There is also an urgent need to enlarge the operations of the existing schemes. At the interregional level, what is required is a full-fledged commercial bank of the South specializing in export credit, an issue we take up later in this chapter.

Regional and subregional development banks A number of development banking institutions have been in operation at the regional, subregional, and interregional levels. Three regional development banks, the Inter-American Development Bank (IDB), the African Development Bank (ADB), and the Asian Development Bank (AsDB), are continental in scope. Some development banks have also been established at the subregional level, for example, the Caribbean Development Bank and the East African Development Bank. These banking institutions are equipped to play an important role in promoting South-South co-operation. While, as now constituted, they are not composed exclusively of countries of the South, and are strongly influenced by their members from the North, they are intended to serve the developing regions in question. Developing countries are important shareholders and have a say in shaping the policies and in influencing the management of these banks. They should insist that these institutions give higher priority–and devote a larger share of their resources–to support for economic co-operation and integration schemes in the region concerned. Also, these countries should propose to these banks for financing projects involving two or more of the member countries.

Regional and subregional development banks should be urged to offer a wider range of financial and technical services in support of regional co-operation, covering such areas as finance for regional and subregional programmes and projects, export-credit and refinancing facilities, and regional clearing and payments arrangements. Recognizing the need to expand the scope of operations in this direction, the IDB has already created a facility to refinance export credits granted by Latin American countries to promote trade in capital goods. Other regional banks should set up similar facilities. The regional development banks should also consider the establishment of consortium arrangements for financing projects and exports that would promote interregional co-operation within the South.

An example of committed support for diverse aspects of South-South co-operation is provided by the Arab Fund for Economic and Social Development. Like the Arab Bank for the Development of Africa, this is a wholly Southern-owned regional development bank, in which all Arab countries who are members of the League of Arab States participate. Its paid-up capital and resources amount to about $5 billion. The Fund has extended project loans and grants for technical assistance which have contributed to developing physical infrastructure and productive sectors in certain member countries, in particular agriculture, industry, transport and telecommunications, energy, water, and sewerage installations. It has paid special attention to projects of interregional importance such as transportation networks, electrical grids, and telecommunications systems. In co-operation with the Arab Monetary Fund, it has also helped to set up the Inter-Arab Trade Financing Facility, with an authorized capital of $500 million. The facility will finance all traded goods and services (excluding oil) within the Arab region.

Multilateral institutions for financing and development assistance While the three main multilateral institutions concerned with financing and development assistance–the World Bank, IMF, and the United Nations Development Programme (UNDP)–could do a great deal to support South-South co-operation, this has not been one of their principal concerns. Their position is not likely to change unless the developing countries show much greater interest and determination in this respect. They should propose in the respective governing bodies new policy guidelines for each of these institutions, directing them to play a much greater and systematic role in extending support to South-South co-operation. At the same time, these countries should suggest projects and programmes requiring such support.

The World Bank should be invited to finance an increasing number of projects and investment programmes involving two or more developing countries, and also to set up a facility for refinancing export credits given by developing countries. The IMF should be asked to establish a facility that would back moves towards the liberalization and expansion of trade among developing countries. The UNDP should, in the context of its activities in support of Economic Co-operation among Developing Countries (ECDC) and Technical Co-operation among Developing Countries (TCDC), allocate a significant proportion of its funds for regional and interregional programmes of South-South co-operation such as the GSTP, economic integration groupings, and commodity producers' associations.

It would be appropriate that the contribution of all multilateral institutions to South-South co-operation should be reviewed annually by UNCTAD's Committee on Economic Co-operation among Developing Countries.

Development assistance Development assistance provided by developing countries–grants to least developed countries, long-term credits at subsidized interest rates, technical assistance–is an important expression of solidarity among these countries. The OPEC countries jointly, through the OPEC Fund for International Development, and the Arab countries through their national institutions (e.g. Kuwait Fund for Arab Economic Development, Abu Dhabi Fund for Arab Economic Development, Saudi Fund for Development, Libyan Arab Foreign Investment Company, and Qatar Development Account) and through multilateral institutions (e.g. Arab Fund for Economic and Social Development, Arab Bank for Economic Development in Africa, and Islamic Development Bank) have been the most important source of this assistance. Mexico and Venezuela set up in 1980 a Programme of Co-operation in Energy for Central America and the Caribbean, to provide concessional assistance to the countries of the region. A few other developing countries like China and India have also operated their own programmes of development assistance.

The surpluses accruing to some oil-exporting countries, which underwrote the bulk of South-South development assistance, are, however, much diminished, and large transfers on concessional terms are no longer likely to materialize. This places a special responsibility on those countries in the South that have strong reserve positions and export-earning capacities to extend official development assistance of varying degrees of concessionality to the poorer countries of the South. Developing countries in a stronger financial position have an obligation to help the more needy members of the South family. The AFRICA Fund is an example of this spirit of solidarity in action. Set up by the Summit of the Non-Aligned countries in Harare in September 1986, the AFRICA Fund has so far raised more than $500 million to be devoted to assisting the front-line states and liberation movements in Southern Africa in their struggle against the Pretoria regime.

The successful launch of the AFRICA Fund is an illustration of the South's potential as well as of the goodwill that exists within the South—and within some countries in the North which have made contributions to the Fund—and its example should encourage the establishment of other multilateral financial schemes for providing assistance to the needy countries.

The South Bank In the longer run, the South's requirements of development assistance and trade finance are such that setting up a bank of the South will become a compelling necessity. The proposal to establish a South Bank as a fully-fledged multilateral institution for development finance has received much attention in the last ten years. As originally conceived, its broad range of activities was to include the financing of development projects, joint ventures, export credits, arangements for commodity stabilization, balance-of-payments financing, and support for regional and subregional payments and credit arrangements.

The governments of developing countries have not yet reached agreement on the establishment of the bank. It is felt in some quarters that the proposal is too ambitious, and that the range of activities envisaged is too wide. There is also concern in some capital-surplus countries about the emergence of a possible ' donor-recipient' relationship and that the bank might become yet another vehicle for channelling their surpluses as aid to other developing countries. This concern needs to be allayed. Indeed, now that Third World surpluses have been reduced, the bank would have to look to much more diversified sources of capital within the South. Furthermore, capital from the surplus countries would for the most part have to be raised on more commercial terms and used to underwrite the more bankable projects submitted for financing. Such commercial capital would, however, have to be blended with capital raised on more concessional terms in order to sustain investments and activities equally vital to South-South co-operation but yielding returns only over the long term.

The scope of the operations of the proposed South Bank needs to be re-examined in the light of a realistic assessment of the volume and sources of finance available in the South and of the terms on which they could be mobilized. It would be prudent to start on a more modest basis than first envisaged, with the support of a broad group of interested developing countries, leaving it open for others to join later. In view of the constraints on resources likely to be experienced, the operations of the bank should be enlarged gradually.

The bank's first priority should be the financing of exports and support for subregional, regional, and interregional clearing and payments arrangements. As pointed out earlier, the developing countries' capacity to grant export credit is extremely limited. Yet today it is virtually impossible to export non-traditional manufactures unless post-shipment credit is provided.

While facilities exist in the international markets for rediscounting export credits, exporters from developing countries face high rates of rediscount which are supposed to reflect the apparently high risk of default associated with credit of this nature. In part, these high rates reflect the limited creditworthiness of countries guaranteeing export credits. It must be stressed, however, that this situation is attributable in part also to imperfections in international financial markets and to lack of familiarity with developing-country export-credit paper. A pooling of resources, and therefore of risks, by a group of developing countries could help to secure access to export credits and rediscounting facilities at more favourable interest rates. Thus, in addition to the initiatives that could be taken by regional development banks and other multilateral development finance institutions, there is a need for a Southern institution that could offer export credit at competitive rates and thereby provide vital support for South-South trade. In particular, such an institution could buttress the functioning of the GSTP.

Once its initial operations have proved to be viable and effective, the South Bank could explore the feasibility of providing longer-term balance-of-payments support as well as investment finance designed to enhance and diversify the production and trading capacities of the South.

In 1987 the ministerial meeting of the Non-Aligned Movement held in Pyongyang recommended that the High-Level Intergovernmental Technical Group should proceed to draft the statutes for the South Bank so that the interested countries could initiate the bank's operation without much delay and invite other countries to join it later. This recommendation has not been followed up. Further progress is vitally linked to the establishment of an effective mechanism for helping the interested countries to reach an early consensus on the scope of activities, methods of operation, and financing of the bank. Consensus on these matters depends very much on political will and solidarity, as well as on a well-organized and sustained process of technical preparation and negotiation.

The establishment of a debtors' forum In its statement of March 1988 on the developing countries' external debt, the Commission called for the establishment of a debtors' forum as a matter of urgency. The need for such a forum continues, in spite of the recent initiatives for dealing with the debt problem, which are discussed in the next chapter. At a minimum, such a forum would enable the debtor countries to consult each other and to co-ordinate their debt-management policies and procedures. It would also enable them to respond collectively to events and to promote the possibilities of concerted action in defence of their common interests. The establishment of a debtors' forum would represent an important reaffirmation of South-South co-operation and solidarity.

In the final analysis, the developing countries' indebtedness can be settled only in a political context. Co-ordination and joint action by the developing countries in question will become even more compelling in the period to come. The debt burden has been choking development in many parts of the South for years. Were the debt burden, and the associated political and economic constraints on the developing countries, to be eased, the conditions for all forms of South-South co-operation would become much more favourable.

Assistance for countries negotiating with the IMF and the World Bank Owing to their financial difficulties, a large number of developing countries have come to rely more and more heavily on financial assistance from the IMF and the World Bank. Many countries are now implementing programmes of stabilization and structural adjustment designed by these two institutions. The stiff dose of conditionality and performance-norms of a far-reaching nature associated with these programmes have caused deep disquiet (see Chapter 5). Not all developing countries are technically well-equipped to negotiate effectively and on an equal footing on these complex issues with the two institutions and to secure the best possible arrangements. To help overcome this weakness, the Group of 24, which co-ordinates the positions of developing countries in international monetary and financial affairs, should set up a standing group of experienced advisers whose services could be provided to any developing country seeking advice in its negotiations with the IMF and the World Bank. UNDP should be invited to finance the utilization of the services of these experts.

Trade

Co-operation in furtherance of trade in the South takes place at present largely within the framework of regional and subregional schemes for trade promotion and economic integration (the levels of intraregional trade in the three regions of the South during 1965-87 are shown in Fig. 4.3). These schemes have very considerable potential for expansion. Detailed programmes in this regard can best be attempted by the various regional and subregional organizations themselves. We limit ourselves to offering a few general suggestions for revitalizing regional and subregional co-operation in trade, while focusing attention on the strengthening of interregional trade within the South.

There are significant advantages to be gained in promoting South-South trade at the interregional level. A broadening of the scope of co-operation among developing countries would enable them to take greater advantage of the diversity in resources, skills, capabilities, and market opportunities to be found in the South. It is thus sound economic sense for the South to plan to expand trade by widening networks of trade preferences to cover all of the countries concerned rather than to limit such efforts to regional groupings. It is quite consistent for preference systems to co-exist at different levels, larger preferences being extended within particular subregional and regional groupings.

Global System of Trade Preferences (GSTP) The Global System of Trade Preferences among developing countries, which became effective in April 1989 after a process of negotiation started in 1976, is a major achievement. A system for promoting interregional trade among developing countries, it is based on the principle of mutual advantage. In order to ensure that all participants benefit equitably, it takes into account differences in levels of industrial and economic development and trade, and contains special provisions to favour the least developed countries. The scheme is seen as complementing existing regional and subregional preferential trading arrangements.

Figure 4.3

Intraregional Trade as Per Cent of Each Region's Total Trade

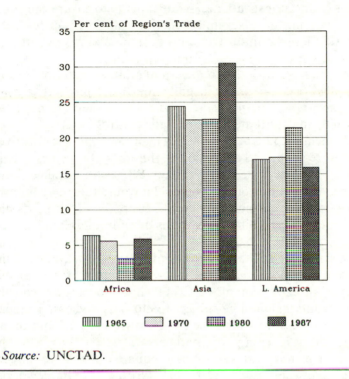

Source: UNCTAD.

The GSTP Agreement establishes a global framework of rules for the reciprocal exchange of concessions as regards tariff, para-tariff, and non-tariff measures covering all types of products, for direct trade measures including medium- and long-term contracts, and for sectoral agreements. The trade liberalization implicit in the first round of negotiations within the GSTP, in which countries exchanged bilateral concessions in April 1988, is not, however, very significant. As of now, the GSTP is largely of symbolic value. It will need to be carefully nursed in order that the expansion of trade among developing countries may acquire a momentum of its own. The challenge is to evolve a coherent strategy so as to ensure that by the year 2000 the GSTP will cover a substantial proportion of the intra-South trade.

In order to make the GSTP more effective in expanding trade, the South needs to give careful consideration to several closely related policy matters:

- Respect for the principle of mutual advantage implies the establishment of institutional arrangements to ensure the equitable sharing of costs and benefits among countries with different levels of industrial and economic development and external trade.
- Once products with the greatest potential for trade expansion are identified and made eligible for trade preferences, arrangements will be needed to ensure that they are not subjected to non-tariff measures of trade control.
- The scheme should be flexible so as not to impair the effectiveness of regional and subregional preferential schemes. This risk could be mitigated to some degree if existing schemes were deepened simultaneously. The GSTP would then help to reinforce existing schemes of bilateral, subregional, and regional trade, and also facilitate an expansion of interregional, multilateral, and bilateral trade.
- Any strategy for the expansion of intra-South trade would have to take into account the long-term nature of such an exercise. The expansion of the GSTP should be negotiated step by step and it should be subject to periodic reviews. The aim should be both to widen the range of concessions and to increase the number of participating countries.
- A strong technical service, with adequate financial resources, needs to be established to support the process of implementation and to promote the scheme's expansion. This service should be able to work out the costs and benefits to members of deepening the system of preferences, and to persuade non-members of the benefits to be derived from participation. It should be given the function of drawing up a timetable and programme of action until the year 2000.

State trading agencies There is considerable scope for increasing co-operation among the South's State trading agencies, both at the regional and the interregional levels. Such co-operation can make it possible to dispense with the services of intermediaries from developed countries, promote countertrade, and diversify trade to include non-traditional items. It can also promote joint activities in: import purchases; export promotion, research, and marketing; warehousing; the use of transport facilities; and training. The establishment of the International Association of State Trading Organisations of Developing Countries (ASTRO) is an important step towards creating the institutional arrangements needed to promote such co-operation. ASTRO should be invited to draw up a comprehensive programme for expanding co-operation among the State trading enterprises of the South in the 1990s.

Countertrade Countertrade between developing countries can be a useful mechanism for overcoming difficulties of payments, export credit, and foreign exchange which might otherwise be serious obstacles to the expansion of South-South trade. It can, again, operate at both regional and interregional levels. However, in order that countertrade may become a major component of the international trade of developing countries, a change in their approach is required. Exports to other developing countries must cease to be regarded as a means of building up a surplus in hard currency. They must instead be looked upon as a means of obtaining the goods and services that the economy needs through a two-way balanced expansion of trade.

So far, the bulk of countertrade between developing countries has been conducted mostly through intermediaries in the North. It is the North that has benefited most from this type of trade, and it obviously has no interest in helping the indirect trading partners in the South to establish direct contacts and develop durable trading relationships. The developing countries need to organize themselves for countertrade, including 'buy-back' arrangements, as this can also pave the way for the growth of more conventional trading relations. Teams of experts to advise them should be established. An information network should also be set up, as is being done by ASTRO. The possibility of establishing an organization that would identify developing countries likely to benefit from such trade and that would act as a broker for countertrade transactions should be explored. ASTRO should be invited to undertake technical studies and bring together interested countries to explore the possibilities of co-operation in this field.

Trade information Beyond policy-induced barriers and structural weaknesses which may limit South-South trade lies a general inertia on the part of authorities and enterprises in developing countries in promoting trade in non-traditional products and with non-traditional partners, particularly with potential partners in other regions of the South. This results from the lack of entrepreneurial initiative compounded by ignorance and prejudice and, not infrequently, by opposition from local vested interests committed to trade with the North.

Improving communications within the South and focusing initiatives for trade promotion on South-South trade would help to overcome such barriers. Detailed, product-by-product investigation of exports and imports taking place between developing countries, as already carried out by UNCTAD and the UNCTAD-GATT International Trade Centre (ITC), should be expanded. The information derived from the research should be incorporated into a computerized network of trade information at the service of the parties to the GSTP and of other developing countries. In addition, meetings should be organized to bring prospective buyers and sellers together.

There exist significant but unrecorded flows of trade between developing countries in border areas. This traffic indicates that there is an as yet insufficiently recognized potential for trade, which should be studied and exploited to promote formal South-South trade.

Co-operation in commodity trade Developing countries have long been adversely affected by the low real international prices of primary commodities of export interest to them, the instability of these prices, the lack of finance for holding stocks, and poor processing and marketing capabilities. In addition, owing to technological advances in the North, the raw material content of many manufactures is tending to diminish, which means a market loss to exporters of primary commodities, and furthermore some agricultural commodities and raw materials originating in the South are being displaced by man-made substitutes produced in the North.

Several decades of effort to stabilize commodity markets through international commodity agreements between producers and consumers have yielded meagre results–and much frustration in the South. In some cases, competition among the producers themselves has aggravated the downward pressure on prices, resulting in additional transfers of resources to the North. The South's commodity producers, particularly in cases where they account for the bulk of world production of, and trade in, the commodities in question, should, therefore, give renewed and urgent attention to setting up producers' associations with a view to managing supplies and/or intervening in the market. Several practical matters merit attention in adopting such a strategy:

- Supply management in commodities can be effective only if it is undertaken by producers accounting for the bulk of world exports. Producer countries which have a significant share of the world market for a particular commodity should be persuaded to join such management schemes, even if their exports of the commodity contribute only a small proportion of their export earnings.
- The concerns of the least developed countries for which the commodities are a principal source of export earnings should be given special consideration in supply-management schemes.
- In determining the price level, the schemes should be sensitive to the concerns of consumers, particularly in the case of commodities where technological developments triggered by high prices can contract the demand for them.

Tropical beverages are produced wholly in the South. Co-operation among Southern producers of cocoa, coffee, and tea could therefore greatly contribute to stabilizing the world markets in these commodities and maintaining prices at remunerative levels. These objectives should be given priority over short-term gains for individual producers. Joint efforts should be undertaken by the producers of these three commodities to introduce rational and fair systems for their international marketing. The Non-Aligned Movement and the Group of 77 should give strong support to these efforts.

If a number of producers' associations are created, they should set up a joint body with a view to co-ordinating action in international markets for a range of commodities. Some pooling of resources and expertise could result from such an initiative. These associations could also undertake joint research to improve productivity and to find new uses for commodities. Processing and marketing is another area where joint action by producers can lead to beneficial results.

Co-operation among commodity-producing developing countries should also extend to consultations and negotiations among themselves with a view to establishing common positions in negotiating international commodity agreements and in dealing with consumer countries.

Industry and business

The appearance of multinational and transnational firms based in the South adds a new dimension to South-South co-operation (see Fig. 4.4). These firms have the potential to become efficient instruments for promoting economic and technological co-operation. They have shown an impressive ability for innovation and for acquiring technological skills, and adapting available technologies.

Experience shows that the technologies offered by Third World firms are often more labour-intensive, more suitable for utilizing local resources, and less costly than similar technologies obtained from developed countries. Moreover, they are more suited to local levels of expertise and skill, and to local infrastructure and environmental conditions. The terms on which these firms transfer technology to others in developing countries appear to be generally more favourable than those stipulated by technology suppliers in the North. In addition, many Third World firms do not insist on having as high a share in the equity capital in joint ventures as transnationals from developed countries usually do. There is also much less fear of their exercising political and economic influence in host developing countries.

Joint production enterprises Joint production enterprises of the South can considerably broaden the range of the Third World's development options. They can facilitate the flow of capital, technology, and management and marketing skills to those developing countries that need them. They can help to exploit complementarities among developing countries and enable countries to specialize in areas where they have a comparative advantage.

Joint enterprises in strategic industrial sectors, such as capital goods, fertilizers, agricultural machinery, pharmaceuticals, energy, and petrochemicals, as well as those manufacturing products for meeting basic human needs, can lead to better use of the productive potential of the countries concerned, and increase their trade. Such joint ventures would reduce the South's dependence on the North and strengthen its bargaining power in dealing with the North and its transnational corporations. The

Figure 4.4

Number of Business Firms in the South with Sales Over
$500 million in 1987/88, by Sector

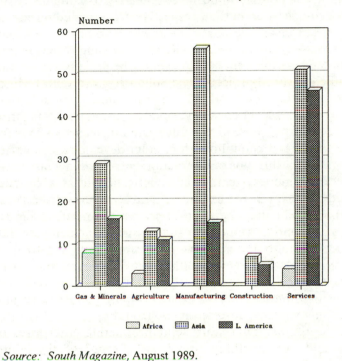

Source: South Magazine, August 1989.

pharmaceutical industry, for example, offers ready scope for joint
ventures to produce generic drugs for basic health needs. These
would yield important economic benefits to countries and, by
lowering the costs of pharmaceuticals, also benefit their people.
They would, at the same time, reduce dependence on the North in
meeting an important basic need in the South.

A useful vehicle for promoting contacts which could lead to
this type of collaboration has been the interregional system of
consultations organized by the United Nations Industrial Development Organization (UNIDO) in support of ECDC. These focus on specific industrial branches and are attended by
representatives of both the public and the private sector. These

and similar consultations should be fostered, as they enable developing countries' representatives to exchange ideas and experiences, as well as to explore proposals for joint industrial projects. Study groups of experts and representatives of various industrial sectors from the South should meet regularly to examine possibilities for co-operation in their respective areas, including co-operation in research and design.

This is also an area in which the more advanced developing countries can help the least developed ones, especially in carrying out specific industrial projects. The Solidarity Ministerial Meetings, also organized by UNIDO, have promoted contacts that have made it possible for least developed countries to obtain loans or grants for the purchase of machinery and to get access to technical assistance and know-how from other developing countries. Opportunities for this type of interaction need to be increased.

Generally, a more systematic effort is needed to assist the least developed countries in the expansion and structural diversification of their production and export base. Joint ventures seem an especially appropriate vehicle for such assistance. Such ventures should be assisted to find markets in the more developed areas of the South. This would give South-South co-operation greater structural balance.

Involving the business sector in South-South co-operation The financial, managerial, and technological capabilities of the business sector in the South—whether public, private, or mixed—should be mobilized more effectively in promoting South-South co-operation.

The fact that co-operation in the business sector has so far been on a modest scale can be attributed to a variety of causes. These include the complacency bred within protected markets, compounded by inward-looking and often erratic fiscal, financial and exchange rate policies. The orientation of parts of the business sector towards the North and their links with transnational corporations have inevitably tended to limit contacts within the South.

In the absence of deliberate policies to promote co-operation, such constraints may persist, particularly where local entrepreneurial resources have yet to mature. None the less, in recent years much more co-operation has been taking place between business concerns in the South. At the regional level, initiatives to encourage co-operation in the business sector are visible in ASEAN, and in the Arab world. In the Latin American region, such steps have been taken in the Ändean Group and elsewhere. For example, LATINEQUIP has been formed by three publicly owned banks of Argentina, Brazil, and Mexico to promote trade and investments in the strategic field of capital goods. The GCC, SADCC, CARICOM, and the CACM are other regional groupings taking active measures to enlarge co-operation in this sector.

Co-operation of this nature needs to be further encouraged, so as to make greater use of the potential in both the public and private sectors. For this purpose it is necessary to reach a broad policy agreement among developing countries, or groups of them, to establish a more favourable environment for joint ventures, investment flows, and technology transfers, and to invite and encourage direct business initiatives. Also, governments should consult with, and seek the involvement of, commerce and industry in matters related to South-South co-operation.

Promoting investment flows within the South The promotion of South-South flows of investment and technology calls for action both by countries with funds for investment abroad and by countries that need foreign investments. The former need to provide incentives to encourage investments to be made in other countries within the South. The latter should introduce arrangements to attract investors from the South. The investment laws in most countries of the South, which were for the most part drafted with investors from the North in mind, are often such as to discourage investors from other developing countries, which do not have the staying power or the global expansion strategies of their counterparts from the developed countries. It would therefore be beneficial for investors from the South to be granted more favourable treatment than is given to foreign investors generally; this would enable Southern investors to compete on fairer terms with companies from the North.

In return, the investing companies should pledge themselves to observe the relevant parts of the norms and standards that the Group of 77 has advocated in the North-South dialogue for transnational companies. This commitment would allay many suspicions, especially among the less developed countries, and pave the way to a genuine sharing of benefits.

Moreover, once such arrangements are adopted to govern the conduct of Third World companies and flows of technology within the South, they can serve as a basis for collective action vis-à-vis transnational corporations of the North. The South may thus unilaterally adopt a protocol defining the terms and conditions it would offer to transnationals and technology exporters of the North.

Improved conditions for business co-operation Developing countries should create a favourable climate for the flow of direct investment from other developing countries, so as to encourage industrial and business co-operation. This may require changes in national laws and regulations and in administrative policy. Priority should be given to providing protection to investors from the South against non-commercial risks. In this context, consideration should be given to the possibility of introducing a multilateral investment-guarantee scheme operated by the South itself. Countries should also conclude agreements for the avoidance of double taxation.

The establishment of, and recourse to, the South's own machinery for international arbitration would go some way towards facilitating the settlement of disputes in connection with trading or investment transactions, or of claims arising out of such transactions, in cases where disputes or claims are due to differences in the business practices, political systems, or customs of the countries of the parties concerned. One arbitrator from the home country, one from the host country, and one from a third country within the region would form the arbitration panel, as is the almost universal practice.

Third World consortia of technical consultancy and design firms and of industrial research institutes should be set up. A network of consultants in the South available to undertake project feasibility studies and other assignments should also be established. High-level expert advisory committees should be set up to provide advice in specialized areas of South-South co-operation. These would be important steps in filling an information gap and in linking the expanding sources of expertise in the South. If these services were available in the South many developing countries would be able to reduce their often exclusive, and expensive, reliance on services from developed countries and their technological dependence on the North.

Decision-makers in both governments and business ought to be encouraged to make greater use of the growing professional capabilities of the South. The United Nations agencies concerned should maintain a roster of experts and consultancy firms from the South, keep it up to date and make it available to governments. Annual reports should give particulars of the number and specialization of these experts whose services are employed by governments of developing countries, as well as of the proportion accounted for by these experts in the total. Moreover, the Group of 77 should ask the governing bodies of the UNDP and other UN organizations and specialized agencies to set targets and adopt effective measures to ensure that experts from the South are used to an increasing extent in their technical assistance activities.

Services for the promotion of foreign investment should be organized on a subregional or regional basis, making use of existing institutions. These should be supported by an interactive database giving particulars of investment laws, regulations, and practices in the South. Links among public and private information-systems for the diffusion and exchange of data concerning manufacturers, technologies, markets, and services should be strongly encouraged.

The efforts to establish an Association of Third World Chambers of Commerce and Industry should be carried forward rapidly and the Association should be given the necessary resources and institutional support by the developing countries. Business conventions and symposia, technology and trade fairs, business clubs, and management and technical training should be used to promote interaction within the business sector. The South-South Partnership Promotion Centre, a non-governmental initiative in the process of formation under the auspices of the African Development Bank, is a welcome development. Its objective is to stimulate the development of private enterprise, including multinational production enterprises and joint ventures, to promote investment in small projects, and to develop trade among developing countries, with the initial focus on Africa and its links with other regions of the South.

In view of the great importance of co-operation among business and industrial enterprises in the South, we recommend that the Group of 77 and the Non-Aligned Movement should jointly establish a standing committee of experts to review the state of

South-South co-operation in this area and to suggest measures for its further development. UNCTAD, UNIDO, FAO, and other concerned international organizations should be invited to assist the proposed standing committee in carrying out its responsibilities.

Services

In the services sector, many developing countries do not have the financial resources, qualified personnel, market size, or technological capabilities that would enable them to make significant progress on their own. This deficiency could be relieved if the development of services were also pursued under agreements for economic co-operation and integration, and if joint activities were promoted. South-South co-operation could provide an important stimulus to the development of national capabilities; indeed, such co-operation is indispensable to the South's efforts to protect its collective interests vis-à-vis the powerful service industries of the North.

Co-operative action in the services field is important in the context of the integration schemes themselves. It can foster increased trade in services among the member countries. Furthermore, an adequate supply of services, in particular telecommunications, banking, insurance, and transport, including shipping, will enhance the overall efficiency of the industrial sector of member countries and so strengthen their competitiveness in world markets.

Policies for increasing co-operation in the services sector should have the following objectives: the creation of an adequate infrastructure, particularly in telecommunications and informatics, and its integration into the global network; the development of producer services and the tightening of their links with sectors of material production and with other sectors; the improvement of the trade balance in services to be achieved by expanding exports of services and rationalizing imports.

Given that the service sector embraces a range of vastly different activities and that co-operation in services among developing countries is still underdeveloped, each regional and subregional grouping should identify priorities corresponding to its specific conditions. They should improve the statistical data on service activities and establish institutional mechanisms and legal frameworks for co-operation. Regular exchanges of information between groupings on experiences, the approaches, and the methods used are to be encouraged. Such exchanges would be beneficial and stimulating not only in the regional context, but also interregionally.

Transport and other infrastructural links

One of the South's colonial legacies is a pattern of transport and communication that is heavily oriented to links with the North. This has been an important obstacle to closer ties between the countries of the South, including those with common borders.

Improved transport, communication, and infrastructural facilities among the countries and regions of the South have throughout been felt to be vital, for they could reduce the South's dependence on the North and create new opportunities for development, industrialization, and integration. Not much progress has, however, been made, largely because of different priorities and the high costs involved.

Encouraging efforts have been made by SADCC to build up or restore transport links in Southern Africa. Its member states have seen this task as important to the process of forging closer economic ties in the region and becoming less vulnerable to South African pressure. In another field, that of electric power, the Arab Fund for Economic and Social Development has played an important role in financing the grid linking developing countries of West Asia and North Africa.

Each region should draw up a long-term plan for building infrastructural links among its countries. The projects should be financed by the countries concerned, which should seek additional funding from multilateral sources like the World Bank (which has so far regrettably shown inadequate interest in such projects) as well as from regional development banks and finance institutions. Building up physical infrastructure should also create opportunities for technical co-operation, transfer of technology, and investment between less developed regions of the South, such as Africa, and those more advanced developing countries that have experience in the construction of roads, railways, bridges, and dams and that can supply the related equipment.

Food security

Food security is vital in the development of the South. Many developing countries that formerly produced enough food for home consumption have become large importers of food, mostly from developed countries. Excessive dependence on food imports is a potential source of instability, as it could expose a country to political pressure. Hence it is necessary for the developing countries concerned to intensify efforts to increase and diversify their own food production and, generally, to expand trade in food products within the South. The South must become increasingly self-reliant in satisfying its food requirements.

Food-exporting developing countries should agree to give priority to the needs of food-importing developing countries in times of scarcity. Developing countries that have chronic food deficits should enter into long-term arrangements with food-exporting developing countries so that they can be assured of stable supplies. Capital-surplus, food-deficit developing countries should be invited to assist other developing countries in increasing their food production, part of the resulting higher output being earmarked for export to food-deficit developing countries; in some instances, provision could be made for payment in the form of manufactured goods, services, or raw materials in return for the food supplies. Joint ventures in farming should be promoted, for example along the lines followed by the Arab Authority for Agricultural Investment and Development.

A long-term co-ordinated programme of the South should be initiated to help Africa deal with its food problems and gain food self-sufficiency, by improving the continent's capacity for food production, modernizing its agriculture, and protecting its natural-resource base on which sustainable agricultural production depends. Such a programme could provide great opportunities for South-South co-operation, in support of people-centred development and national and collective self-reliance in Africa.

Risk-pooling arrangements, such as the regional holding of food stocks, can reinforce national efforts to achieve food security. Already, the members of ASEAN and SAARC have agreed to a limited pooling of food stocks to meet emergency needs in their regions. In Latin America, the treaty on regional assistance negotiated under the auspices of SELA in 1988 provides the framework of a regional system for dealing with food emergencies. We invite other regional and subregional groupings to give high priority to the establishment of similar schemes of mutual assistance, so that member countries facing critical shortages of food have a ready source of support.

In the longer run, consideration should be given to linking the regional schemes to form an interregional system. This would expand the resource base, diversify the commodities held in stock, and reduce risks. If the system were given the capacity to raise some capital, it would be able to buy food from surplus countries participating in the system in years of good harvest, thereby introducing an element of price support into the system.

There is a need for greater co-operation in agricultural research at the regional and subregional levels, for example research into rainfed agriculture in dry areas and into pest control. Interregional co-operation also needs to be emphasized, inasmuch as the techniques used in some developing countries that have dealt successfully with their food problems might be usefully applied, perhaps with adaptation, in other parts of the South. These experiences are generally much more relevant to social and environmental conditions in the South than the experience of developed countries. The Group of 77 should seek the help of FAO and of the International Fund for Agricultural Development (IFAD) in facilitating co-operation among agricultural research institutions in the South. Full advantage should be taken of the network set up under the Consultative Group for International Agricultural Research (CGIAR).

In the years to come, the demand for food will rise in the South. As the population is growing, the area of agricultural land per head is diminishing, and there are also mounting stresses on the soil and ecosystems. In view of these trends, attention needs to be given to using advances in biotechnology in order to secure longer-term food security by improving the productivity, profitability, and sustainability of the South's farming systems.

This is an area especially suitable for South-South co-operation. Because of the complex nature of research in this field, the best approach for developing countries is to pool their resources and work jointly on projects of common interest, including genetic enhancing centres and gene banks. Co-operation, particularly within regions and subregions in the South, holds much promise on account of their common genetic bases and ecosystems. Further, it is only through collaboration among themselves that developing countries will be able to resist the pressure from the North and the transnational corporations that rely mostly on the gene pool from the South in their global drive to exploit biotechnology for their commercial advantage.

Science and technology

Science and technology are exerting an ever growing influence on the development prospects of the South. The developing countries need to co-operate in strengthening their scientific and technological capabilities for the purpose of harnessing the growing potential of science and technology for their development objectives. South-South collaboration is important for scientific and technological education, for higher training, for scientific research, and for the building-up of technological capabilities.

The developing countries also need to stand together in facing the developed countries in multilateral negotiations. In dealings with governments and corporations from the North on matters of technology, the adoption of a common approach would similarly be to the advantage of developing countries.

The issues of access to science and technology have been under international discussion for years, mostly in the United Nations bodies. Strategies and guidelines for the development of science and for technological transformation in developing countries have been adopted. These are useful and should be drawn on by developing countries in working out their own plans. To set in motion a more vigorous process of co-operation, a three-pronged approach is suggested:

- Giving high political visibility to the issues and sensitizing leaders and public opinion in the South to the nature of the opportunities and challenges offered by modern science and technology. A possible instrument for these purposes would be a charter on scientific co-operation among developing countries.
- Identifying a number of areas of scientific research and technical innovation which are of immediate concern to the South and in which joint activity, both within regions and between regions, would generate significant benefits for the developing countries.

- Carrying out a set of activities that would demonstrate the value of co-operation and help to strengthen the foundations for greater collective self-reliance in science and technology.

The Third World Academy of Sciences was founded in 1983 as an international forum bringing together distinguished men and women of science from the South. Its main purpose is to promote basic and applied sciences in the Third World, to facilitate contacts among scientists from developing countries, to strengthen their research, and to further relations between their scientific institutions. Under the sponsorship of the Academy, a Third World Network of Scientific Organizations has been set up. The efforts of the Academy and the Network deserve strong support from governments of the South.

As noted earlier, special attention should be devoted to the higher training and education within the South of scientists, engineers, and technicians from developing countries. Priority should be given to setting up jointly funded, specialized training and research institutions, which would provide able scientists from developing countries with attractive opportunities to work in the South and for the South. In this context, the initiative, backed by the 1989 Summit of the Non-Aligned Movement, to set up twenty centres for science, high technology, and environment in different parts of the South, merits special support and encouragement.

The Third World Academy of Sciences has established an extensive programme of fellowships to facilitate contacts and exchanges between research scientists and between scientific institutions in the South. Governments and scientific organizations in the South that are in a position to host such exchanges should offer research facilities to scientists from other countries of the South and finance the local costs of their visits. This would contribute to the development of a commonwealth of scientists of the South interacting with each other.

Thousands of scientists from the South work in the North. Many of them continue to be concerned about the South's progress. Their practical support could be of value to the South in many directions. Contacts should be established with them, and their assistance should be sought in the training of scientists, improvement of institutions, and in research in developing countries. Their advice on science and technology issues, including those related to negotiations and dealings with the North, should be sought on a continuing basis. Schemes should be set up to encourage and finance regular working visits of expatriate scientists and technologists to their home countries.

The South urgently needs to examine jointly the implications for its economies and societies of current advances in science and technology, especially in such frontier disciplines as biotechnology and microelectronics, and in the use of new materials, robotics, and fibre optics. This is an area where a global view is called for; it is therefore well-suited for interregional consultations and co-operation. Such joint analysis would be of value to individual countries when they have to choose between various technology options and adjust the rate of introduction of new systems to ensure compatibility with their economic, social, and cultural conditions. It is also essential for sensitizing and guiding the developing countries in their collective thinking and in their responses to new challenges, including those originating from political and technological decisions and developments in the North. Third World joint action should be considered on global scientific topics such as the greenhouse effect, the ozone layer, the human genome, and fusion research.

Existing projects and centres for joint research and development should be used or new ones initiated for the purpose of applying some of the new frontier technologies. Biotechnology and informatics, especially software applications, deserve special attention because of their significant implications for development prospects in the South. The use of solar energy, the uses of biomass in tropical and subtropical ecosystems, and the control of tropical diseases offer great scope for joint R&D programmes and for the sharing of benefits among developing countries. A number of institutes and laboratories in the South are already working in these areas, but mechanisms need to be established, with governmental support, that would encourage team-work, collaboration, or complementary research.

South-South co-operation is essential to promote the establishment of innovative firms, involving two or more countries, in such critical areas as biotechnology, new materials, informatics, energy generation including nuclear plants, and the production of scientific equipment and capital goods. To this end, collaboration between relevant firms, universities, laboratories, and other repositories of knowledge in these fields in the South should be encouraged through credit, tax exemption, and other incentives.

Regular exchange of information and experience among the countries of the South should be organized on technology transfer and adaptation. National technical-information centres for adaptive development and research of imported technologies should be set up and linked through a network. Systematic exchanges among developing countries should be arranged on their experiences in technology transfer from the North and its adaptation to local conditions and needs. The transfer of science and technology among the countries of the South should also be promoted.

The establishment of the Centre for Science and Technology of the Non-Aligned and Other Developing Countries in India is a welcome event. The Centre can play an important role in identifying those core activities in scientific and technological research which may be jointly sponsored and in co-ordinating work in these areas. In co-operation with the Third World Academy of Sciences and with regional, subregional, and national scientific research institutions in the South, the Centre should draw up an operational programme for co-operation in, and co-ordination of, scientific and technological research within the South, to be coupled with a programme to promote the application and use of research results in the productive sector.

Environment and development

Environmental issues have been on the international agenda for more than two decades. At the intergovernmental level, the developing countries have not, as a group, devoted adequate attention to these issues and have yet to work out a comprehensive joint position. They have allowed the North to take the initiative in raising and defining issues, and in proposing action.

The environmental agenda is laden with political, economic, and social implications for the future of all developing countries. It is a global set of issues to which they must respond collectively, in negotiating and interacting with the North. They also need to act collectively in the regional context in managing shared resources and in dealing with common problems. By working together they would be in a better position to find more effective answers to environmental issues they face individually.

The search for an appropriate environmental strategy must begin in each country but with sensivity to the concerns of neighbouring countries. Subregional groupings are appropriate forums for working out and implementing joint programmes designed to protect the environment and the natural-resource base. The exchange of experience in the adaptation and use of traditional knowledge can be useful in introducing environmental sensitivity in the application of modern technologies to agriculture and in the management of ecosystems and natural resources.

The management of shared water resources is an instance where bilateral, subregional, and regional environmental co-operation in the South is required. The prevention or reduction of floods, siltation, and erosion, the management of irrigation systems, the generation of energy, and the conservation of sources of energy–all these call for close co-operation within groups of developing countries. Several co-operative schemes for the management of river basins are already in operation in some developing regions, and there is a great deal of experience that can be valuable to other parts of the South where the rational management of shared water resources–including rivers that flow through two or more countries–is sorely needed.

Experiences with the management of common resources, especially in similar ecosystems, may be usefully shared within and between regions. Ground rules should be established that would govern the uses of the environment and resources in cases where their use may affect adjacent countries. However, specific policies and programmes will have to be carried out on a subregional basis, as is already happening in many places. In regional seas or coastal areas, the management of Exclusive Economic Zones, offshore oil exploration, and pollution control offer significant opportunities for co-operation. The management of tropical forests, the prevention of desertification, and the conservation of wildlife, genetic resources, and generally of ecosystems are also appropriate matters for collective approaches.

There is also a need for co-operation in the use of remote-sensing techniques to assess natural resources and in the use of the resulting data. Without working together in this area, developing countries will not be able to reduce their present heavy dependence on services and data from the North.

The management of their energy systems and needs is a critical determinant of the developing countries' ability to evolve a sustainable process of development. Adequate availability of energy is at the very core of this process. But both the production of energy and its consumption in various forms have become a key cause of environmental degradation and a factor contributing to climate change.

It is essential for the South to take a comprehensive and long-term view of energy issues. This need is commonly ignored in the standard, sectoral approaches followed by most governments and in intergovernmental deliberations. As noted in the discussion on science and technology, the developing countries need to pool their resources in carrying out research into ways of increasing the supply of energy from new and renewable sources, including biomass and solar energy. They should also co-operate in the search for approaches and techniques that will make it possible to use energy more efficiently in industry, agriculture, and transport, and in homes. In addition, they should adopt a common position in negotiating with the North a global plan for the development and sharing of technologies that would help to conserve energy and to control pollution arising from energy use. Such a plan should also help the South to gain prompt access to new technologies for energy production.

Information and communications

In the earlier sections frequent reference has been made to the need for improved information and communications within the South, as an essential ingredient for an efficient functioning of many of the proposed mechanisms and schemes. However, the point deserves added emphasis.

The importance of collective solidarity in the South should be impressed upon the people with a view to securing their support for South-South co-operation. Efforts should be made to disseminate regular information and news on the situation in the South and to publicize through the media various forms of South-South co-operation to the general public.

At the same time, the existing co-operation among the media of developing countries should be greatly intensified and diversified, and the necessary infrastructural links improved. Action on these lines could greatly contribute to the forging of horizontal links within the South, to reducing dependence on the North-based global information services, and to diversifying sources of information in developing countries.

Information is now a crucial determinant of the pace of social and economic change. Very often, the manner in which the data are collected, classified, and organized has far-reaching implications for the use that is made of these data. The South has to act collectively so as to minimize its dependence on Northern sources for data flows in critical areas. Thus, the developing countries have to work together to set up networks linking national data-banks in various sectors.

In general, South-South co-operation can be greatly enhanced by efficient, rapid, and cost-effective information links and flows, which are becoming realizable thanks to advances in information and communication technologies. As a number of South-owned communication satellites are now in orbit, specialized regional and global information networks of the South could be set in place.

People-to-people contacts

Intergovernmental and interinstitutional co-operation and links in the South need to be supplemented by broad-based inter-actions between civil societies and peoples of developing countries.

In this context, great importance attaches to the promotion of cultural exchanges, sports events, and other social contacts. This type of interaction and co-operation would build solidarity and bridges between peoples of developing countries, and would contribute to mobilizing public opinion in support of South-South co-operation.

Likewise, special attention should be given to establishing co-operation among organizations representing the self-employed, neighbourhood groups, and non-governmental voluntary organizations that have sprung up throughout the South, for these have valuable experience and expertise to share on how to get organized and how to deal with daily problems of economic, physical, and environmental survival in developing countries. Of particular importance are voluntary organizations in which women participate. Indeed, women represent a key social force for South-South co-operation at the grass-roots level, for they are able to find easily a common language across borders and continents, united by the similarity of their experiences and roles in society.

Revitalizing Regional and Subregional Economic Co-operation and Integration Schemes

Until now, South-South economic co-operation has taken place mainly within regions and subregions. As noted above, most of the activities undertaken within these groupings were affected adversely by the development crisis of the 1980s and many are consequently at a low ebb. Regional economic co-operation will continue to be an essential dimension and a major building block of South-South co-operation.

Accordingly, and though we have dealt above with a large number of issues which concern regional and subregional co-operation, we wish to stress that any programme of action for the South in the years immediately ahead must have as a principal objective the revitalization of the existing regional and subregional bodies and mechanisms. This must start from a thorough review by those bodies themselves of their problems and prospects. Each grouping or scheme of economic co-operation should review its agenda of action and critically examine its options, in the light of current circumstances and trends, and set immediate priorities and targets, as well as longer-term objectives for its work.

The Commission has not attempted to address these issues in detail, as that is better undertaken by the regional bodies themselves. It will, however, highlight some questions that seem to require their attention, and offer some suggestions which could be helpful to them in considering ways of reinvigorating regional and subregional co-operation.

A basic handicap for regional organizations has been inadequate support from their member countries, which appear to be giving low priority to South-South co-operation. It is clearly essential that this attitude should be reversed if the schemes are to gain the necessary strength. Preferential trading arrangements are functioning under the following regional and subregional schemes: ALADI, Andean Group, ASEAN, Bangkok Agreement, CACM, CARICOM, CEAO, Council for Arab Economic Unity, GCC, PTA, UDEAC. SADCC and ECOWAS are actively considering the implementation of similar arrangements. A determined effort should be made by the governments of countries which are members of regional groupings to increase support for the existing schemes and to adopt national economic policies that would make them more effective. Thus, any relevant controls on trade and foreign exchange imposed during the crisis of the 1980s should be gradually eased, the range of products covered by preferences extended, and the preferences deepened. To this end, negotiations should be started with a view to dismantling a whole range of non-tariff barriers and other trade restrictions that now inhibit the expansion of trade within various groupings.

Secondly, the governments concerned should endeavour to redress the structural imbalances that tend to impair the functioning of the schemes. Where a group's membership comprises economies at different levels of development, such imbalances are probably inevitable. To concentrate merely on the issues of trade financing and credit will not remove these structural features of the imbalances. For this, it is essential to devise national investment programmes aimed at enlarging the export capacity of countries facing such trade imbalances. Thus the integration groupings need to enter into agreements that provide wider market opportunities in the other member countries. Recent initiatives by ALADI and CARICOM to extend special concessions to less advanced member states have had a positive influence on regional trade and are to be commended.

In the long run, trade expansion can be sustained only if it is accompanied by the regional planning of investment in selected areas. Parallel efforts have to be made by the integration institutions to identify possibilities for efficient import substitution within their groupings. ALADI has recently begun negotiations on a trade-oriented programme of regional import substitution. Such exercises can yield a significant number of trading possibilities and bring prospective trading partners into contact with each other.

During periods of global recession, when countries are obliged to scale down imports, intraregional trade has been the first casualty. Regional groupings should therefore consider how their facilities could be used in such circumstances to promote intra-group trade as a countercyclical device to compensate for reduced import capabilities.

Co-ordination in planning and evaluation Most groupings do not have arrangements for evaluating and co-ordinating their members' macroeconomic policies (e.g. fiscal, inflation, employment, and exchange rate policies) and for assessing how national development plans relate to the process of economic integration. Regular opportunities for discussions among the appropriate officials and the exchange of documentation would go some way to filling this gap.

Attempts to harmonize policies and co-ordinate plans are now under way in such groupings as the Arab Maghreb Union, ECOWAS, GCC and UDEAC. An agreement under which member states would launch their multi-year development plans at the same time may serve as a useful prelude to attempts at plan co-ordination. Economic research institutions in member countries could assist these efforts by building or refining existing regional macro-models; these can provide a basis for evaluating plans for integrating trade and harmonizing production. The regional secretariats should build up their technical ability to analyse and evaluate national development plans and macroeconomic policies, with particular reference to the way in which they relate to those of other countries within the grouping.

The ultimate goal should be some degree of harmonization of plans to ensure that national policies do not conflict and that production capacities reinforce each other to strengthen the economy of the region as a whole.

Promoting co-operation between different groupings More effective links between different co-operative schemes, within the same region, and on an interregional basis, are most desirable. Arrangements for regular consultation, interaction, exchange of experience, and mutual technical assistance among those involved in schemes of co-operation and integration (governments, secretariats, enterprises, banks, etc.) are certain to be of benefit to all. Within each grouping or scheme, a special office should be established to be responsible for relations with other organizations involved in South-South co-operation, and in general to survey the relevant activities regionally and world-wide, and to seek opportunities for improved links and co-operation.

The special role of larger and more advanced countries The achievement of a degree of coherence in economic policies among the members of a regional grouping depends mainly on the behaviour of the larger and more advanced members. Their commitment to regional co-operation and to a fair distribution of its fruits, with particular attention to the needs of the least developed members, is crucial to success in co-operation. A gradual opening of their markets to partner countries would have significant results in regional trade. Their willingness to assume a degree of responsibility for the financing of the development of smaller and less developed members would provide a further stimulus to regional co-operation. In acting in these directions, they would be putting into practice some of the very precepts that the developing countries have been urging on countries in the North.

Using regional forums for settling local conflicts Regional conflicts, including armed conflicts, have proved harmful to South-South co-operation in many regions. It is encouraging, therefore, that in a number of cases developing countries have taken initiatives to help settle conflicts in their regions. The improvement of East-West relations should tend to diminish the superpowers' involvement in conflicts in the Third World. Developing countries should use the new, more auspicious climate to make more vigorous efforts to settle their conflicts and preserve peace within their regions.

Regional and subregional organizations for economic co-operation are hardly appropriate instruments for settling and managing conflicts, but they could provide a setting for consultations to ease tensions and even act as a channel through which members not parties to a dispute could offer their good offices.

The Need for a South Secretariat

The South is not well organized at the global level and has not been effective in mobilizing its shared expertise and experience or its bargaining power. As a consequence, it is at a great disadvantage in its relations with the North. This weakness is also prejudicial to the process of South-South co-operation.

This deficiency is now being felt more acutely. On the one hand, this is due to the difficulties that the developing countries have been experiencing in working together and in assuming a group stand. Furthermore, because of objections from the North,

they can no longer count on the level of technical support traditionally provided by the UNCTAD Secretariat to the Group of
77. On the other hand, the South has more at stake in the global
arena, as the agenda of issues becomes wider and more complex
and as the North, much better equipped for international negotiations, becomes more disposed to using its weight in dealing with
the South.

Many issues, in such diverse fields as trade, the international
monetary system, finance, technology, services, and the environment, and with far-reaching implications for the South, are negotiated in multilateral bodies. Their range and technical
complexity–and the multiplicity of forums in which negotiations
take place–impose a negotiating burden far beyond the capacity
of most developing countries. The existing arrangements for consultations among them–occasional meetings at the political level,
backed by meetings of ad hoc working parties and groups of officials from capitals–are inadequate to assess alternative options,
to co-ordinate their strategies, or to evolve common negotiating
positions in the various forums.

The rapidly changing global context poses further difficulties.
Current advances in science and technology have profound economic, social, and political consequences. Far-reaching shifts are
taking place in the economic structures of the developed countries, both East and West, and in these countries' relationships
with each other. They are evolving new approaches for dealing
with the South, in relation to multilateral institutions, the management of an increasingly globalized world economy, environmental change, and many other issues. The developing countries
need to be actively concerned with all these matters. It is only collectively, and through the effective organization of their collective
strength, that they can hope to safeguard their interests and prevent the North from determining unilaterally how these issues are
disposed of.

While the central common interests of the countries of the
South are as strong as ever, the increasing diversity within the
South demands careful attention to ways of accommodating different and sometimes even conflicting interests. In this situation
both technically sound assessments and continuing interaction
among countries are called for, with the object of smoothing dif-

ferences and working out agreed positions that advance the common interest.

The South's present arrangements for technical support, consisting of the modest office of the Chairman of the Group of 77 in New York and of ad hoc working parties and groups of the Group of 77 and the Non-Aligned Movement are now widely recognized to be totally inadequate for coping with these multifarious tasks. This inadequacy is highlighted by the fact that the South has to face a well-organized and united North. The developed countries not only have powerful domestic and regional institutions, but in the case of the West can also rely on the services of the OECD, which has a large secretariat with a high-calibre professional staff, efficient facilities, and ample financial resources. In addition, representatives of the leading industrial countries meet regularly at the summit level to consider a wide spectrum of topical issues and to co-ordinate their countries' policies.

In the light of these considerations, the Commission is firmly of the view that the developing countries should establish a well-staffed secretariat of the South that would provide continuing institutional support for analysis, interaction, negotiations, and follow-up action–the technical foundation for their collective action. The secretariat should deal both with the issues of South-South co-operation and with North-South relations and should become an intellectual powerhouse for the South's collective advance. Its establishment would give fresh momentum to the process of strengthening the solidarity of the South in the service of its efforts to create a better future for all its people.

As we visualize it, the South Secretariat should be at the service of the Group of 77, the Non-Aligned Movement, and the newly established Summit Level Group for South-South Consultations and Co-operation, and of the South in general, in charting directions for South-South co-operation and in working out technically sound approaches to the whole range of North-South issues. We believe that a well-organized secretariat could perform a valuable catalytic function in the South's global endeavours.

We list below a few functions which the South Secretariat should perform, while keeping in mind the likely limits on its resources, manpower, and experience at the initial stages and the need to build up its capacity and methods of work over a period of time.

Technical, intellectual, and organizational support The South Secretariat should provide technical, intellectual, and organizational support for joint initiatives and actions of the developing countries, and assist them in their efforts to deal with issues under discussion in various international organizations. In this context, the secretariat should:

- Provide research and intellectual support for negotiations and discussions on South-South co-operation. One objective in the early stages should be to improve the process of consultation for accommodating differences and for developing more effective forms of co-operation in the South.
- Seek to establish its credibility as a source of sound thinking on development issues and to demonstrate its ability to formulate a common approach for the South. On this premise, it should work out responses to the dominant approaches of the North and of the multilateral institutions controlled by the North.
- Generate and refine analyses, ideas, and policy options, based on the situation, needs, and views of the South, for the purpose of assisting the South to formulate its strategies on North-South issues and the management of global interdependence, and provide technical support in negotiations upon request.
- Support follow-up work and assist in execution where decisions are to be implemented.
- Publish an annual review of South-South co-operation, which should eventually become an authoritative work of reference and source of information.

Nucleus of a global South network The South Secretariat should perform a role in collecting and disseminating information. For this purpose, it should encourage contributions to its work from a wide range of sources in the South–academics, political parties, trade unions, NGOs, business groups, and community organizations–and should promote interaction among them. By relying on modern means of communication and data processing, it should help build a Third World communication and interaction network. It should set up a strong information, documentation, and data centre. And it should act as a clearing-house for information about technical capabilities and technologies available in different countries, and for the exchange of ideas and experiences. It is in this context that we recommend that the South Secretariat should take a lead role in launching a programme for the development of human resources in the South.

Advanced means of information storage and communication can greatly assist the new institution. These should be used to link institutions in different parts of the South in an interactive global database and ECDC/TCDC information network. Modern office-management and information technologies make possible relatively simple and efficient global linking, which will enable close and continuous interaction to be maintained with the whole of the South.

In view of its limited size, and in order to enhance its effectiveness, the secretariat should work with other appropriate institutions in the South and secure their support as a means of supplementing its resources. When necessary and possible, specific tasks, research, and projects should be commissioned from institutions. Ad hoc or standing working groups or advisory teams on given topics should be set up to assemble the best expertise from the South.

Place of contact The South Secretariat should act as a place for interaction between developing countries' representatives. It should help them to meet informally, as well as arrange formal meetings as necessary. In general, it should foster a habit of working together, a role in which the OECD has been markedly successful in the North, notably through its system of working parties, which ensure that documentation, proposals, and ideas are widely discussed among decision-makers in member countries.

Observer post The South Secretariat should also act as an observer post, analysing and interpreting events and trends on the world scene, and signalling and warning of their potential implications for the South.

Lobby for the South The South Secretariat should be active in articulating the South's position and canvassing support for it in the North, paying particular attention to political parties, trade unions, development NGOs, and other groups which can influence policy in the North. It should also work closely with countries and groups in the North that are sympathetic to the South or have complementary interests.

Commitment to the South, high-quality leadership, effective management, and the professional excellence of its staff would be paramount for the success of the South Secretariat in meeting the many demands from its large constituency. We recommend strongly therefore that its executive head should be a person of high international standing, and its senior professional officers should be chosen for their technical excellence as well as for their commitment to the cause of the South. While the activities of the secretariat would no doubt evolve over time, a minimum staff of twenty to twenty-five professionals will be required at the beginning, so as to ensure the necessary level of effectiveness. The secretariat should be subject to the supervision of an advisory board of distinguished personalities from the South.

We recognize that adequate and assured financing is vital to the functioning of the South Secretariat. We have no doubt that the necessary resources can be found within the South to finance its work, as the experience of our Commission has demonstrated. While it will take some time to work out the long-term arrangements that would assure the level of finance commensurate to the needs, we are optimistic that, as the secretariat's work proceeds and demonstrates its value to the South, the necessary resources and support will be forthcoming. In addition to the regular budget, special funds could be established on an ad hoc basis for particular activities and to enable governments or non-governmental sources to support work that is of special interest to them.

Finally, while we very much hope that it will receive widespread support, we do not believe that the establishment of the South Secretariat should depend on unanimity among the countries of the South. So long as there is substantial enough support to make its setting-up feasible, a start should be made. The quality of the secretariat's work will in time be the best guarantee of support from all countries of the South.

A PROGRAMME OF PRIORITY ACTION FOR SOUTH-SOUTH CO-OPERATION

South-South co-operation will be of very great importance to developing countries in the years ahead. Its scope is vast and it has to be pursued as a long-term undertaking. The set-backs of the 1980s now require that immediate efforts should be made to impart a fresh momentum to the South's collective work. These should start with action in a few key areas, progress in which could have catalytic effects and help to put South-South co-operation on a more secure path for the future.

As a prerequisite for the priority action programme, we wish to underline the importance of three matters for the future of South-South co-operation and of the South as a group:

* The proposal to establish the South Secretariat requires immediate action. We believe that the secretariat could act as a vital pillar of the South's efforts to expand co-operation within the South and to secure a fairer system of global relationships through negotiations with the North.
* The participation of heads of state or government in regular institutionalized consultations is a very important step towards the South's improved organization. Therefore the Commission welcomes the decision by a group of heads of state or government of developing countries to set up a Summit Level Group for South-South Consultations and Co-operation.
* The attitude of the North towards South-South co-operation has ranged from lukewarm support to benign neglect, to veiled discouragement, down to overt opposition. There are some quarters in the North that see South-South co-operation as a threat and also resist any attempt by the South to organize itself to promote its interests. We believe that the North's attitude is a matter that should be raised with the North at the highest level and that the South should seek a clear policy commitment of support for its efforts to help itself through South-South co-operation. The South should endeavour to have it accepted widely within the world community that diversified links and co-operation among developing countries

are desirable as a contribution to peace, to the well-being of all, and to the successful functioning of the world economy.

The programme of priority action we propose incorporates a number of suggestions made earlier in this chapter. They are selected and restated here as a call to action to the governments and peoples of the South:

- The success of South-South co-operation is dependent on supportive national policies and, ultimately, on the support of the people of the South. Each developing country should reflect in its development plans and national policies an explicit commitment to South-South co-operation. It should give to one government ministry or department responsibility for co-ordinating action within the country arising from the commitment to South-South co-operation. In addition, each country should set up a national committee to advise the government, to mobilize public opinion in support of South-South co-operation, and to promote people-to-people contacts in the South.

- As part of the efforts to develop the South's human resources, fuller use should be made of the South's educational institutions in meeting the needs of countries with inadequate facilities of their own. Priority should be given to the identification and development of selected Centres of Educational Excellence, particularly in the fields of basic sciences, engineering, medicine, management, and public administration. It is equally necessary to create a Foundation for South Fellowships to facilitate the movement of students, teachers, researchers, and other technical personnel among developing countries.

- In the area of financial co-operation, priority attention should be given to the strengthening of regional and subregional clearing and payments arrangements as well as export credit facilities. A co-ordinated stand of developing countries in the multilateral financial institutions and regional banks in order to obtain their support for these arrangements is highly advisable. At the same time, ways and means should be sought whereby these institutions and banks could play a more active role in financially supporting trade and other forms of South-South co-operation.

- The establishment of a debtors' forum, as proposed in the Commission's statement on debt of March 1988, remains urgent. Early action in this respect is strongly recommended.
- The proposal to establish a South Bank should be implemented. A start should be made with a narrower range of functions than originally planned. A broad group of developing countries whose association with the project would give it international credibility should take the initiative in establishing the bank, but its membership should be open to all developing countries.
- The framework for facilitating and promoting all forms of South-South trade created by the Global System of Trade Preferences should be purposefully used. Expansion and deepening of the GSTP should receive urgent priority. Action should be taken to devise a timetable and a programme of action to ensure that by the year 2000 a significant proportion of the trade among developing countries is covered by the GSTP. A regular process of review and negotiation needs to be set in motion.
- With a view to improving their position in world markets through supply management or other means, commodity producers within the South should urgently consider reinforcing existing producers' associations and setting up new ones. In particular, producers of the three tropical beverages—tea, coffee, cocoa—should work out a comprehensive programme of co-operation among them. The Group of 77 and the Non-Aligned Movement should provide strong support to these initiatives.
- Co-operation among business enterprises of the South should be promoted at the bilateral, subregional, regional, and interregional levels. All developing countries should introduce legal, technical, and fiscal measures that encourage joint ventures and the conclusion of agreements for the transfer of technology among Southern enterprises. They should give preferential treatment to investment and technology flows from other developing countries. A code for the operation of Southern multinational enterprises and for the transfer of technology should be adopted, setting out the rights and obligations of all parties. Business and industry in the South should be brought into the mainstream of South-South co-op-

eration; the establishment and effective functioning of the Association of Third World Chambers of Commerce and Industry should be made a priority. The Group of 77 and the Non-Aligned Movement should set up a Standing Committee consisting of government representatives as well as businessmen to keep enterprise co-operation under regular review.

- A process should be initiated for the review of food security and related issues on a continuous basis and for co-ordinating policies and action with respect to food security at the subregional, regional, and interregional levels. Special attention should be paid to developing joint research and productive enterprises in agro-industry and food production. Food-exporting developing countries should agree to give priority to the needs of food-importing developing countries in times of scarcity. Within regions or subregions, arrangements should be made to co-ordinate national food-stocks and establish jointly managed emergency food reserves. The South should jointly evolve a long-term programme to help Africa meet its food needs and step up food production.

- The South should develop a strategy for scientific co-operation focused on issues of major concern in which research and innovation could offer tangible benefits through the pooling of resources. The Centre for Science and Technology of the Non-Aligned and Other Developing Countries should be invited to draw up, in co-operation with the Third World Academy of Sciences and other scientific institutions in the South, a programme for co-ordinating scientific and technological research in the South in identified core areas. Particular attention should be given to fostering joint research and development in key areas of high technology such as biotechnology, informatics, and materials sciences. Southern institutions with a high level of research and facilities should be identified for training scientists, engineers, and technicians from other countries in the South under programmes of co-operation.

- Measures should be taken to make schemes for subregional and regional co-operation more effective. The existing preferential trading arrangements should be strengthened and new ones created. Controls on trade and foreign exchange should be rolled back, product coverage extended, and non-tariff barriers removed. Clearing and payments arrangements should be revitalized. These initiatives should be complemented by the regional planning of investment in selected areas. Each regional and subregional group should critically examine its options and draw up a more up-to-date agenda of action, identifying immediate priorities and targets to the year 2000, as well as a longer-term plan extending to the year 2020.

We believe that the conditions for South-South co-operation have become more favourable and that the need for such co-operation has become more compelling. We are convinced that if the South takes up the challenge seriously and comprehensively—as suggested in our Report—South-South co-operation can add an important dimension to international political and economic relations by the end of this decade.

North-South Relations and the Management of the International System

5

ONE WORLD: INTERDEPENDENCE AND NORTH-SOUTH RELATIONS

The central message of this Report is that, to get ahead, the South must primarily rely on itself. If underdevelopment is to be conquered, the countries of the South must mobilize the potential of their people and their resources for accelerated, equitable, and sustainable growth. And they must work together to multiply the impact of their domestic effort through solidarity, co-operation, and collective self-reliance.

But this message should not obscure the reality that the possibility of development in the South is closely tied to an improvement in its relationship with the North. The South needs the North as a market for its exports, as a supplier of essential imports for consumption and production, as a source of technology and of capital. Additionally, the South requires more co-operation from the North for its efforts to achieve self-reliance. Collective self-reliance is not autarky; it does not mean opting out of economic relations with the North. Scientific and technological innovation—originating mostly in the North—is opening up undreamt-of possibilities for human progress; the spread of global relations is a source of economic, social, and political dynamism. The issue for the South is not whether to cut its links with the North, but how to transform them. The relationship must be changed from exploitation to shared benefit, from subordination to partnership.

We believe this is a feasible objective because the North also needs the South. The well-being of the North and the stability of the world as a whole cannot be consolidated without ending poverty in the South. Several factors have made this increasingly apparent in the last decade.

Social tensions have been rising in many parts of the South, and in some countries are approaching explosive dimensions.

Demographic trends have made the young a growing proportion of the population, while improvements in education and communications have dramatically raised their aspirations and expectations. When economic stagnation frustrates these hopes, the result is bitterness and tension. The alienated young are joined by equally bitter adults whose livelihoods have been destroyed. Initially, the target of the discontented will be their governments, but swelling unrest may not always be contained within national borders–or within the South. Tension and conflict in the South have not been produced only by economic factors. But, there is evidence that the lack of economic opportunity, particularly for the young, is an increasing element in the turbulence within the South, and is reinforcing the strains caused by other factors.

The North cannot hope to remain insulated from social and political upheaval in the South; the upheaval will spill over, inexorably, in various ways. This is evident, for instance, from the steady flow of refugees from countries of the South to the United States and Western Europe. The ranks of those fleeing from zones of conflict or persecution are now joined by others who, seeking a better life, enter countries in the North–legally or illegally. There cannot be either genuine peace at the global level or stable and secure prosperity in the North unless the South can accelerate its growth, overcome underdevelopment, and build a better life for its people.

The North also needs the South for good economic reasons. Developing countries have become increasingly important in the world economy. Before the onset of the crisis of the 1980s, they accounted for over one-fifth of global GDP, a share comparable to that of the EC. Their weight as export markets had grown accordingly; by that time they were taking about one-fourth of the total exports of the developed countries. They provided a market for nearly 40 per cent of US exports, and for half of Japan's. Recovery and sustained development in the South will therefore enlarge the demand for the North's exports–to the North's advantage. Faster growth in the South will spur international flows of trade and investment, foster growth and employment in the North, and help to reduce payments imbalances among industrial countries.

The weight of the South in the world economy was demonstrated by the crisis of the 1980s, which caused it to reduce its imports sharply, leading to a substantial diminution of its role as a market for exports from developed countries. Had the South's ability to import in 1984-87 been at the same proportionate level as in 1981-83, the South's purchases from the North would have totalled nearly $1500 billion; in the event, because of the crisis and the contraction of imports, they fell below $1200 billion. The cumulative loss in exports to the industrialized world in those four years was more than the value of a whole year's global exports of the United States.

The resumption of development in the South is equally important in another area of central interest to the developed world: the protection of the global environment. Poverty is a major degrader of the habitat, and the state of the environment in the South is of critical importance to the health of the global ecology. Thus, the promotion of sustainable development in the South is demonstrably in the interest of the North as well, a point by now increasingly recognized by the influential environmental lobby in the North.

The overexploitation of the habitat, land, and water resources that results from the pressure of population is a direct consequence of the insecurity of life in poverty. The containment of the population explosion in the South—a matter of growing concern to public opinion in the North—is to be sought through development in the South and through a fairer distribution of income. While family planning measures are vitally necessary, they are more effective as economic security and living standards improve. Poverty must be eradicated, for only then will it be possible to create the conditions in which people are more likely to see virtue in smaller families.

These considerations add to the ethical argument for a joint North-South effort to overcome poverty and underdevelopment. A world in which a large proportion of the people is without enough food while a small proportion indulges in superfluous consumption; in which massive waste coexists with pervasive deprivation; in which the majority of the people have little control over their fates and futures, but are essentially at the mercy of trends, processes, and decisions in the centres of power of the industrialized world—such a world cannot be morally acceptable. Indeed, a substantial body of opinion in the North holds that such a state of affairs is indefensible.

The bases—political, economic, environmental, and moral— exist, therefore, for building a new international consensus on development.   Interdependence in the contemporary world, the inescapable fact that we share a fragile global habitat, the South's importance in international economic, political, and security relations—all these make growth and development in the South a condition for sustained expansion of the world economy as a whole, for the preservation of the environment and, above all, for the safety of the present and future generations. For its growth, the South needs an international setting supportive of its efforts. This calls for a profound restructuring of the economic relationships between rich and poor nations and of the manner in which the international system is organized and operates.

This chapter will review the present state of North-South relations and of the international system. It will then outline a vision of the global system of the future which, we believe, would further the South's development—and be in the interests of the world community as a whole. It will next propose the kind of changes that, from the point of view of the South, can contribute to the building of a more rationally managed and development-oriented international system. It will indicate, lastly, the kinds of efforts, processes, and means through which those changes can be realized.

NORTH-SOUTH RELATIONS AND THE INTERNATIONAL SYSTEM AT THE CLOSE OF THE 1980S

Structural Changes in the Global System

In Chapter 2 we argued that the most striking feature of the 1980s was the sharp deterioration in the international economic environment for the great majority of developing countries. This took place in the context of radical readjustments and structural changes in the world economy, with far-reaching implications for international economic interdependence. This transformation involved essentially:

- The rapid expansion of transnational enterprises as the main producers of goods and services for international trade, with a growing proportion of international transactions taking place among branches of the same firm or among related firms.

- A related expansion of the role of private banks in creating international liquidity, which became uncoupled from the growth of international trade in goods and services. The banks' international transactions escape supervision by central banks and hence national macroeconomic regulatory policy lost much of its efficacy.
- A resulting excessive growth of indebtedness in both developed and developing economies, including the public and the private sectors, and domestic as well as foreign debt.
- Changes in the relative importance of factors of production, which implied a move away from material/energy/unskilled labour-intensive products and processes and towards knowledge-intensive products and processes; this trend meant a loss of comparative advantage for developing countries.
- Related changes in the importance of sectors of production in the developed countries, implying a shift away from agriculture and industry and towards services, and rapidly expanding internationalization in the production of, and employment and trade in, services.
- Growing instability, unpredictability, and fluctuation in the functioning of the international economy, notably in interest rates and exchange rates, and growing uncertainty in capital markets.
- Significant institutional changes: at the national level, increasing deregulation, privatization, and reliance on market forces; at the international level, the collapse of the international monetary system established at Bretton Woods and the erosion of the multilateral trading system embodied in GATT.

As a result, the links among sectors of the international economy–notably among debt, trade, and finance, and among the commodity, money, and stock markets–multiplied. Instability and difficulties in one sector spread quickly, often in magnified form, to the others. The need for international economic co-ordination became more imperative, and its absence increasingly harmful. Developed countries have institutional mechanisms to cope with uncertainties. Developing countries have no such devices. They–the weakest members of the international economic system–are the main victims of the lack of rational management of the world economy. Furthermore, the deterioration of the external environment accentuated their vulnerability to external shocks, as previously available buffers–financial flows from world capital markets and compensatory finance from international financial institutions–disappeared or shrank.

The worsening of the environment for development is related to the way in which international economic relations are structured, to the way in which they are changing, and to the inability of the global system to manage these changes. The reform of those relations and of their management is a prerequisite both for creating an environment favourable to development and for introducing rationality, and a measure of predictability and certainty, into the global economic system.

The Collapse of the North-South Dialogue

The North-South dialogue, started in 1974 with the aim of negotiating changes in the global economic system in order to make it more equitable and more supportive of development, has now completely broken down. This does not mean, however, that no international negotiations are proceeding. But the negotiations that have taken place, notably the Uruguay Round on trade, have been called by the North, with an agenda devised to further its global interests. They have been imposed by the North on the South.

The North-South dialogue acquired some momentum between 1974 and 1979. It was undoubtedly spurred by the fear of the developed countries that the newly found assertiveness of the South after the rise in oil prices in 1973 could lead to a damaging confrontation. For so long as that threat was perceived as possible, the North kept the dialogue going; when it subsided, the North withdrew.

To be sure, the negotiations between 1974 and 1979 produced some progress. The United Nations General Assembly adopted in 1974 the Declaration and Programme of Action on the Establishment of a New International Economic Order, formally acknowledging for the first time that economic injustice was as much a threat to world security and peace as were military and political tensions and conflicts. In 1976 at UNCTAD IV in Nairobi, the developing countries won acceptance for the ambitious Integratcd Programme for Commodities; this envisaged a regime of international intervention to stabilize commodity markets, backed by a new financial institution, the Common Fund. The years that followed saw other gains, notably the adoption of the Charter of Economic Rights and Duties of States, the Convention on Multimodal Transport, the Agreement on Restrictive Business Practices, the decision of the governments of certain developed countries to write off the official debts of the poorest countries, and the agreement on guidelines for debt rescheduling adopted in the course of the regular negotiations conducted by debtor developing countries with official creditors in the Paris Club.

But most of these gains had little substance beyond declaratory value. When specific aspects of the New International Economic Order came to be discussed, the developed countries won the major strategic advantage from the beginning; they ensured that the negotiations would take place in different forums, thus fragmenting them, straining the negotiating capabilities of the South, and allowing procrastination in the adoption of agreements capable of being implemented. An attempt was made at UNCTAD V in Manila in 1979 to initiate wide-ranging negotiations that would take account of the fact that the issues were interrelated. But this was rejected by the North, by then much less fearful of oil power.

In effect, meaningful North-South negotiations ended at that conference in Manila. The Cancun Summit of twenty-two Heads of State and Government, which took place in 1981, co-chaired by the President of Mexico and the Prime Minister of Canada, was an effort to find political support for a sustained process of North-South negotiations. But it did not succeed. By that time there had been an ideological shift in the governments of some leading countries of the North. In addition the governments of most of the countries of the North had become preoccupied with fighting inflation at home, and gave no priority to agreeing on a new basis for North-South economic relations or to defining the nature, scope, and prospects of interdependence links in the world economy.

At UNCTAD VI in Belgrade in 1983, the UNCTAD Secretariat and the Group of 77 made another attempt to revive the North-South dialogue on the basis of a revised rationale: the need to reactivate development in the South as an essential means of stimulating the global economy and reinforcing recovery in the industrialized countries themselves. This was, again, turned down by the North, which argued that recovery in the North was already under way and would in due course spill over to the South. It further claimed that to try to stimulate the economies of the South directly would only create inflationary pressures; it argued that the South should undertake adjustment, i.e. belt-tightening, until the spillover took place. Thus Belgrade not only confirmed the impasse in the North-South dialogue but brought dramatically to light that any shared commitment to it had vanished.

Equally unsatisfactory is the absence of coherent international management of the environment. The countries of the South are today the victims of the deleterious environmental effects of policies and patterns of development in the North. These include such global phenomena as the thinning of the ozone layer, nuclear radiation, and the greenhouse effect, as well as such direct acts as the dumping of hazardous wastes and the location of polluting industries in the South. Attempts by the developing countries to bring the global commons–in particular the oceans and outer space–under effective international jurisdiction have been defeated in practice by the lack of co-operation of the developed countries. The situation is made worse by the pressure on developing countries resulting from the debt burden. They must at all costs increase their receipts of foreign exchange to service the debt. Equally, the fall in commodity prices leads to pressure to increase production and step up exports. The result is, on the one hand, that developing countries are forced to overexploit their resources, harming the environment, and, on the other, to accept environmentally damaging deals with the North, e.g. deals for the disposal of toxic wastes.

One feature which has characterized the world economic scene in the last ten years or so and which is potentially very damaging to the long-term development prospects of the South is the increasing monopolization of technological progress by transnational corporations in the North. At the same time as the sweeping pace of technological innovation in key new fields is revolutionizing society and offering breathtaking possibilities for human advancement, the principle of science as the shared heritage of mankind is being systematically eroded. Knowledge is becoming increasingly privatized, and the South is being excluded. Transnational corporations control the flow of technology; they decide where to locate productive operations and on what terms they will provide services and transfer technology, being guided entirely by considerations of their world-wide corporate interests that are often in conflict with the interests of host developing countries. Developing countries find themselves increasingly unable to predict, let alone regulate, these flows.

A Special Session of the UN General Assembly on Development Co-operation was held at the end of April while we were finalizing our Report. Its results represent a limited response to the persistent call of the developing countries for a revitalization of the North-South dialogue.

The Declaration adopted covers many of the issues addressed in our Report. We welcome the recognition given in the Declaration to many of the serious problems facing developing countries which require urgent action. We regret, however, that this recognition did not translate itself into concrete commitments to action at this time of crisis for many developing countries and, that as a result, no formal follow-up mechanism was agreed. Such agreement, limited as it was, was more on what to say than on what to do. We are confirmed in our view that there is a need for continuing concerted action of the kind recommended in this Report to secure renewed efforts towards a North-South Action Programme. We can only hope that the Declaration will help to set the stage for such action through a new phase of the North-South dialogue and the revitalization of international economic co-operation for development in the forthcoming relevant multilateral conferences.

Recent developments

The closing years of the decade of the 1980s featured other international developments whose impact on the South is still largely uncertain. Reference has already been made to the growing awareness in the international community of the common interest in taking up the global environmental challenge. While the intellectual arguments in this respect have been rehearsed for a long time, there is now sufficient political consciousness and support in the North to make the environment a promising subject for global co-operation. In order that this co-operation may materialize,

however, there must be an explicit recognition by the North that
the protection of the environment is a matter of global concern,
that the responsibilities for, and costs of, its protection, should be
shared equitably, and that protective measures cannot be taken
at the expense of the development of the South.

Other trends in the international scene, as discussed in Chapter 1, are the reduction in East-West tensions and the resumption
of disarmament negotiations. These developments are welcome,
and together with the economic and political reforms in Eastern
Europe, they offer opportunities as well as challenges. The situation is complex, for the potential positive effects of the changes
have to be balanced against possible drawbacks, and the ultimate
implications for North-South relations are still unclear.

Insofar as reforms in the USSR and Eastern Europe spur economic progress in the countries concerned, the effect in the medi-
um-to-long term on the world economy, and particularly on
world trade, could be beneficial. This change in turn could produce a more favourable external environment for the development of the South. However, in the present international context
many uncertainties remain.

To begin with, the USSR and Eastern Europe cannot be a
source of large-scale transfers of resources to the Third World.
Indeed, their own demand for Western capital is increasing which
will mean that they would absorb some of the surplus savings of
the West, including that part which otherwise would have been
available for investment in the South. Despite assertions to the
contrary by Western sources, we remain deeply concerned over a
probable diversion of both attention and resources from development.

If progress is made towards disarmament and arms control,
there should be international agreement that part of the savings
on armaments expenditure be set aside for agreed international
purposes–particularly environmental protection, food security,
and meeting basic needs in the South. The South must therefore
be alert to the need to press forcefully the case for a link between
disarmament and development; otherwise, the much vaunted
'peace dividend' will elude its reach.

Enterprises in Eastern Europe, now having greater economic
freedom to enter into foreign transactions, will no doubt seek
more competitive sources for capital and other imports. Specifi-

cally in the case of trade, this new approach could place some developing countries at a disadvantage vis-à-vis Western suppliers. However, in the short run the stated objective of the USSR of greatly increasing its imports of consumer goods could open up opportunities for countries of the South in a position to export such goods, particularly consumer durables and light manufactures, at competitive prices. The bilateral balancing which was formerly a feature of trade between Eastern European and developing countries limited the scope for trade. Should the Eastern European countries progressively multilateralize their trade and payments arrangements, the scope for trade is likely to expand, but the change may also create some transitional problems for developing countries hitherto heavily dependent on markets in the USSR and Eastern Europe with special payment arrangements.

If, thanks to economic reforms, the standard of living in the Eastern European countries rises, their consumption of labour-intensive products will increase in the long run. A trade regime in those countries that enables developing countries to supply an increasing proportion of the consumption of these goods would considerably improve the trade prospects for the Third World. However, in the short run, the countries of the South may face more intense competition in some of their traditional export markets in the North from the Eastern European countries.

As indicated, the ending of the Cold War may facilitate the settlement of at least some regional conflicts in the Third World. However, as tensions ease between the two superpowers, a situation may arise in which they feel they can operate more freely to promote what they consider as their essential interests in areas they regard as strategic–or indeed support each other's policies in such areas –irrespective of the interests of countries in these areas. To forestall this situation, a strengthening of multilateral political and economic institutions is essential.

In the long run the participation of the Eastern European countries in the IMF, World Bank, and GATT should contribute to a more balanced multilateral approach to global economic issues. As importers of capital and technology, and as exporters in need of expanding their share in world markets for their products, these countries have a common interest with the countries of the South in a basic reform of the global economic system. The

USSR, like the developing countries, is a major producer of primary commodities; its support for the Common Fund for Commodities could materially strengthen efforts to reduce the instability and uncertainty characterizing world commodity trade.

THE VISION: A RATIONAL AND DEVELOPMENT-ORIENTED INTERNATIONAL SYSTEM

The need–and the opportunity–for a fundamental reshaping of the international system are apparent. It is also clear that the South must play a crucial role in such a reshaping. Just as there cannot be genuine development in the South without a better international environment, so there cannot be a truly stable system of global relations without development in the South. Accordingly, the salient features of the international system we envisage are two-fold:

- It should provide the framework for a rational, coherent, and democratic management of international economic and political relations that can ensure peace, stability, prosperity, and human dignity within the global community as a whole.
- It should embody as a central objective the support of the efforts of the countries of the South to resume growth and to undertake a process of sustainable and self-reliant development.

To achieve these objectives, what is required is a fundamental reform of the international financial, monetary, and trading systems, including the establishment of contingency mechanisms for resource flows to ensure the orderly continuation of development efforts in the face of unforeseen shocks and uncertainty. The post-war international system needs an overhaul of its mechanisms for political consultation and of its multilateral economic institutions to accomodate these two objectives and to meet the challenges arising from changes in the USSR and Eastern Europe. Such a reformed global system would also necessitate the establishment of a fair international regime for science and technology and of structures for the equitable management of the global environment.

In the reform of the international financial system, the central need is to set up durable arrangements for the transfer of adequate resources from developed to developing countries so as to accelerate development in the South. This issue was not adequately addressed in the design of the Bretton Woods system, notwithstanding the establishment of the World Bank. In the long run, the countries of the South should endeavour to cover their capital needs from their own resources. However, until these countries are able to achieve a self-sustaining momentum of growth, and particularly for the poorest and least developed countries, flows of long-term development finance from the North will continue to be needed. The new global financial system should therefore include a mechanism for providing development finance to the South with the security and continuity that bilateral aid, private direct investment, and commercial financial flows have so far been–and will no doubt continue to be–unable to provide. In the short run it should also include provision for a substantial reduction of the burden of servicing external debts. The cause of global well-being and prosperity would be best served if the surplus savings of countries like Japan and the Federal Republic of Germany were channelled towards productive uses in the developing countries rather than to increase consumption in the rich countries.

The reform of the international financial system is, in a fundamental sense, inseparable from the reform of the international monetary system. A reformed monetary system must:

- provide for the establishment and management of an international reserve asset
- introduce greater stability of exchange rates and international interest rates
- provide adequate international liquidity on terms that take account of the needs of all countries, including the special needs of developing countries
- facilitate and be consistent with the mechanisms for resource transfers referred to above

The long-term goal of the international community should be to transform a fundamentally restructured International Monetary Fund into a genuine world central bank.

The reform of the international trading system should be oriented towards creating a global rule-based system built on the principles of transparency, multilateralism, and non-discrimination. It should lead to improved access to markets for developing countries and enable them to expand their share of world trade in products in which they have a distinct comparative advantage; it should, in addition, provide increased support for the growth of trade among developing countries themselves. The promotion of sustained development in the Third World should be a central objective; the new system should consequently maintain the principle, recognized by the Contracting Parties to GATT, of differential and more favourable treatment for the exports of developing countries and limited reciprocity. It should also include arrangements to secure stable and remunerative returns for the commodity exports of developing countries; these should include arrangements for the stabilization of both prices and earnings. The long-term objective must continue to be to set up an International Trade Organization, with a much wider mandate than the GATT and paying particular attention to the trade and development needs of developing countries.

The objectives we have set out are closely linked to the need to reduce the harmful effects for developing countries of uncertainty and unpredictability in the flows of long-term capital, in exchange rates and interest rates, and in trade flows. Until developing countries achieve a reasonable level of development, it is fair that the international community should accept responsibility for devising mechanisms to shield them from the disruptive consequences of volatility in world markets.

In the field of science and technology, the aim should be to introduce an international regime that allows the South a fair chance to share in the benefits from the revolutionary advances that are now being made. The North will continue to be the principal locus of scientific and technological innovation for a long time to come. For its part, the South must be able both to develop science and technology in its own right and to have access to the results of scientific and technological work in the North, including work in the advanced areas of technology, on favourable terms.

Closely related to this, the aim of developing countries in the environmental field must be to secure the adoption of a global strategy for sustainable development in the context of a redefined notion of global interdependence and shared benefits and costs. What is required is an international regime of duties and responsibilities for the rational management of the planet and for making it safer for human habitation.

Lastly, in the context of the reform of institutional arrange-ments, there must be a reconsideration of the role of the United Nations in the management of the international system and in decision-making on world economic and social issues. The United Nations should play a pivotal role. For this purpose, the capabil-ity of the UN system to make comprehensive reviews of the func-tioning of the world economy and the prospects for development must be strengthened and made credible. Institutional reform is thus needed, with the aim of setting up a focal structure for eco-nomic decision-making within the UN system which would set strategies, policies and priorities for the entire system and review and evaluate developments in its specialized agencies and other related bodies. This reform should also include changes aimed at democratizing and increasing the effectiveness of the United Na-tions in dealing with global security and regional conflicts.

THE PROPOSALS: POLICIES, STRATEGIES, PROCESSES, AND INSTITUTIONS

The bases for a new international development consensus–a pact of global solidarity between South and North–are in place, and increasingly evident to any impartial observer. However, the North, its governments and its decision-makers, by and large re-fuse to acknowledge them. This attitude reflects, on the one hand, the extent to which official Northern thinking has come to be do-minated by the ideological notion that attempts at managing the world economy are, by definition, bound to be pernicious. As in-dicated earlier, this has not prevented the governments of the North from making efforts to co-ordinate their macroeconomic policies in some areas, such as exchange rate management. On the other hand, it reflects the power of special interests in the North for whom improved economic conditions in the South are either irrelevant or may even be unwelcome in view of their immediate financial or commercial impact.

The urgency of the case therefore calls for renewed efforts to mobilize opinion in the North. It is necessary to set up arenas and forums in which exchanges and negotiations can take place, to identify governments and groups with which agreement can be sought in specific areas, to define objectives and set priorities among them so that the initially possible may open a sequence of steps towards the ultimate goals. The South must strive for a revival of the North-South dialogue on a more meaningful and realistic basis. For this purpose, the South must be clear about its central proposals for reform and about the process that might lead to their being adopted and implemented. The following paragraphs present some elements of a possible set of proposals and attempt to outline the steps ahead.

Debt, Capital Flows, and Resource Transfers

Paramount among the issues on which action is urgent is that of debt. Achieving a durable solution to this problem has become an absolute prerequisite for any resumption of growth, not only in the heavily indebted countries, but in most parts of the South. The creditors have so far stuck to a case-by-case approach, refusing until very recently to consider debt reduction except for the least developed countries, and pressing the debtor countries to hold down their expenditure in order to generate trade surpluses with which to service the debt. This strategy has served the banks well: a crisis has been averted. But it has completely failed to free developing countries from the predicament in which they are trapped. They need a substantial reduction of their burden of debt servicing in order that they may be left with sufficient resources to achieve a level of growth that would enable them to service their debt soundly in the future.

The time has come therefore for effective multilateral action to scale down the debt and reduce the burden of debt service to tolerable levels. In most cases, the debt crisis has turned out to be a crisis of solvency rather than merely of liquidity. In all historical experiences of generalized difficulties, the burden of debt on the debtors was reduced–either de facto or by agreement–by reducing the capital owed or the interest payments or both. This approach must also prevail in the present debt crisis. The point must be accepted once and for all that the external debt of the developing countries is not repayable in full, and that its full nominal value will not be paid. The Brady initiative is only a cautious first recognition of this realistic proposition. The official position of the creditor banks and governments of developed countries remains that any reduction is a matter for voluntary decisions by the banks.

The upshot is that debt has become a form of bondage, and the indebted economies have become indentured economies–a clear manifestation of neo-colonialism. This state of affairs cannot go on. The debt and its service must be reduced to a level that allows growth to proceed at an acceptable pace.

The implementation of the Brady initiative clearly reveals its limitations. The conditions for its use are unduly restrictive: the plan applies solely to the debt owed to commercial banks. The currently available pool of $30 billion is clearly inadequate to achieve a significant measure of debt reduction. There is no official target for debt reduction, nor are there even agreed criteria for determining whether the amount of debt reduction is adequate for particular countries. And the banks fully retain the right to choose between debt reduction and new lending, the latter being in many cases intended only, or mainly, to maintain the service of the old debt without any alleviation of the debt burden as such. Unless these arrangements involve substantial reductions in the net transfer of capital from developing to developed countries, allowing vigorous growth to take place, they will do no more than add to the debt burden for the future.

What is needed is a concerted approach to achieve a substantial reduction of debt and debt service simultaneously. Negative transfers of resources–from poor to rich–should be ended, and the service of the debt should be related to the ability of the economy to pay and to grow. The amount of debt service that a country can bear–and is required to pay–should be linked to the level of resources it needs to keep income per head rising at a rate of at least 2-3 per cent a year. The necessary level of resources can be determined with reasonable accuracy through macroeconomic analysis for individual countries. The policies for achieving this target could then be negotiated, taking into account the various forms of debt and the circumstances of the debtor country concerned. The central point, though, is that the reduction of debt and of debt service should be the subject of multilateral intergovernmental negotiation.

We reaffirm the need for an International Debt Conference with the participation of the debtor governments, the governments of the creditors, and the international financial insti-

tutions, whose mandate would be to arrive at a binding
international agreement on a framework solution. The international financial institutions must evolve a medium-term programme regarding the net financing needs of debtor countries
consistent with the accepted growth objective. The international
political community must assume its responsibility in this area.

Any global agreement on the South's external debt must make
specific provision for the case of the least developed countries,
whose needs are not addressed in the Brady initiative. Their total
debts are not large in absolute terms. However, in most cases, in
relation to the size of their economies and to the volume of their
foreign trade, they represent a very heavy burden. For example,
in 1988 the total external debt of the severely indebted low-income countries was equal to 111 per cent of their combined GNP
and to 488 per cent of their combined exports; the corresponding
proportions for the seventeen highly indebted countries were 54
per cent and 300 per cent. As can be seen, for countries whose
economies are in a state of crisis, this constitutes an insurmount-
able obstacle to any attempts at reviving growth and development. The debt burden of the three regions of the South is
presented in Figs. 5.1 and 5.2.

A major new step is now needed. This should involve, in the
first place, the full write-off of the bilateral official debt of the
least developed countries–as already done partially by Canada,
Denmark, Finland, France, the Federal Republic of Germany,
Italy, Luxembourg, the Netherlands, Norway, Sweden, Switzerland, and the United Kingdom. It should also involve the extension of debt cancellation to other low-income countries that may
be less poor but are still heavily indebted, and the refinancing on
concessional terms of the nonconcessional bilateral official debt,
as well as of the multilateral debt, of all countries concerned. The
participation of the IMF and the World Bank in operations to reduce debt and debt service should be increased. The establishment by the World Bank of a debt reduction facility for
low-income countries that have access to Bank's resources only
through its soft-loan affiliate, IDA, is welcome, but the sum of
$100 million being made available to the facility is insufficient. A
substantial increase is needed.

Figure 5.1

External Debt as Per Cent of GNP, 1980-88

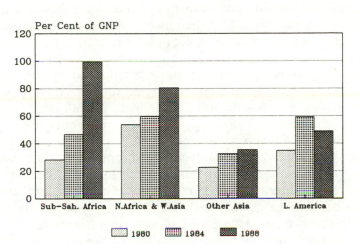

Figure 5.2

Debt Service as Per Cent of Export of Goods and Services,
1980-88

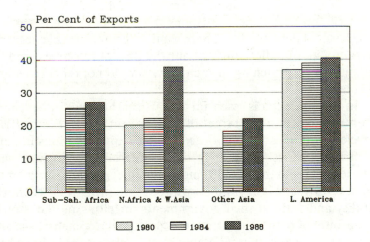

Source: World Bank, *World Debt Tables, 1989-90.*

Even after a substantial reduction in the debt burden of the developing countries, there will initially be a need for large capital transfers from the developed countries if growth is to be resumed on a sustained basis and a self-reinforcing process of capital accumulation started. The countries of the South should then be able to generate capital for their own development, but given the present crisis, particularly in the poorest countries, a transitional stage in which external resources are needed is unavoidable. Past experience shows that these cannot be supplied by the private sector. In the 1970s the bulk of external financial flows to developing countries took the form of commercial bank loans. The severe limitations of that approach are now only too clear. Excessive reliance on commercial flows is dangerous, as they are uncertain, unpredictable, and can fall sharply when most needed, thus accentuating cyclical fluctuations. Furthermore they are not, on the whole, available to the poorest countries, for these are considered to be insufficiently creditworthy, nor are they provided for investments in physical and social infrastructure such as roads or irrigation systems, schools, or hospitals. Such investments are crucial for development, but, because they do not yield direct or immediate profits, they do not qualify for commercial loans.

What is needed therefore is an international system that will provide an adequate volume of external capital to the developing countries on terms and conditions that do not create unsustainable levels of debt service. There should be a reasonable degree of certainty and predictability about the flow of resources, and the conditionality attaching to such flows should not reflect ideological bias.

In this context it is essential to reaffirm the need for developed countries to attain the target of 0.7 per cent of GNP for official development assistance adopted by the United Nations in 1968. A few countries–Denmark, the Netherlands, Norway, and Sweden–have, to their credit, more than met global targets for aid for several years. They did so without impairing their economic vitality and without their governments forfeiting public support on account of their commitment to global development. Some developing countries such as Kuwait and Saudi Arabia have consistently far exceeded the target. The performance of all these countries serves to question the validity of the economic and political difficulties cited by larger countries to justify their own failure. Those that have failed include the United States, whose aid to GNP ratio slipped from 0.24 per cent in 1980-84 to 0.21 per cent in 1988, the Federal Republic of Germany (down from 0.46 to 0.39 per cent), and the United Kingdom (down from 0.37 to 0.32 per cent). The gap between target and performance for the developed countries as a group widened between the 1960s and the 1980s. The need to reverse this trend and move closer to the target should be a central element in any forthcoming negotiations.

The aid requirements of the least developed countries deserve priority attention. At the 1981 United Nations Conference on the least developed countries most donors had agreed to provide 0.15 per cent of their GNP to these countries. In 1988, donor members of the Development Assistance Committee of the OECD achieved almost 0.09 per cent, little more than half of the target. It is imperative that international efforts be intensified to double official development assistance (ODA) to the least developed countries by 1995 and to increase the level of ODA to these countries to 0.20 per cent of donors' GNP by the end of the 1990s.

It is equally important to enlarge the share of multilateral assistance in financial flows to developing countries. International financial institutions, notably the World Bank and the regional development banks, must be given a much larger role in meeting the requirements for development finance. These institutions have the responsibility to promote a more rational and equitable allocation of global savings. However, both for want of resources and because of the ideological prejudices of some developed countries, they have not been playing this role. Between 1983 and 1987, the net transfer of resources (new loans less capital repayments and interest payments) associated with World Bank lending was almost insignificant. In 1988 it turned negative for the first time, so that the Bank was receiving from the developing countries more than it was lending to them–a topsy-turvy situation which negates the Bank's role as a development finance institution.

Recent trends point to increases in the resources available to the multilateral institutions as part of a general increase of their capital. However, they have also made the use of these resources by developing countries increasingly conditional upon the adoption of adjustment policies of doubtful value. The expansion of the role of these institutions should therefore be accompanied by a depoliticization of their operations, in order to ensure that the conditions they impose on borrowing countries are not based on ideological premises. Also necessary is a change in their decision-making structures to make these more representative of developing countries.

Particular significance attaches to the enlargement of the concessional component of multilateral assistance. The poorer countries of the South, which cannot afford credit on normal commercial terms, will have to depend primarily on concessional assistance from multilateral sources in the years to come. This calls, among other things, for increases in the resources available to the multilateral sources of concessional assistance, i.e. IDA, IFAD, and the soft windows of the regional development banks. In the light of prospective requirements these sources should be enabled to maintain a minimum annual real increase of 15 per cent in their lending to developing countries. We welcome the agreement among the donor countries for the IXth replenishment of IDA resources. However, while the needs of countries eligible for loans from IDA have greatly increased, the resources made available are no higher than those of IDA VIII. This is clearly unsatisfactory. Moreover, in view of the difficulties and delays invariably associated with the negotiations on the funds for each IDA cycle, future replenishments should cover a minimum period of five years as against the present three years.

In addition, the World Bank should revive the Third Window instituted for a short period in the 1970s to provide loans on terms intermediate between those applicable to IDA loans on the one hand and regular World Bank loans on the other. The need for this Third Window is again strong. IDA's resources have not been increased. The pressing needs of sub-Saharan Africa call for a larger allocation of IDA funds to this region. That will leave a number of poor countries outside Africa with high debt-service obligations whose needs IDA will not be able to meet adequately.

Regional development banks must play an enlarged role. These banks are better equipped than the World Bank to take into account regional differences within the South. Albeit with variations, developing countries have a more influential voice in those institutions than in the World Bank and the IMF. Because of this higher Southern influence, the North tends to question the quality and operational capabilities of the regional banks. This issue should be brought into the open in negotiations with the North. The real position and problems should be assessed and, if necessary, a short-to-medium-term programme agreed to strengthen their technical capabilities. A larger mandate should then be internationally agreed for these institutions to include, in addition to project finance, programme finance, balance-of-payments support, and finance for regional and interregional trade. Their resources should be expanded accordingly.

Direct foreign investment Direct investment from abroad may become increasingly important in meeting some of the capital requirements of developing the South. However, it should also be recognized that the flow of investment from the North to the South has decreased in the last decade. On the other hand, South-South investment flows could increase. The question therefore is how direct foreign investment should be internationally managed so as to avoid the disputes that marked the relations between host countries and transnational companies in the 1960s and 1970s. The establishment by the World Bank of the Multilateral Investment Guarantee Agency (MIGA) was an important step towards removing some of the main apprehensions of the transnationals. The new agency offers possibilities to developing countries which should be explored in each case, particularly in so far as it can facilitate foreign investment by Southern enterprises within the South. With respect to Northern transnationals, though, the need remains for international action to meet the concerns of developing countries. In effect, what is required is an international framework to regulate the activities of transnational corporations in developing countries.

A starting point for building such a framework would be the introduction of a code of conduct for transnational corporations. Since the time when negotiations on a Code of Conduct for Transnational Corporations began at the United Nations in 1976, significant progress has been made on a number of its draft provisions, and the technical-support work for the Code as a whole has been practically completed. The next step will have to be a political commitment on the part of both developed and developing countries to implement the proposals, which, on the whole, are clearly in their common interest.

Joint ventures and other forms of association among small and medium-sized firms in the industrial countries and the business sector in the South might provide new channels for the transfer of managerial skills and technology, for investment flows, for the opening of new markets, and for closer and constructive North-South relations.

Closely related to this topic are the attempts at introducing international rules to control restrictive business practices. Such practices as those barring a Northern company's subsidiary in a developing country from exporting to a particular market are common, and developing countries have no means of checking them. Agreement on a set of principles and rules was reached in UNCTAD in 1980, but these make no provision for penalizing violations and, most decisively, do not cover restrictive business practices among subsidiaries of the same transnational corporation. Hence, the effectiveness of these rules and principles is very doubtful, as was found by an intergovernmental panel of experts convened in 1981 to review the operation of the provisions in question. The need to introduce an effective form of international regulation of restrictive business practices thus remains. It should be pressed by the South, particularly as the trend towards monopolization and mergers is on the increase in the North.

South investment in the North

The resources available for national development in the South are eroded when capital from the South is invested in the North. This happens not only through illegal movements of capital; it happens in the case of any transaction whereby resources originating in an economy in the South are remitted to the North to be invested in bonds, shares, productive assets, real estate, and the like. The IMF estimates that the stock of foreign assets of capital-importing countries–excluding offshore banking centres–amounted at the end of 1985 to $511 billion, and that capital outflows from those countries between 1974 and 1985 totalled about $250 billion. These are probably underestimates because of definitional problems; but the outflow still adds up to about 40 per cent of the increase in the South's external debt in that period.

The individual who sends his money abroad is no doubt seeking greater security or a higher income and acting rationally in his own interests. But for a country short of capital, the outflow of resources amounts to self-inflicted damage–and is clearly against the national interest. It reduces domestic investment as well as the tax base of the economy. Even though the returns earned from investment abroad might be higher than those obtainable from domestic investment at the private level, the social returns on domestic projects will in all likelihood exceed private returns.

It is clearly desirable that the resources of developing countries in need of funds for domestic investment should continue to remain there, and that efforts should be made to have capital that has gone to the North repatriated. Investment in the North is made easier, and encouraged, by the increasing interdependence and transnationalization of the world economy, and as such it has a structural basis. However, it has been further facilitated by the premature removal of foreign exchange controls and of restrictions on the movement of capital–as part of the adjustment programmes promoted by the IMF and the World Bank in the name of economic liberalization. A well-designed system of controls on foreign capital transactions can reduce the outflow of capital from the South.

Governments in the North can make a contribution to stemming the drain of financial resources from the South by co-operating under treaties of mutual legal assistance with Southern governments in identifying and instituting judicial proceedings against those responsible for illegal movements of capital from the South.

The most important factor influencing the outflow of capital is, however, the extent to which the economies of the South offer, or do not offer, credible possibilities for profitable investment. Nationals are less likely to send their capital abroad if their home countries are able to control inflation, keep the exchange rate steady, and provide stability and certainty in the investment regime. In the end, what matters is the dynamism of the South's economies. A resumption of growth is thus a condition for a long-term solution to the problem of capital outflow. In the short term, curbs on capital movements appear indispensable to keep it under some control and to blunt the harm it does to many economies in the South.

The International Monetary System

The growth of the world economy needs liquidity, just as an engine needs lubricants. It should be available in adequate amounts to all countries. Recent trends have tended to concentrate international liquidity in private hands–the banks and other financial institutions of the North. While there is sufficient liquidity within the world as a whole, its growing privatization puts the South at a great disadvantage.

In the discussions on international monetary reform in the 1960s, considerable emphasis was laid on bringing the creation of world liquidity under international control so that it could respond better to global needs. In 1969, the IMF created a new reserve asset in the form of Special Drawing Rights (SDRs) as an immediate means to increasing liquidity. But interest soon waned after the Bretton Woods system broke down, fixed exchange rates gave way to floating rates, and the international banking system started expanding vigorously. The IMF has made too few allocations of SDRs and taken no major steps to make SDRs the principal reserve asset of the world monetary system.

Subsequent events have shown, however, that there is a need for considerable official financing even with floating exchange rates. And this need is likely to grow as countries seek to reduce the fluctuations in their exchange rates resulting from the operation of market forces. At the same time, the hazards of relying on the traditional methods of liquidity creation–the balance-of-payments deficits of reserve-currency countries and conditional liquidity provided by the private financial sector–have not diminished. The instability and unpredictability that go with reliance on these methods are not conducive to orderly growth in world trade and output. Fiscal and monetary discipline in the North is essential. The use of several national currencies as international reserve assets needs to be phased out.

In addition, world conditions hardly allow developing countries to build up external reserves through trade surpluses. At the same time, they need larger reserves of foreign exchange because of the increased instability and uncertainty of their international economic transactions. Hence, immediate action to enlarge developing countries' access to liquidity is clearly needed.

A regular annual allocation of SDRs during the next few years would provide some relief to developing countries. However, since SDRs are allocated to countries in proportion to their quotas in the IMF—the richer the country, the higher the quota—this relief is unlikely to be very substantial. Thus there is a strong case for giving a modest amount of SDRs on a regular basis exclusively to developing countries so as to ensure a more balanced international distribution of liquidity. This objective would be achieved if developed countries agreed to surrender some of their share of SDR allocations to the IMF in favour of developing countries.

The long-term objective should remain that of making the SDRs the main reserve asset for the international monetary system. To the fullest possible extent the creation of liquidity should be placed under the control of the international community. The reformed monetary system ought to impose symmetrical obligations for adjustment on both surplus and deficit countries. It should have adequate powers to ensure effective surveillance of international financial markets and on the macroeconomic policies of major economic powers whose actions have far-reaching implications for the functioning of the global economy. Moreover, the reformed system must show adequate concern for the trade, investment, and development needs of the countries of the South.

Another crucial aspect of international monetary reform is exchange rate management. The move from fixed exchange rates to floating rates is probably irreversible. However, there has been growing concern about the high volatility and prolonged misalignment in exchange rates since the shift to floating rates in the early 1970s. Several developed countries have devised effective national and international arrangements for dealing with the consequences of excessive uncertainty and unpredictability in exchange rates. Futures markets in currencies, interest rates, and currency swaps are among these arrangements. The institution of the European Monetary System with its exchange rate mechanism and the arrangements now being envisaged to establish a monetary union among the members of the European Community represent another attempt to minimize damage caused by excessive fluctuations in exchange rates.

For various reasons, developing countries are unable to protect themselves from the effects of prolonged misalignment and excessive movements in the exchange rates of the currencies of major developed countries. They therefore have a strong interest in effective international arrangements to reduce the scope for misalignment and volatility. One way would be to introduce a system of target zones for the currencies in which most of the world's trade is conducted, whereby their exchange rates would be allowed to move only within an agreed range. Achieving this objective is bound to be a long and complex process, as it is linked to the co-ordination of the macroeconomic policies of the leading developed countries. The trend towards the deregulation of financial markets encouraged by the prevailing economic philosophies in these countries has tended to hamper such co-ordination. However, as already indicated, there is now a growing recognition in the developed countries that it is needed, though co-ordination has yet to be institutionalized. It is clearly in the interest of developing countries that this process should be strengthened.

How will the international monetary system evolve over the longer term? One strong possibility is the formation of currency blocs built on the US dollar, the West German mark or the European Currency Unit, and the Japanese yen. But it is difficult to visualize how such a development would affect the world economy. Nevertheless, we consider that developing countries are entitled to a say in the way exchange rate arrangements are decided and operated because these have world-wide repercussions. They should press for more effective international surveillance of exchange rate arrangements among major developed countries and of their macroeconomic policies.

So far as international interest rates are concerned, the aim must be to bring them in line with historical levels. Present levels are totally incompatible with a sustained resumption of investment in the developing countries. There is simply no way in which productive investments financed by international borrowing at the current rates of interest can yield a reasonable return. Investment in the South is therefore bound to be squeezed hard as long as interest rates remain as high as they are. The reality, however, is that a lasting reduction in international interest rates will not take place without action to narrow the United States budget deficit– action which it has consistently failed to undertake. Pending a general decline in interest rates, mechanisms have therefore to be devised to insulate developing countries from the effects of unusually high rates.

Compensatory finance There has been a general recognition by the world community in the post-war period of the need for contingency provisions, by way of mechanisms for compensatory and supplementary financing, to be built into the operations of international financial institutions to cushion developing countries against a sudden reversal of their economic prospects. The establishment by the IMF in 1963 of a Compensatory Financing Facility (CFF) to provide assistance to developing countries facing unexpected shortfalls in exports was a limited response to this need. In the 1970s, the scope of this facility was expanded to include the financing of contributions to international buffer stocks of primary commodities and to cover unexpected increases in the cost of cereal imports.

The increased uncertainty and fluctuations in the world economy in the 1980s–and the continued vulnerability of developing countries–amply justify a further widening and deepening of the Compensatory Financing Facility. Unfortunately, the trend has been in the reverse direction. The CFF was originally designed to provide quasi-automatic financial support for developing countries whose export revenue fell sharply. Its initial conditionality was very low. Until the 1970s, the access limits which govern how much a country may borrow were also gradually increased. However, in the 1980s, under the ideological pressure of some developed countries, the IMF substantially tightened the conditions associated with support under this facility.

In 1988 the IMF merged the CFF in a new Compensatory and Contingency Financing Facility (CCFF). This has the merit of covering a wider range of external shocks than falls in export earnings and increases in cereal import bills. For example, it can also assist countries to meet unexpected increases in interest payments on external debt. But the new facility lowered the limit on drawings from 83 to 65 per cent of a country's IMF quota, and also made the conditionality more severe. Under the earlier CFF, countries could draw up to 50 per cent of quota without having to subject themselves to adjustment programmes prescribed by the Fund. By contrast, under the new facility almost all support is conditional upon the Fund's approval of adjustment policies. Compensatory drawings have been further tightened by the introduction of phasing. All these features involve a far more restrictive approach than the semi-automaticity originally

associated with compensatory financing. The facility as it now
stands is extremely complex and does not provide a reasonable
assurance of support when a country is driven by external shocks
to turn to the IMF.

It should be a priority of a reform of the international financial
system to remove the conditionality now attached to compensatory financing and to return the scheme to its original conception
of quasi-automatic offsetting of losses of foreign exchange receipts suffered by developing countries through factors outside
their control.

Conditionality and structural adjustment The preceding point
is linked to the more general issue of conditionality in the relations
between the developing countries and the international financial
institutions. The 1980s witnessed a sharp increase in
conditionality associated with their provision of finance to
developing countries. The two Bretton Woods institutions–the
IMF and the World Bank–were pace-setters in this regard.
Cross-conditionality–the practice whereby the conditions
imposed by one institution are also imposed by the other–is now
a practically universal fact of life. It has left developing countries
with almost no discretion in determining their economic policies.
Although both institutions now officially endorse the concept of
growth-oriented adjustment, the truth is that, as discussed in
Chapter 2, their increased involvement in the domestic policies of
developing countries in the 1980s did not promote either growth
or equity in the South.

Here, international reform must be guided by two sets of considerations. On the one hand, it has to be recognized that only appropriate macroeconomic policies can restore countries to
economic health; on the other, it must be accepted that, to be
workable, a policy package must be country-specific, i.e. suited to
a country's particular circumstances, and free of ideological bias.
It must also be recognized that devising and carrying out structural reform is a complex operation. Differences can and do arise
in working out and agreeing on the best mix of policies. Hence, the
mechanisms for setting the performance norms a country should
satisfy and for monitoring how it implements agreed policies must
ensure that both the standards and the evaluation of performance
are based on an objective analysis of its situation and are not influenced by the ideological prejudices of the providers of funds.

The international credit mechanism is at present a highly political mechanism. Creditors–including the international financial institutions–are in a stronger bargaining position, which allows them to impose their views on borrowers. Only a depoliticization of the process through the introduction of an independent international evaluation of development performance can inspire the respect and confidence of both donors and recipients. The setting-up of a panel of experts, independent of the international financial institutions but operating as an advisory committee to them, and assisting them in making appraisals of the situation of recipient countries, can be an important step in this direction. It is also most desirable that the World Bank and the IMF should set up high-powered regional Advisory Councils to advise them on the broad framework of their policies and programmes. The effectiveness of international financial institutions will be irreparably compromised if inflexible ideological prejudices combined with economic muscle continue to influence their priorities and functions.

Furthermore, adjustment-oriented conditionality for developing countries should be decided in the context of global schemes for policy co-ordination and surveillance. In that way the need for adjustments in the economies of the developed countries as well would be recognized; these arguably exhibit as a group even more pronounced imbalances than developing countries. A more symmetrical effort undertaken by the international community as a whole would remove the unacceptable unilateral nature of present conditionality and adjustment.

The International Trading System

The prevailing approaches, rules, and disciplines of the world trading system, embodied in the General Agreement on Tariffs and Trade, are based on the notion of open, multilateral, transparent, and non-discriminatory trading. However, there is now a distinct tendency towards the formation of large trading groups of developed countries which are linked by close economic relations and which at some point decide to unify their markets. The most notable instances are the Canada-United States Free Trade Agreement of December 1987 and the 1987 Single European Act which commits the countries of the European Community to the

creation of a unified market by the end of 1992. While these arrangements will evidently entail freer trade within the respective
groupings, their impact on the rest of the world and on the global
trading system as a whole is unclear and in some important respects worrying.

It is argued that the removal of trade barriers in these groupings will lead to higher efficiency and productivity as a result of
competition. The ensuing increase in income would raise the demand for imports from the rest of the world, provided tariff protection was not increased. The trade-creating effects, in this view,
would exceed the trade-diverting impact of the unified market.

The issue is particularly important in connection with the EC,
which is a major market for both commodities and manufactures
from the South, including most of the least developed countries.
In the late 1980s the EC as a whole accounted for nearly one-
fourth of all exports from developing countries and for almost 60
per cent of those of sub-Saharan Africa.

The main form of protection applied by the EC countries to
imports from outside the Community–notably from the South–is
non-tariff. The increased income resulting from intra-Commu-
nity competition is therefore unlikely to lead to a substantial rise
in Community imports. Even on the assumption that the average
level of external protection will be maintained, trade diversion is
likely to take place, as less efficient suppliers within the Community, who are not affected by barriers, will be preferred to more
efficient suppliers outside the Community to whom the barriers
apply.

Further, there is a strong chance that effective protection will
in effect increase, as import-competing products from EC members begin to be traded freely within the Community. This is particularly important in agriculture and in textiles, both sectors of
major interest to developing countries in terms of exports.

More generally, the possible effects of the Single European
Act on the South must be viewed in the context of current European Community policies. Here the situation gives rise to very serious concern. EC trade policies involve a high level of
discrimination against imports from the South. This is, to be sure,
mitigated by the Generalized System of Preferences and by the
special provisions of the Lomé Convention. However, both the
coverage of the GSP and the relief it offers are limited, and fur-

thermore subject to unilateral termination by the EC on grounds of 'graduation', i.e. the withdrawal of concessional treatment with respect to a developing country that 'graduates' from a lower to a higher level of economic development. The Lomé Convention, in turn, offers limited concessions on commodities that come within the scope of the EC's Common Agricultural Policy. For example, subsidized production of beet sugar in Western Europe has done irreparable harm to Third World producers and exporters of cane sugar. Tight restrictions on imports of animal feed and vegetable oils into EC countries have also been gravely detrimental to Third World producers, while seasonal quotas for some products add to the downward pressure on prices. If steps are not taken to eliminate these restrictions and liberalize trade, the Single European Act might in effect lead to the creation of a 'Fortress Europe'. Recent signs are far from encouraging.

The EC is strongly advocating selectivity in the application of safeguards, that is, temporary import barriers imposed in order to protect domestic industries at risk. If this proposal is accepted, the consequential restrictions would be used essentially against imports from the Third World rather than against those from other developed countries. It has been an accepted international principle so far that safeguards should be applied to imports from all sources, not selectively.

The EC is also demanding protection for intellectual property owned by nationals or companies of its member states–trade marks, patents, and the like–in Third World countries as well as for services performed there by EC firms. However, it has given no indication of a commitment to phase out the Multi-Fibre Arrangement which limits textile imports from the South or to ease tariff and non-tariff barriers affecting other Third World exports.

A possible approach to this problem would be for the Community to accept the principle that external protection should be set at the lowest level obtaining among its member countries. This raises the thorny question of removing agricultural protection, and is likely to be resisted by both the more developed European countries that have a large agricultural export sector and by the EC's less developed newer entrants, which see their competitive advantage within the Community precisely in agriculture.

In any case, the increasing trend towards the establishment of regional trading blocs raises important issues for the future of the international trading system. The South should be alert to the danger that these developments could result in narrowed access to developed-country markets for its exports. The international community should agree that the design of unified markets should make reasonable provision for preserving, and indeed expanding, the preferential access of developing countries to these markets of the North.

There is little question that sustained growth in the South will necessitate a substantial expansion of Southern exports to the North. As world trade is unlikely to grow as fast as it did during the 1945-79 period, this will require more deliberate action by developed countries to open their markets to Third World products. A reformed international trading system must therefore embody a recognition of the need to promote a rise in the share of imports from developing countries in the total consumption of primary and manufactured products in the developed countries.

The question of access is particularly important for exports of manufactures. In consequence of the recent intensification of protectionism in the developed countries, developing countries' exports have been subjected to discriminatory restrictions precisely in those sectors where they have a clear comparative advantage. These restrictions take several forms: explicit departures from GATT, such as the Multi-Fibre Arrangement concerning textiles and clothing; 'grey-area' measures, such as Voluntary Export Restraints and Orderly Marketing Arrangements, which bypass GATT rules and principles; or the more transparent tariff barriers within the rules of GATT, which discriminate not between countries but by sectors or by the degree of processing. Whatever the form, and whether old or new, protectionism in the North affects a very large proportion of the exports of processed products and manufactured goods from the South. Tariffs imposed by industrial countries on labour-intensive products that are of considerable export interest to developing countries continue to be much higher than the average. Action to redress this unacceptable state of affairs should be a priority in a reform of trading arrangements.

More specifically, trade in textiles and clothing must be freed from restrictions and become once again subject to GATT rules and disciplines as a matter of urgency. Equally, sector-specific quantitative restrictions which affect, for instance, steel, leather goods, footwear, and consumer electronics, and which discriminate against, and so limit, manufactured exports from many developing countries, must be eliminated.

A satisfactory outcome of negotiations in some of these areas is linked to reaching a comprehensive agreement on safeguards. Non-discrimination in their application is a sine qua non of such an agreement. Over the last few years, there has been a convergence of views on several aspects of safeguards, including: the desirability of adequate transparency, consultation, and multilateral surveillance; limited duration; and the progressive liberalization of application. Agreement on these aspects should be pursued vigorously. On the other hand, the introduction of selectivity in the application of safeguards would be a retrograde step, and should be resisted.

The reformed trading system must restore observance of the principle that developing countries qualify for differential and more favourable treatment and it must incorporate effective arrangements to ensure that the principle is put into practice. It is recognized that, as these countries progress and their trade situation improves, they should progressively accept the full obligations of the world trading system. However, this evolution should not be unilaterally imposed by the industrial countries, but should be determined multilaterally on the basis of objective criteria.

A reformed regime for international trade will therefore need to deal with a vastly enlarged and more complex set of inter-related issues and interests. New institutional arrangements are thus required. We believe the time has come for the world community to take up again the idea of an International Trade Organization. However, this should involve the creation of a framework that can deal with the new needs of the world trading system in a comprehensive and integrated fashion. The mandate of the new organization should include both a regulatory role in the world trade system and the promotion of development.

Agricultural trade Trade liberalization in agriculture by the leading developed countries could have a number of consequences for the agricultural and food situation of developing countries. It could significantly improve the access to markets in developing countries and export prospects for many agricultural commodities. A reduction in agricultural protection and subsidies could lead to price increases in world markets. In the medium term, these may provide a stimulus to food production in developing countries, leading to a reduction in food imports.

Increases in world agricultural prices can be expected to have net benefits for developing countries as a group. However, their distribution can vary substantially among individual countries. Countries with food deficits, many of whom are in the low-income group, can suffer income losses as they have to pay higher bills for food imports. It is therefore necessary to ensure that their interests are protected in the process of liberalizing agricultural trade. Increased food aid, special allocations for emergency relief, and compensatory financing can help to mitigate their short-term burdens. Equally important will be increased international technical and financial support for stepping up food production in the South.

The liberalization of agricultural trade can also have an important effect on developed countries' policies with respect to the holding of food stocks. The stability of world food markets has come to rest vitally on the large buffer stocks held by a few developed countries. These countries carry extensive stocks not for the purpose of stabilizing world food supplies but rather as a result of their programmes of price support and subsidies for their own farmers.

In a changed world setting, developed countries, especially the USA and those in the EC, may not continue to play the role of buffer-stock-holders for the world. A very dangerous situation could therefore arise if harvests fail in important grain producing countries, particularly if large countries also begin to rely on world markets for supplies. Poorer developing countries could face acute difficulties in such circumstances. It is therefore necessary to think of new international arrangements to avoid the risk of greater instability in the world food system.

In developing countries, it is necessary that the process of liberalization of agricultural trade should take into account the need to give sustained encouragement and incentives to their agricultural sector in order to modernize it over a period of time.

Trade in commodities Commodity trade is of crucial importance for the development prospects of the countries of the South, as most of them still earn the bulk of their foreign exchange by exporting primary commodities. In Chapter 2 we drew attention to the slide in commodity prices which has added to the debility of a large number of developing countries. A renewed effort towards halting the prolonged crisis in commodity markets in ways that will prevent its recurrence is urgently needed. The setting-up of mechanisms for regulating the international commodity economy should be one of the issues at the top of the agenda of the world community. The crisis in commodities is as dramatic and as devastating as the debt crisis, and the rationale for concerted action is as strong. In this context, the essential objectives of UNCTAD's Integrated Programme for Commodities remain valid, namely improvement of the terms of trade for commodity-exporting countries, stabilization of commodity prices, compensation for shortfalls in commodity export earnings, and commodity development through increased productivity, domestic processing, and participation by developing countries in marketing and distribution.

The improvement of the South's trade performance depends on the creation of dynamic comparative advantages based on the transformation of economic structures, technological change and improvement of the terms of trade. Within this context of transformation, efforts to secure stable, remunerative prices for commodities must be based on the concept of supply management. Market forces can deal with serious imbalances between supply and demand only through long and painful boom-bust cycles in production and prices. Cyclical downturns in commodity markets have very adverse effects on the longer-term productive capacity of producer countries, while consumer countries might suffer from high commodity prices in cyclical upturns. Appropriate schemes for supply management, which could benefit both groups of countries, are now urgently required to restore more balance to international commodity markets, recently characterized by persistent excess supply and depressed prices.

Supply management should be supplemented by the adequate provision of compensatory finance for short-term falls in earnings from commodity exports. We have already touched on the negative evolution of the IMF's Compensatory Financing Facility.

The EC's STABEX scheme has less restrictive conditions than the IMF's CCFF, but it is considerably smaller and applies only to the Group of African, Caribbean and Pacific States (ACP) linked to the Community under the Lomé Convention, although a similar facility, COMPEX, has recently been introduced for the non-ACP least developed countries. In the medium term, the international community should examine the feasibility of expanding the scope and coverage of commodity-related compensation schemes. Additionally, the compensatory financing facility of the IMF should be liberalized along the lines indicated earlier in this chapter. There must be a mechanism for a co-ordinated operation of all the existing schemes of compensation.

For the longer term, it is essential that the Common Fund for Commodities established under the auspices of UNCTAD should operate actively in both its intended areas: price stabilization designed to reduce the amplitude of fluctuations, and commodity development. Price stabilization has to be a central immediate objective, while commodity development must be pursued as a long-term strategy for increasing the value added to the raw material and diversifying the commodity sector. Developing countries should request the Common Fund to intensify efforts to introduce support schemes for price stabilization through its First Account. Similarly, commodity development activities to be funded through the Second Account should be started. These include research and development projects to find new uses for commodities; marketing and processing facilities to increase the producers' share of what consumers pay for the final product; and diversification into new commodities. The Common Fund authority should also give early attention to ways of mobilizing additional resources for Second Account activities, and explore the feasibility of collaborating with other financial institutions.

Trade in services This is another area of paramount importance for the development prospects of the countries of the South. Services such as transport, communications, banking, insurance, health, and education have always been regarded as critical for development. The argument is by now well-rehearsed that the application to trade in services of the rules traditionally applied to trade in goods could seriously undermine the South's ability to promote and regulate its service industries so as to improve its development prospects. Developing countries agreed to participate in the negotiations on trade in services in the context of the Uruguay Round only after the Punta del Este Ministerial Meeting of GATT members in September 1986 had reached agreement on three points:

- Negotiations on trade in services would be conducted in an ad hoc juridical frame of reference separate from the negotiations on trade in goods, leaving the question open whether an international regime for trade in services was indeed needed, and, if so, whether it should be within the GATT framework, or be the subject of a separate Code of its own.
- Development in Third World countries would be regarded as an integral part of the objectives for negotiations. These would be designed to promote the economic growth of all trading partners, and particularly of developing countries, through expansion of trade in services under conditions of transparency and progressive liberalization.
- The framework would respect the policy objectives of national laws and regulations applying to services.

These guidelines remain central to the interests of developing countries. The recent advances in information and communications technologies have now added an altogether new dimension to the role of services in the development process. The new 'producer' or 'business' services–those used by enterprises as inputs in their own production of goods and services–have a profound impact on the competitiveness of a wide range of economic processes and products, for instance by computerizing inventory management or quality control. The ability to take advantage of new technologies in organizing productive processes therefore has a critical influence on the development prospects of an economy as a whole.

In the longer term, an excessive dependence on imported services could seriously weaken the development process. An underdeveloped domestic services-sector would imply weak links between producers and users of services, which could adversely affect the ability of the economy to innovate, absorb, and assimilate new technological changes and to benefit from learning by doing. Moreover, since tradeable services–those that can be bought abroad, e.g. engineering, insurance, software–constitute a growing share of value added, heavy reliance on imported services would lead to an increasing proportion of value added being transferred abroad. Also, poor domestic capacity in the South's services sector would provide added scope for transnational corporations to appropriate the bulk of income from the provision of services.

Foreign firms can make useful contributions to the development of domestic service-industries in developing countries. Thus there is considerable room to expand flows of trade and technology. However, this does not justify an uncritical acceptance for the services trade of the GATT rules applicable to the goods sector. Indeed, GATT rules, developed at a particular historical juncture in the context of trade in goods, are quite inappropriate for a regime of trade in services. If the primacy of the development objective is accepted with the proposals for liberalization as a basis for a multilateral arrangement for services, a new conceptual framework must be sought. This must facilitate the use of the technological and economic capabilities of foreign firms in a way consistent with the development needs of the Third World.

To be consistent with the objective of promoting development, any multilateral framework for services must provide for adequate and increasing opportunities for the growth of a strong producer-services sector in developing countries. Failure to develop domestic capabilities in knowledge-intensive service industries could in the long run seriously jeopardize development. Simultaneously, the new regime must also facilitate the growing participation of developing countries in the world export trade in services. Finally, it must also support an expansion of trade in services among the developing countries; co-operation in this area could lead both to the expansion of trade and to accelerated development in developing countries.

The proposals for liberalizing trade in services are concentrated in capital- or technology-related services, in which developed countries have a pronounced comparative advantage. Labour and labour-related services, in which developing countries have a comparative advantage, are not yet an accepted subject of negotiations. Thus, situations in which persons from the North cross frontiers in order to produce and deliver services to consumers are characterized as trade in services, but situations in which the persons from the South want to do the same are described as immigration. It is essential for developing countries that such asymmetries be removed and that negotiations on services are balanced in coverage to include labour services. Such barriers as immigration laws and consular practices, which impede the export of labour services from developing countries, should therefore receive the necessary attention in the negotiations.

GATT and foreign-investment regimes In pressing for the inclusion of trade-related investment measures (TRIMs) as a subject of the Uruguay Round negotiations, capital-exporting developed countries sought to establish a new set of multilateral rules for private foreign investment which would ultimately severely cramp the ability of the capital-importing countries to regulate such investment in accordance with their own national development priorities. The developed countries' objective was to design a multilateral system that would further strengthen the role and expand the presence and power of their transnational corporations.

Although investment rules go beyond GATT's traditional concern about impediments to trade imposed at national borders, an attempt was made to justify the use of GATT to lay down these rules. It was claimed that, in an increasingly interdependent world, the distinction between investment flows and trade flows had been blurred and that GATT ought to be concerned with at least those aspects of investment policies that have a bearing on trade flows. It was argued that particular attention ought to be given to trade-related investment measures considered to have significant trade-distorting effects.

A multilateral investment regime designed to promote the interests of capital exporters in general and of the transnational corporations in particular would clearly have serious adverse effects on the development prospects of host countries in the South. There are very sound economic reasons why developing countries need to regulate the inflow of private foreign investment and to subject these investments to conditions and performance requirements based on their development needs and priorities. Given the vast imperfections in both product and factor markets in most developing countries, flows of foreign investment whose volumes and pattern are determined solely by the corporate objectives of foreign investors would not produce an efficient or optimum outcome from the standpoint of capital-importing countries.

In economic theory, trade-distorting practices are viewed against the background of the ideal of perfect competition. Yet the world markets for capital and technology hardly bear comparison with the competitive ideal. In their dealings with transnational corporations, developing countries have to contend with market structures characterized by significant elements of market power and monopoly and a complete lack of transparency in the behaviour of transnational corporations. In this setting, it is a travesty of the facts to describe as trade distortions measures adopted by host countries to minimize the harmful and maximize the favourable impact of foreign investments on their national economies. In a world of monopolies, transfer pricing, and internationalization of economic processes, measures to regulate investment are not necessarily trade-distorting.

Clearly, all countries need screening procedures to block unacceptable and counter-productive activities or projects and to modify the terms of their operations in order to make them consistent with their development objectives. If a proper balance is to be maintained, the integrity of the development objective must be the prime consideration. Equal attention must be paid to those aspects of the behaviour of transnationals–restrictive business practices, restrictions on the free flow of technology, market-sharing arrangements–that impede the realization of the objectives of the developing countries in regard to trade policy and development.   Any equitable multilateral arrangements must then also include acceptance by the transnational corporations and the governments of developed countries of their own responsibilities to curb the restrictive practices of those corporations and to facilitate the freer transfer of technology to Third World countries. A great deal of work has been carried out in various international forums towards evolving suitable norms in these fields, but the opposition of the capital-exporting countries has blocked further progress.

A good case can be made for greater transparency, predictability, and non-discrimination in the application of the investment regulations enacted by the developing countries. Such features would make it easier to assess objectively the costs and benefits of various investment proposals. But insistence on them as part of a multilateral arrangement that would leave transnational corporations wholly free to operate in any manner they liked would only compound the inequities of the present system. There is no justification for GATT limiting, through multilateral rules, the negotiating scope of governments of developing countries while leaving untouched the policies of the transnational corporations in vital areas where they impinge on the development prospects of the host countries. This would make GATT the champion of those corporations at the expense of the South.

It is generally agreed that data on TRIMs are sparse and imprecise, and the extent to which investment measures have a direct or indirect effect on trade is debatable. There are a number of unresolved problems of definition and measurement. It is also well-known that the issue of TRIMs is very complicated, involving as it does domestic policy-making in such a sensitive area as investment. For all these reasons, great caution is necessary; to rush to put in place a multilateral set of rules without careful and balanced consideration of all relevant issues and interests is most undesirable.

Science and Technology

The countries of the South are almost entirely buyers in the international market for technology, in which the sellers enjoy an oligopolistic position. Developing countries lack in various degrees the information and the negotiating capability to secure fair and equitable terms when importing technology. Moreover, the intellectual property system (governing patents, trade marks, copyrights, etc.) further strengthens the position of the technology-holders of the North by granting them monopolistic rights in the markets of the South. It limits the access of the South to the advances of world science and technology. If the South is to benefit from these advances, this situation, with its legally built-in restrictions on technology transactions, needs to be altered.

The promotion of technical change and of an environment conducive to innovation is no doubt of interest to the world community as a whole. However, the diffusion of new technologies to the developing countries with a view to accelerating the tempo of their development must be an equally cogent international concern. Developing countries need active assistance to catch up with the rest of the world, or at least to shorten the distance that now separates them from it. Technological transformation is a key to their rapid progress. Any new international regime for the protection of intellectual property rights should recognize the urgent need of developing countries to leap-frog technologically. The development of their domestic technological capacities is therefore of critical importance.

Considerable progress towards facilitating the South's access to technology was made during the 1970s in negotiations in UNCTAD on an International Code of Conduct on the Transfer of Technology and on a revision of the intellectual property system. Progress was later made in the World Intellectual Property Organization (WIPO) on the revision of the Paris Convention for the Protection of Industrial Property. By the early 1980s only two substantive matters remained to be settled in the UNCTAD code - the clause governing restrictive practices and the provision concerning applicable law and dispute settlement. Mutual concessions by North and South on each of these could have finalized the negotiations. Before that could happen, further negotiations were blocked by the North. Similarly, the revision of the Paris Convention has been stalled for several years.

The North has since used the recent acceleration of technological advances to press for a reversal of earlier negotiations. It has proposed stronger national laws and stricter international agreements to protect its innovations. The technologically advanced countries thought fit to launch a GATT-based initiative (the negotiations on the so-called 'trade-related aspects of intellectual property rights', or TRIPs, in the Uruguay Round) to secure a tighter and expanded international system for enforcing respect for intellectual property rights. The objective clearly is to install a system that would oblige developing countries to restructure their national laws so as to accommodate the needs and interests of the North. This initiative seeks to expand the scope of the system governing intellectual property rights, extend the lifetime of the granted privileges, widen the geographical area where these privileges can be exercised, and ease restrictions on the use of granted rights. The North is thus insisting on enlarging and strengthening the monopolistic rights of their sellers of technology and thereby distorting free trade in technology; and yet, it is asking in the same forum for a greater liberalization and opening-up of trade in goods and services. If successful, this attempt will have significant adverse effects on the pace of the generation, absorption, adaptation, and assimilation of technical change in the developing countries.

The new technologies are difficult to develop. Substantial investments in research and development are required to transform scientific discoveries into technological innovations. But once these innovations have been made, they are easy to imitate and use in production processes. While they are relatively less capital-intensive, they are highly skill-intensive. Once a critical mass of research and development capabilities has been reached, the new technologies offer wide opportunities for speeding up economic progress, leap-frogging over intermediate levels of technological change. In order to take advantage of them the developing countries need great flexibility in shaping their national laws on intellectual property. These should help them to achieve national development objectives by giving them the freedom to determine what to include and what to exclude from patentability, the duration of rights, and the procedures for compulsory licensing and licence of rights in the public interest.

Improving the access of the countries of the South to technologies and promoting their domestic technological capabilities should therefore be components of any balanced and equitable regime for science and technology. Curbs on the restrictive practices of transnational corporations and the adoption of positive measures to help the Third World to acquire new technologies should figure prominently in any new international system.

The revolutionary impact of modern advances in science and technology on society, the economy, the habitat, and the human condition generally has highlighted once again the concept of knowledge and science as a shared heritage of the world's people. New technologies can be instrumental in protecting the physical environment, preventing irreversible soil erosion, and guaranteeing the adequate replenishment of natural resources. Technologies for the use and protection of water and land for the prevention of desertification, and for reforestation are essentially means to preserve life on the planet as a whole, since the environment is an indivisible global good. These technologies are indeed international public goods, whose benefits should be shared equitably. The new global arrangements for economic relations and for the fair sharing of the benefits of science and technology that we envisage would embody the recognition of these technologies as international public goods, and include mechanisms to subsidize their acquisition by developing countries. Concessional treatment is also needed in respect of technologies that could be applied in meeting the basic needs of the peoples of the South, i.e. in such fields as food, health, pharmaceuticals, housing, and education.

New technologies, while offering immense possibilities, also present potential threats. Purely commercial considerations can distort priorities for technical innovation and product development. The case for international regulation and monitoring of the direction in which these technological changes proceed, of the use of their results, and of the impact of their application is very strong.

These considerations should inform the new international regime for science and technology which should be negotiated between the North and the South. Such a new regime should cover the following aspects:

- There should be a link between total international aid and aid for science and technology. Donor countries should agree to provide a given percentage of their ODA as an additional sum to finance R&D activities in the recipient country.
- The regime should provide for the transfer of relevant technology from the North on terms consistent with the development interests of the South. Financing should not be tied; there should be controls to check transfer pricing: the ability to export should not be restricted; and there must be freedom to diffuse the technology within the country. The negotiation of an International Code of Conduct on the Transfer of Technology to Developing Countries and revision of the Paris Convention should be completed in a spirit of accommodation between North and South. Holders of patent rights must accept corresponding obligations to facilitate the development of links for the absorption of technology by the developing countries.
- Centres of technological information should be established in countries in the South to facilitate access to scientific literature; these centres should have comprehensive collections of scientific and technological books and journals either provided by governments of the North or supported by bilateral or multilateral aid.
- Technologies that help to preserve the environment and conserve natural resources should be treated as international

public goods. Technologies with potentially dangerous social consequences should be internationally monitored and controlled.

- The United Nations agencies, in particular UNIDO, UNESCO, the International Atomic Energy Agency (IAEA) and the UN University, should play a more prominent part in building up a scientific infrastructure in their areas of competence, with a view to contributing to scientific and technological progress in the South. The UN Commission on Science and Technology should identify the priorities for international policy in this area. Scientific centres for agriculture–CGIAR, the International Centre for the Improvement of Corn and Wheat (CIMMYT) in Mexico, the International Centre for Insect Physiology and Ecology in Kenya, and the International Centre for Biotechnology and Genetic Engineering in Trieste and Delhi sponsored by UNIDO–provide models of institutions engaged in applied research. In basic research, the experience of UNESCO and the IAEA in relation to the International Centre for Theoretical Physics (ICTP) in Trieste should be explored with a view to setting up other centres of advanced research and training, sponsored by United Nations bodies in disciplines relevant to their interests. The decision to set up, with the financial support of the Italian Government through UNIDO, three new research centres in Trieste–one for high technology and new materials, one for pure and applied chemistry, and one for earth sciences and the environment, which together with the ICTP will constitute the International Centre for Science–is a welcome development in this direction.

- A network of research and training institutes for the development and application of high technology should be established in the South. Their establishment should be supported by the multilateral financial institutions, notably the World Bank. The proposal by the Trieste Centre for creating twenty new centres around the world provides a basis for developing such a network.

Environment, Oceans, and Energy

The protection of the environment is a matter of global concern calling for global measures. However, the manner in which the North is attempting to define the issues introduces an element of potential North-South conflict. This must be avoided, since the only possible way forward is through global co-operative efforts.

With regard to the depletion of the ozone layer due to the emission of chlorofluorocarbons (CFCs) and the destruction of rain forests, the North is in effect demanding that the South should give priority to environmental protection over development objectives. It is also attempting to put in place mechanisms for Northern monitoring and control over development policies in the South that could have environmental implications.

This is unacceptable on several counts. Singling out developing countries as a main source of the threat to the global environment obscures the fact that the ecological stress on the global commons has in large part been caused by the North. The North, with only 20 per cent of the earth's population, accounts for 85 per cent of the global consumption of non-renewable energy. Its burning of fossil fuel–coal, oil–is by far the most important source of gases harming the atmosphere, particularly carbon dioxide, which causes the greenhouse effect (see Fig. 5.3), and sulphur dioxide, which produces acid rain. Similarly, the threat to the earth's ozone layer from the emission of chlorofluorocarbons is largely the outcome of the consumption patterns of the North and is attributable to the wide use of such products as refrigerators and aerosols. And the threat to marine life in the world's oceans is again largely due to the industrial effluents and toxic wastes originating in the countries of the North, and to over-fishing by their fishing enterprises.

The North has already used much of the planet's ecological capital. It will have to take important measures to adjust its patterns of production and consumption in order to mitigate the clear threat to the earth's environment. It will also have to reduce its consumption of certain key natural resources, such as non-renewable fossil fuels, to accommodate the industrialization and economic development of the South.

Figure 5.3

Emissions of Industrial Carbon Dioxide in 1985, by Region

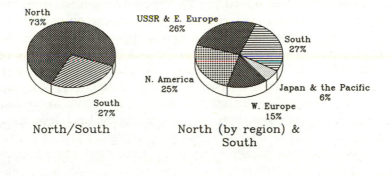

North/South   North (by region) &
                     South

Note: Industrial carbon dioxide emission is defined as carbon dioxide
released by fossil fuel combustion and industrial processes.

Source: Based on World Resources Institute, *World Resources 1988/89.*

In earlier chapters we have set out what we believe the South
should do, in its own interests, to safeguard the environment. But
the South cannot accept that its development should be arrested
in order to conserve the environment. The real choice is not between development and the environment, but between environment-sensitive and environment-insensitive forms of
development. The former calls for large-scale investments which
the South can hardly make unaided.

We believe that it is in the North's own interest to assist the
South in safeguarding the environment. Technical and financial
assistance from the North will be essential to enable the South to
use its natural resources in an efficient manner compatible with
the protection of the environment. Similar assistance will be required to reduce the pollution of the global commons that industrialization and urbanization in the South will inevitably entail.

Should the North be prepared to finance a substantial part of
the cost of switching to environment-sensitive patterns of growth
and consumption in the South, a negotiated agreement could

provide for reciprocal obligations on the part of the governments of the South. A concerted attack on global poverty has to be an integral part of the efforts to protect the environment. Measures taken in this connection must of course respect the sovereignty of national governments and their right to determine their national development policies freely. A new, environment-related form of conditionality –to be added to that imposed on the South by the international financial institutions–is utterly unacceptable.

The South's commitment to a global approach is signified by the proposal made by India at the Non-Aligned Summit in Belgrade in September 1989 for the establishment of a Planet Protection Fund under the auspices of the United Nations. The proposal envisages annual contributions to the Fund at the rate of 0.1 per cent of GDP by all countries, except the least developed. The Fund would be used for developing or purchasing conservation-compatible technologies in critical areas which could then be brought into the public domain for the benefit of both developing and developed countries. Additional resources for the Fund could be mobilized, for instance through a levy on the consumption of pollutants in the North. This type of tax is well known at the national level, taxes on petrol for automobile engines being a prime example. Its extension to the international field would be testimony to the North's commitment to a global effort to protect the environment.

Important steps towards introducing a global approach to some of these issues are the adoption in 1988 of United Nations General Assembly resolution 43/53 on the Protection of the Global Climate, the conclusion of the 1985 Vienna Convention for the Protection of the Ozone Layer and the 1987 Montreal Protocol, and the creation of the Intergovernmental Panel on Climatic Change by the United Nations Environment Programme and the World Meteorological Organization.

A global approach also informs the Declaration of The Hague, signed in 1989 by twenty-four Heads of State and Government or their representatives, which deals with the subjects of climate change, the warming of the atmosphere, and the deterioration of the ozone layer. The Declaration states the principle that developing countries have a right to fair and equitable compensation for the burden they may bear in carrying out decisions taken to protect the atmosphere, in recognition both of their development needs and of their lesser responsibility for the deterioration of the atmosphere. Much will depend on the operational guide-lines and the mechanism devised to implement this principle.

The oceans and the United Nations Convention on the Law of the Sea A particularly important topic of international environmental policy is the treatment of oceans. The enormous wealth of the world's oceans and their potential for hastening economic development led developing countries in the late 1960s to propose that this wealth should be declared part of the common heritage of humankind.

The United Nations Convention on the Law of the Sea of 1982 offers a comprehensive institutional and legal framework for the embodiment of this principle. It provides an internationally agreed regime for the management of the oceans, based on the principle of equity in the use of their resources. It gives to coastal states permanent sovereignty over natural resources within an Exclusive Economic Zone of 200 nautical miles. It establishes an International Seabed Authority to regulate the exploitation of the international waters, sea-bed, and subsoil, notably sea-bed mining. The Authority has the power to levy an international tax or royalty on the exploitation of these resources, and developing countries participate as equals in its decision-making.

The Convention establishes a structured relationship between ocean-mining companies and the International Authority, which in effect goes beyond issuing a code of conduct for multinational corporations. It provides for regional co-operation, especially in the management of living resources and in the protection of the marine environment, as well as for the establishment of regional centres to advance marine sciences and to facilitate the transfer of technology. The first such centre has been set up in the Mediterranean, and similar centres are to be set up in the Caribbean and Indian Ocean regions.

The Convention reserves the use of the high seas, the international sea-bed area, and marine scientific research for peaceful purposes, and provides a system for the settlement of disputes. While the relevant articles need further interpretation and progressive development, they provide a basis for the denuclearization and demilitarization of ocean regions such as the Indian Ocean, the Mediterranean, the sea of Japan, and the Southern Ocean.

The Convention is a legal instrument which integrates development, the environment, and the issues of disarmament and peace in the overall goal of sustainable development. It is necessary that all states should ratify the Convention on the Law of the Sea and bring it into force as soon as possible. A forum should be created within the United Nations system for the discussion of ocean affairs in an integrated manner, in line with the recognition in the preamble to the Convention that the problems of the oceans are closely interrelated and should be considered together. Other conventions and treaties dealing with marine affairs should be harmonized, wherever required, with the Convention on the Law of the Sea. These should include in particular the treaty banning nuclear weapons and other weapons of mass destruction from the sea-bed.

The problems which may arise in the management of the international sea-bed may differ from those arising in the management and possible exploitation of other global commons such as Antarctica and outer space. However, any international regime in these areas must also be based on their acceptance as part of the common heritage of mankind. Regulation on the basis of agreements involving only a small group of technologically developed states should be clearly rejected. It is necessary that the 1959 Antarctica Treaty, which expires in 1991, should be succeeded by a new treaty inspired by a vision of the continent as part of the global commons–and of the common heritage of all countries.

An international regime for energy Fluctuations in the international supply and price of energy, notably oil, have a profound influence on the world economy. The sharp increase in prices in 1973-74 made oil a key factor in most countries' balance of payments, inflation, and growth. The economic slow-down in the developed countries in the mid-1970s was related to the 'oil shock', as was the recession which began in the 1980s. Higher oil prices, while dramatically boosting the foreign exchange surpluses of the oil-exporting countries of the South, also placed a heavy burden on the South's oil importers. The reversal of the price trend in the 1980s, notably from 1986 onwards, also had significant effects on both oil producers and consumers. Volatility in prices has continued to be a feature of the world oil market.

So far, a global energy/oil crisis has been averted because of improvements in the energy efficiency of the economies of the North, and because of the modest rate of growth of the large countries of the South. A higher growth rate in these countries would stimulate a rising demand for oil and eventually put further pressure on energy supplies. The likely entry of the countries of Eastern Europe into the world market for petroleum, in consequence of a reduction of supplies from the USSR, adds to the uncertainty of the world oil market.

An agreed international regime for energy is therefore necessary, so that the development of the South is not impeded by the failure to provide for an orderly expansion and fair allocation of exhaustible energy resources. The South would need to be actively assisted to develop substitutes for fossil fuels and also to adopt techniques for conserving energy to the maximum extent possible.

The global economy needs a regime for energy that would be both stable, in that it would minimize disruptive fluctuations in supply and prices, and fair to both producers and consumers, assuring reasonable and remunerative prices as well as predictable access to supplies. The two objectives are interrelated, since fair prices will encourage an orderly expansion of production and so minimize the occurrence of both gluts and shortages. The scramble for supplies which marks periods of scarcity would be eliminated, and all countries would be assured of supplies to meet their needs.

The Reform of International Institutions

It must be an important aim of the South to secure for the United Nations a pivotal role in the management of the international economic system. With the easing of world political and military tensions, the demands on the United Nations in its primary traditional role–to preserve international peace and security– can be expected to subside, allowing it to give a higher priority to economic and social issues. Furthermore, the increasing globalization of the world economy poses problems for the solution of which no international set of mechanisms exists. In view of the growth in the activity of transnational corporations and other transnational actors, and of the greater prominence of transnational issues–the environment, the global commons, the uses of outer space, the international traffic in narcotics, among others–it is urgently necessary to strengthen international institutions and arrangements so that the new challenges can be faced in an effective and equitable manner.

Strengthening the role of the United Nations in the management of the world economy is, moreover, a natural extension of its original mandate to preserve international security. Peace and security cannot be realized unless peoples and nations are free from underdevelopment and deprivation. Poverty is itself tantamount to insecurity: insecurity produced by the threat of hunger, malnutrition, and disease for the millions who scrape a subhuman living in the drought-affected Sahel or in the slums of Latin America or Asia; insecurity for nation states resulting from vulnerability to fluctuations in external markets, from unbearable debt obligations, from externally imposed conditionality, from unequal bargaining power at the global level. True peace and security in the world cannot be achieved unless the international economic order becomes more equitable, rational, predictable, and development-oriented. Accordingly, it seems opportune to explore various ways in which the United Nations, at a high political level, might periodically take an overview of world economic issues and monitor developments in the international economy, paying special attention to the implications which significant trends and movements have for development.

Equally essential to an improvement in global economic management and decision-making is the reform of the voting structure of the principal multilateral financial institutions. The demand should be pressed firmly that the present rules–which give effective control of the IMF and the World Bank to the larger contributors, i.e. the developed countries–should be reviewed and modified so as to give increased weight to the South. The weighted voting system of the recently established Common Fund for Commodities should also be examined, with a view to designing arrangements that, while providing for a more egalitarian distribution of voting influence, would at the same time be acceptable to the international community as a whole.

We suggest that, under the auspices of the United Nations, a summit of leaders of a representative group of developed and developing countries should be convened periodically to review the world economic situation, the prospects for development, and the environment. A main objective should be to explore the interrelationship of the various components of the world economy, notably the monetary system, finance, and trade, their links with international political and security matters, and their impact on the development prospects of the South. This summit should recommend guide-lines for action by various specialized agencies of the United Nations and other major actors on the global scene.

Disarmament and North-South Relations

Disarmament is an instrument for achieving a more peaceful and secure world and has a direct bearing on North-South relations and on development issues. As we have argued above, the enhancement of common security in the global system is inseparable from the movement of the countries of the South away from poverty.

Disarmament has a bearing on development and North-South relations in yet another sense. The world has been witnessing what promises to be a historic change in international attitudes towards collective security. There is a growing recognition by the superpowers of the need to adhere to agreed principles and rules in the conduct of strategic relations, and progress is being made towards the elimination of nuclear weapons and the reduction of the arsenal of conventional weapons. This could open up enormous possibilities for global development efforts. As the Palme Commission emphasized, there is considerable experience of the conversion of military to civilian production. Scientific and technological innovation in the military sphere can be redirected towards the creation of techniques and instruments for improving economic efficiency, expanding food production, combating disease, and preserving the environment. More specifically, some of the resources used to produce weapons and maintain large defence forces in the North can now be used for the war against poverty. China and the Soviet Union are already on record as favouring the diversion of military resources to economic and social development.

A substantial part of the resources to be released by the reduction in defence budgets in the developed countries should be used to create a Peace and Development Fund. A significant proportion of the Fund's resources should be applied to assisting developing countries in meeting their technological needs through wide-ranging programmes for expanding their stock of skilled manpower through: scholarships; fellowships; the establishment and expansion of higher education facilities, including centres of excellence; on-the-job and in-firm training; and contacts among scientists and technologists and institutes of higher learning. Innovative mechanisms should be developed to improve the South's scientific and technological capabilities, particularly in satisfying the basic needs of the world's billion poor, and to protect the environment. The possibility of combining this initiative with the proposed Planet Protection Fund discussed above should be explored. Humanity has a chance to begin the noble process of beating swords into ploughshares; we hope it will be taken.

A Special Issue: The Illicit Traffic in Drugs

The illicit traffic in narcotic drugs is not a North-South issue; there is no conflict of interest to be resolved through bargaining. However, the eradication of the traffic calls for a concerted international effort, because few countries are totally unaffected—or can expect to remain unaffected—and because many countries, North and South, are now caught in the web of the global traffic in drugs.

So far, the approach of the governments of the North has tended to concentrate on attempts to make governments of the South prevent by force the cultivation and processing of the crops in question, and to curb the international marketing of the illicitly manufactured drugs. This approach ignores the elementary fact that the basic stimulus for this trade is provided by its enormous profitability, rooted in rising demand in the North. Such crops also yield very high returns, exceeding by many orders of magnitude the returns from any alternative conventional crop. The peasants who grow them will therefore deploy a range of strategies to be able to continue their cultivation even in the face of police and military force.

This enormous differential in returns is largely due to the poor state of agricultural development, marked by very low productivity of conventional crops, in the regions concerned. The problem is compounded by the persistence of low and unstable export prices for agricultural commodities. The only long-term response to the problem of drugs from the supply side lies therefore in increasing the level of productivity of, and the income generated by, conventional agriculture–in other words, in promoting a dynamic process of agricultural development backed by viable international arrangements to provide remunerative and stable prices to producers of primary products. This link was recognized in the declaration issued by the Drug Summit Meeting of the Presidents of Bolivia, Colombia, Peru, and the United States which took place in February 1990 in Cartagena, Colombia. However, it must be followed up with concrete action by the international community, including making available resources adequate to the task.

Any action on the part of governments of the South to stamp out the production of narcotic drugs needs to be accompanied–to be effective–by appropriate measures in the North to reduce the demand for drugs and the consequent profitability of the drug industry world-wide.

People-to-People Relations and the North-South Agenda

Many of the proposals we have made in this chapter call for negotiations between the governments of the South and of the North, since they can only be implemented through the action of governments. But there is also a vast field of relations between the South and the North that do not necessarily involve governments. The proliferation of organized non-governmental activity in both North and South, together with the revolutionary advances in communication and transport, has made links and contacts among groups and individuals a dynamic source of international initiatives and change. These trends provide important opportunities for the South to advance its vision of the new global system and to start translating it into reality.

Links among grass-roots organizations of the South and the North are valuable as a way of enhancing international understanding, overcoming differences in approaches and perceptions, and generating a favourable environment for international co-operation. They also enable the South to find important allies in its quest for international reform. Many public-minded interest groups in the North have been active in supporting the case for a restructuring of the international system. It is in the South's interest to make efforts to widen this community and build larger coalitions of support in the North.

Moreover, the direct involvement of non-governmental organizations in the South and the North in collaborative activities can be a valuable source of inputs for the development efforts of the South. Experience shows, in particular, that non-governmental North-South joint ventures in the field of research and development can provide groups and individuals in the South with strategic support for significant advances.

These contacts should therefore be encouraged and expanded through a systematic policy of fostering people-to-people links and initiatives at the North-South level.

THE NEXT STEP: A GLOBAL PROGRAMME OF IMMEDIATE ACTION

The difficulties and setbacks of the North-South dialogue to date have already been examined. The South has to work for the resumption of global negotiations, but this will be a time-consuming process and will also require careful preparation. In the meantime, it is necessary to make use of all appropriate forums for dealing with pressing issues of importance, in the knowledge that any success there will create a better climate for pursuing negotiations on the long-term questions.

The South should therefore seek to have negotiations started immediately, in whatever forums are currently appropriate, with a view to preparing the ground for dealing with the most urgent issues facing the South and the world economy generally. The aim must be to work out a Global Programme of Immediate Action that could be adopted by the North and the South. The following paragraphs summarize the rationale and the main priorities of such a programme.

A Six-Point Global Programme of Immediate Action

There is today a new combination of powerful political, economic, ecological, and moral considerations which justify a Six-Point Global Programme of Immediate Action to combat world poverty, in the interest of sustainable development worldwide and the promotion of global peace and security. This Programme needs to address some urgent issues, whose resolution will help to revive growth in the Third World and also be a first step towards a more basic restructuring of the international system, the aim being to ensure a more equitable management of global interdependence, in the interest of both developed and developing countries. The Programme should have the following objectives:

- Action to stop the net transfer of resources from the South to the North, to remove the overhang of the external debt of developing countries, and to scale down their debt service to levels that would allow growth to be sustained at a rate that would yield annual increases in per capita income of at least 2-3 per cent.

- The establishment of multilateral arrangements for protecting the global environmental commons and ensuring sustainable development. These arrangements should recognize that poverty must be overcome in order that the environment in the South may be protected, and should respect the freedom of governments to set their own national priorities and policies.

- Doubling the volume of concessional transfers of resources to developing countries by 1995, priority being given to transfers through multilateral institutions (IDA and the soft windows of regional development banks); the additional resources are to be devoted to food production, the provision of other basic needs, population control, energy security, and other environmentally sensitive areas.

- The establishment of independent international mechanisms for evaluating the requirements of developing countries, the norms and indicators for performance, and the criteria and conditionality appropriate to each country. These mechanisms, acting in an advisory capacity, could help considerably to depoliticize the negotiations between international financial institutions and developing countries, the laying-down of performance norms and the assessment of performance.

- A time table for lifting protectionist barriers that adversely affect the growth of developing countries' exports to the developed countries, bringing the textiles trade under normal GATT disciplines, and removing various 'grey area' restraints affecting developing countries' access to markets in the developed countries. Provision should be made for the stabiliza-

tion and support of the international prices of primary
commodities of special export interest to developing countries;
there should be a commitment to negotiate international
agreements for these commodities, and international assistance should be made available to developing countries in diversifying their commodity sectors.
- The incorporation of contingency provisions in international
  arrangements with a view to protecting developing countries
  against excessive fluctuations in international interest rates,
  exchange rates and terms of trade.

If a programme on these lines is to be realized, political initiative at the highest level will be needed, in order to impart the necessary momentum. The leaders of the South's nations should
meet and agree on a programme for immediate action; and then
use their influence to convene a global summit to discuss it with
the leaders of the North. These North-South discussions could, at
the same time, reopen the process of negotiation for a longer-term,
fundamental reform of the international system.

The South on the Threshold of the Twenty-First Century

6

We stand only a decade away from the beginning of a new century and a new millennium. In a very swiftly changing world it is not possible to chart with any certitude the likely course of the economies and societies of the South beyond the year 2000. There are many uncertainties about the future, and the discontinuities with the past may be pronounced.

The future is not foreordained. It will evolve from the interplay of many forces. It will be the outcome of contending interests and new ideas, of human creativity and organization. It will be conditioned by existing and new problems, and by the way in which the world–both North and South–responds to them and deals with the dilemmas and conflicts that are bound to arise.

The South must not remain a passive bystander in this process of change. It must seek to exercise the maximum influence on the course of events, inspired by its vision of the kind of world it wants and guided by the long-term interests of its people.

The people of the South, being the great majority of the inhabitants of the planet, have a right to do so. They also have the capacity–political, economic, intellectual–to shape this historical process to a significant degree. But to be effective this capacity must be purposefully mobilized.

We do not claim to have made an exhaustive study of all the formidable challenges the countries of the South might face in the period ahead. In particular, we have not dealt with international political issues. However, throughout our work we have been conscious of the implications of some powerful trends which could have a profound bearing on the ability of the societies of the South to meet the challenges and seize the opportunities of the twenty-first century. Because of the inevitable time-lags in economic and social processes, there is a need for early policy action if these opportunities are to be exploited and undesirable outcomes minimized.

In the preceding chapters, we have made a series of suggestions–on the reform of national policies, the revitalization of co-operation among developing countries, and the restructuring of the global economic system. We believe that many of these suggestions will retain their relevance well into the coming century. Their effective implementation will enhance the ability of the countries of the South to meet more vigorously the challenges that lie ahead, challenges which must be met if the aspirations of the people of the South for a life of dignity, self-respect, and freedom from want and exploitation are to be realized.

We conclude our Report with this epilogue which draws more explicitly the attention of the peoples and governments of the South to some key concerns which, in the Commission's view, could have a vital bearing on the future of the societies of the South in the twenty-first century.

DEVELOPMENT: FIRST THINGS FIRST

Most nations of the South will have to deal with the consequences of a fairly rapid growth of their population and labour force for many decades to come. People who will join the labour force fifteen years from now have already been born. Thus a decline in the birth rate, essential though it is for the longer-term sustainability of the development process in the South, can have only a modest impact in the foreseeable future on the demand for food and other basic goods, and for new productive jobs to keep the labour force fully employed.

Most developing countries will need to expand their economies at a fairly rapid rate to satisfy the legitimate aspirations of their people. The South needs strong economic growth, including advances in both agriculture and industry, to provide a decent livelihood for all those entering the labour market. This process of growth will entail a significant increase in the use of natural resources, to which the international community will have to adjust if the South is to attain its development goals without harming global ecological stability.

A critical factor in how the South itself confronts the challenge is its choice of development patterns and life-styles. Neither the demand side nor the supply side of these patterns can simply be a replica of the past or a blind copy of the consumerist models of the advanced industrial societies of the North.

As a result of continuing poverty and widening disparities, many developing countries face an increasingly explosive social, economic, and political situation. The poor majority will not continue to accept docilely the proposition that they must be reconciled to their misery year after year. The challenge before the societies in the South is the removal of extreme poverty, which still affects the great mass of the people in many countries, while in others it is entrenched in sizeable marginalized groups in rural and urban areas. This can become a reality only if they give priority to the meeting of basic human needs through people-centred strategies for development.

Life-styles for a few which are incompatible with the level of development and resources of a poor country can give rise to serious political and economic tensions, leading to the collapse of the basic consensus on development that is essential for pursuing consistent and efficient growth-oriented policies. Economic growth and the meeting of basic needs have to go together.

A progressive rise in the standard of living is a legitimate aspiration of the people of the South. However, this does not imply development strategies whose aim is merely to mimic the wasteful life-styles in the North. The South's development strategies should instead aim, as a priority, at satisfying basic human needs and at closing the distance between South and North in food, education, health, safe drinking water, and a healthy and secure environment.

It is in this context that the Commission's emphasis on the priority goal of first meeting the basic needs of the mass of the people and a firm commitment to the removal of poverty and hunger assumes special significance.

The South must make full use of modern science and technology to realize its development goals. Science and technology can be powerful instruments for regenerating the economies of the South, and particularly for revitalizing the countryside, and can thereby help to ward off excessive migration to urban areas. In the more populous countries, dispersed, broad-based, and regionally balanced development is particularly important to avoid the unplanned and unregulated growth of massive urban agglomerations which become increasingly chaotic and ungovernable.

These are attainable and realistic goals for the South, but time is not on its side.

TOWARDS ENHANCED DEVELOPMENT EFFECTIVENESS

Development is a process of profound structural transformation. It cannot simply be imported. By now, there is ample evidence that successful development is vitally linked to the resilience of the economy, polity, and civil society, all functioning in a spirit of harmony to promote shared goals and objectives. Thus the success of the South's struggle against its poverty and underdevelopment will depend on the ability of the South to reform and regenerate its economies, polities, and societies in line with its basic development goals.

It is obvious that the economies of the South will need to display a high degree of technical dynamism to achieve their development goals. They will also require high rates of domestic savings to cover the investment needs of an expanding economy. But the processes through which savings and investment are mobilized and the associated development patterns can be either integrative or disruptive. In particular, the extent to which science and technology and high rates of capital accumulation become instruments for the emancipation of the people of the South will depend on:

- the values and norms which inspire the leadership and the governing institutions of the society, as well as the mass of the population
- the capacity of the political system to reconcile social conflicts and to direct the processes of social and economic change in conformity with the needs of the civil society
- the ability of the economic system–which determines the allocation of resources among competing uses, the distribution of income, and the weight to be attached to present as against future consumption–to balance rewards for enterprise, initiative, and creativity with support for the underprivileged and deprived sections of society

There are no ready-made models the South can adopt to enhance its development effectiveness. To be sure, in developing countries the issues of markets, incentives, the climate for investment, and entrepreneurship have to be addressed if the growth momentum is to be sustained. It is, however, necessary to recognize that the establishment of a market economy is not a turn-key operation. Reforms need to be carefully sequenced. Nor can the market provide all the answers to the formidable social problems that inevitably arise in the process of rapid change. There is need for social safety-nets to soften the adverse impact of market processes on income distribution and the well-being of underprivileged sections of society. Moreover, all reforms have to be related to the larger social goal of enabling all people to live a life of dignity, and ending the marginalization and alienation of a large mass of people.

Clearly, the reform of economic mechanisms in the absence of political reforms offers no assurance of success. But neither can the reform of political and economic mechanisms deliver solid results if there is no attempt to realign the values and norms upheld by the leadership and other dominant actors in the society. Impatient reformers often forget that governments can change policies but cannot change societies–at least not overnight.

The value system and the political and economic mechanisms consistent with the development needs of the societies of the South cannot be evolved in the abstract. A country's institutional mechanisms have to be related to its history and its culture, as well as to the democratically expressed needs and aspirations of its people. Thus the institutional patterns have to be country-specific. It is imperative that each nation of the South should undertake a critical self-examination to ensure that its institutional health is sufficiently sound to be able to respond to the vigorous demands likely to be made on it in the twenty-first century.

In general terms, the countries of the South need to evolve a value system that prizes creativity, innovation, and the spirit of enterprise and is at the same time moved by concern for the underprivileged and the unfortunate. Poor societies cannot afford to waste scarce resources. Therefore the utmost emphasis on efficiency has to be built into economic processes. But all economic processes are ultimately meant to serve the interests of human beings. Hence an abiding concern with social justice must go hand in hand with the pursuit of economic efficiency. It is only through a commitment to social justice that the call to dedicated collective effort for development can be sustained, its objectives given a high moral purpose, and the spirit of human solidarity kept alive. The massive social and economic reforms needed to remove the scourge of mass poverty can succeed only if backed by a spirit of high idealism, self-sacrifice, and dedication. A self-sustaining economy within a stable society is inconceivable in the long run if the society is not imbued with the integrative and cohesive spirit of social justice. In particular, the progress in improving the status accorded to women and in removing the discrimination currently practised against them in social, economic, and political affairs will be a most important test of the South's commitment to development with equity.

Modern social history suggests a host of instruments for reconciling the twin requirements of efficiency and equity, involving acceptably moderate trade-offs between the two. Each society in the South must seek to evolve its own instruments, suited to the genius of its people. There is a need for innovative approaches–extending beyond the domains of both the market and the traditional welfare State–that will maximize the creativity of each individual in the process of development.

However, the role of the State in the management of development will remain essential even if the market is chosen as the primary instrument for resource allocation. Economists have long recognized that market forces alone cannot be relied upon to yield optimum rates of savings or to safeguard the interests of future generations. Market processes are likely to lead to underinvestment in such areas as education and health–areas in which the benefits to society at large exceed the returns to investors. Lastly, competitive markets cannot be taken for granted. Markets need a regulatory framework–for instance, to ensure effective freedom of new entry, access to information, and prevention of monopolistic practices–for allocating resources with reasonable efficiency.

It is therefore necessary to create State structures reflecting broad public purposes or improve existing ones. The State, while articulating the basic social concerns, must, however, provide incentives and not curb the initiative of the various actors of civil society–producers and consumers–in acting as responsible members of a civilized, caring society.

Earlier in our Report, we have emphasized that the present governmental structures in many developing countries are much too fragile and ineffective as instruments of development. In many countries, the State has underachieved precisely because it has tried to do too much, too soon. Administrative capabilities are exceedingly scarce in many Third World countries. In such conditions, the withdrawal of the State from some activities may well enhance its effectiveness as an instrument of development. The available administrative resources can then be concentrated on areas where intervention can be economically and socially most productive.

Simultaneously, systematic efforts must be made to reform the tax system in order that it may provide an expanding volume of resources for covering essential public expenditure without eroding the incentives to work and save or stifling entrepreneurship. The sound management of public enterprises, with a judicious blend of autonomy and accountability, is also an urgent necessity. Equally important are efficiency, responsiveness, and integrity in public administration. Commitment to the rule of law and respect for fundamental human rights are also an important part of the process of modernizing the State in the interest of people-centred development. The other critical requirement is that the people themselves should be involved in the process of development, and should have the opportunity to influence it. Their voice must be heard. Leaders who refuse to listen to any but their own voices soon exhaust their leadership potential. Participatory development is thus a must. All these elements are vital for constructing durable national structures in which the State and civil society reinforce each other in effecting the social and economic transformation of the South.

Politics in the management of development cannot be wished away. But if it is to be creative, politics must be the servant of social sympathies. It must be an instrument for purposeful social change rather than a ticket to power and privilege or another lucrative profession.

OVERCOMING THE KNOWLEDGE GAP

We live in an age in which the role of science-based technologies as a major determinant of the pace of social and economic change, as well as of global power structures, has become even more pronounced. In the past, there were great civilizations in the South that were fertile in scientific ideas, but the bulk of new knowledge now originates in the developed countries of the North. Sometimes, new technologies hurt the interests of the South–for example, when they replace the raw materials exported by the South with synthetic substitutes or when they make it possible to substitute capital for labour, thereby destroying the South's comparative advantage in labour-intensive manufactures. Even when these technologies can be beneficial to the South, their Northern producers seek to exact a stiff price by way of royalties and fees.

Unless the South learns to harness the forces of modern science and technology, it has no chance of fulfilling its developmental aspirations or its yearning for an effective voice in the management of global interdependence. All its societies must therefore mount a determined effort to absorb, adapt, and assimilate new technological advances as part of their development strategies. Simultaneously, their technological, economic, and social structures must acquire a built-in inducement and capacity to generate new technologies in accordance with their development needs.

The foundation for the build-up of scientific and technological capabilities in the South is an educated and skilled labour force, with ample opportunities for continuing education and updating of knowledge and skills throughout the productive career. To achieve this, all countries of the South should give priority to providing a high standard of education to all children between the ages of 6 and 15 years, with basic sciences and mathematics being given the importance that is in keeping with the requirements of the modern technological age. The tree of knowledge can flourish only if it is securely planted in the educational system.

Moreover, given the shortage of resources and the competing claims on them, it is essential that the educational system should be geared to opportunities for productive work. Education and training unrelated to the society's development needs lead to unemployment, frustration, and alienation among the educated, with highly disruptive effects on social and economic stability.

Productive enterprises in the South–in the public as well as the private sector–have a major responsibility for contributing to efforts to overcome the South's knowledge gap. They must create an environment that places a premium on technological innovation and creativity. There must be built-in inducements and pressure mechanisms to promote technical change and to encourage a spirit of enterprise and innovation.

For its part, the State, through its various agencies, must provide both adequate resources and a policy environment conducive to the pursuit of creativity and excellence in scientific and technological endeavours, and to the speedy incorporation of new knowledge into economic processes.

The South has clearly no choice but to master modern science and technology. But scientific and technological research is very expensive. Even the rich countries of Western Europe have found it necessary in several cases to pool their resources. With resources being as scarce as they are in the South, the need for South-South co-operation, at subregional, regional, and interregional levels in some critical areas of science and technology can hardly be over-emphasized.

Many new technologies, such as biotechnologies and micro-electronics, can readily be applied in a wide range of economic activities in the South. Some other new technologies may be less relevant to its immediate needs, but even in these cases the South must have a critical mass of scientists and technologists operating at the frontiers of these technologies. Nobody can predict with confidence all the future applications of new technologies. And if the South does not pay adequate attention to them now, the longer-term consequences may be disastrous, even though the immediate costs may be negligible. For neglect of new technologies may permanently foreclose the future development options of the South and thereby deepen its dependence on the North. South-South co-operation is the only effective strategy for avoiding such an outcome and for ensuring that modern science and technology become instruments for the regeneration and self-reliant development of the South.

PROTECTION OF THE ENVIRONMENT

The world shares a single environmental system. Three-fourths of humanity live in the South. The South has to be vitally concerned about safeguarding the life-support systems of the planet. The North is responsible for the bulk of the damage to the environment because of its wasteful life-style. However, poverty is also a great degrader of the environment, and an effective strategy for the removal of poverty is, in the final analysis, a strategy for protecting the environment. But different development strategies have different environmental implications.

The South's development strategies must take explicit account of the finite character of the world's natural capital. The concept of sustainable development serves to draw attention to the need for compatibility between growth and the preservation of the environment and to warn against a narrow-minded and short-sighted approach to development and economic modernization. There is ample evidence that a mindless preoccupation with modernizing at any cost can do irreparable damage to ecological systems. Degradation of land and water and deforestation already constitute a serious threat to the sustainability of the development process in many developing countries.

Since it takes a long time for measures to protect the environment to yield results, the countries of the South must not lose any further time in building environmental concerns into all developmental processes. These concerns should receive prominent attention in development strategies and planning, and environmental costs should be reflected in national accounts. Society has to be mobilized in support of life-styles that do not put excessive pressure on scarce natural resources. Strategies for the utilization of land and water must prevent their overexploitation. Energy intensities must be kept within prudent limits. Patterns of urbanization that make it impossible to ease to any meaningful extent the environmental strains of mega-cities must yield to more regionally balanced and decentralized patterns of urban development. Lastly, the environmental impact of uncontrolled population growth has to be fully appreciated both by government and by society at large. Environmental issues should become an essential component of all educational programmes.

Ecologically viable patterns of development will in many cases need more resources in the short run than conventional development strategies. But this cannot be an argument for not taking a serious view of environmental degradation. To do so would amount to condemning the South to an insecure future in the twenty-first century. As concerned citizens of this earth, the people of the South must do all that is within their power to protect the environment. The South must not shirk its responsibilities towards future generations.

We recognize that a situation in which the South absorbs and internalizes all environmental costs and pursues rational pricing and tax policies that penalize the polluters–through the proper pricing of energy, for example–while the North fails to do so would place the South at a great competitive disadvantage in international markets. Its economies could collapse under the weight of such unequal competition long before the beneficial impact of their environmental-protection policies materializes. If this happens, it will be most difficult to sustain the support of public opinion in the South for such policies. It is therefore essential that countries in the North assume their full share of the cost of protecting the global environment, and take tangible steps to accommodate the inevitable increase in the South's demand for commercial energy and its need for both capital and environmentally friendly technologies, in order that it may achieve the goal of accelerated development while ensuring environmental protection.

It would be unacceptable if, out of concern for environmental damage, the North were to impose new conditionalities on the debt-ridden and resource-starved economies of the South, while the Northern countries continued their present environmentally unsound patterns of living. It would be indefensible if measures for the protection of the planet and its environment were to involve the perpetuation of the poverty and underdevelopment of the South.

THE NEED FOR AN EFFECTIVE POPULATION POLICY

We are greatly concerned that the population in many countries of the South is growing at an explosive and, in the long run, unsustainable pace. The present high rates of population growth increase the burden of dependency and reduce the resources available for raising productivity to what is sufficient just to maintain subsistence levels. In several countries, the pressure of growing numbers on the limited fertile land is accelerating the degradation of land and water resources and causing excessive deforestation. Rapid population growth is also a principal factor in the uncontrolled growth of vast urban agglomerations. In many large cities of the South, islands of affluence are surrounded by sprawling slums in which the evils of poor housing, polluted air and water, bad sanitation, and widespread disease are compounded by the activities of drug peddlers, smugglers, and other undesirable elements.

In the long run the problem of overpopulation of the countries of the South can be fully resolved only through their development. But action to contain the rise of population cannot be postponed. The present trends in population, if not moderated, have frightening implications for the ability of the South to meet the twin challenges of development and environmental security in the twenty-first century.

It takes time before even well-designed policies can have a material impact on the birth rate. It is therefore necessary that countries with high birth rates should act without delay and adopt policies which will have an impact on population growth in a reasonable period of time.

Measures to raise the social, economic, and political status of women are fundamental to the success of population policies. It is equally essential to universalize access to elementary education, priority being given to the education of girls. Simultaneously, cost-effective health care measures must be put into operation, seeking in particular further reductions in infant mortality rates; this will reduce the social pressure on families to have as many children as possible as a way to insure against a high rate of child mortality. Family planning services must be made available to all at affordable cost. And all these activities have to be an integral part of policies for poverty alleviation, so that the poor do not need to pursue the type of survival strategies that consciously or unconsciously promote improvident maternity. The societies of the South must willingly accept a firm commitment to responsible parenthood and the small-family norm.

We are conscious that we are dealing with issues that touch on some of the deepest human emotions. The pronatal sentiment has strong roots in most traditional societies. Willing acceptance of the small-family norm therefore necessitates the active involvement and support of local communities and responsible guidance and encouragement from civic and religious leaders.

The task is indeed formidable, but the consequences of inaction can be disastrous. The South must summon sufficient political will to overcome the various obstacles to the pursuit of a sensible policy on population.

THE SOUTH AND THE MANAGEMENT OF GLOBAL INTERDEPENDENCE

The concept of global interdependence describes a fundamental trend in the modern world. The interrelationships among countries have multiplied and diversified to an unprecedented degree. International flows and transactions tightly enmesh all national economies, while transport, communication, and information networks span the globe. The biosphere reacts globally to man's intrusions irrespective of where they originate.

The trend towards the globalization of economic, social, and political processes which is now firmly established is likely to be further accelerated in years to come. The integration of global markets for money, finance, and technology, and the predominance in these markets of transnational enterprises based in the North, have far-reaching implications for the world economy, as well as for the South.

Some of these implications are so fundamental as to mark a historic departure from the past. Many events and processes within national borders, traditionally considered as strictly the business of the sovereign State, have influences on the rest of the world and are now clearly of concern to the international community. The extent to which countries are internationally accountable for their national behaviour and policies has become an important issue in modern life.

Conversely, the influence of the external economic environment on national fortunes has become so much more pronounced that the notion that countries are fully sovereign in respect of their internal policies has lost much of its practical validity. It is increasingly difficult for countries to insulate their economies and societies from processes, actions, and decisions in the broader global setting. The ability of governments to control events within national borders is drastically constrained by the external environment. Developing countries are inevitably in the most vulnerable position in the face of these trends.

The rapid integration of the world economy has so far taken place in an unregulated, haphazard manner. While imbalances and fluctuations have increased as a result of the larger number of transactions and agents, there are no global mechanisms to moderate their international transmission; on the contrary, shocks and disturbances are magnified. Uncertainty, instability, and unpredictability in the world economy have dramatically increased.

Furthermore, global interdependence is not symmetrical: the South is not an equal partner of the North but is in a position of subordination. In international economic relations the South is not allowed a fair share but is exploited. So far from participating in decision-making at the world level, it is in fact excluded. It has little influence on its external environment; it is by and large at its mercy.

Thus, the task that the new context poses for the global community is two-fold: on the one hand, to devise international economic and political structures and arrangements for dealing effectively with the host of new issues raised by growing interdependence; on the other, to incorporate the developing countries both in the fair sharing of the benefits of interdependence and in the systems through which it is managed. This is indeed a momentous challenge for humankind.

One of the central conclusions of this Report is that the destiny of developing countries and their economies and societies will become even more dependent on the external environment in the period to come, and in a number of new, diverse, and complex ways.

In view of their weaknesses and vulnerabilities, it is therefore of critical importance for all developing countries to try to secure an adequate degree of institutionalized protection of their independence and freedom of action through a multilateral regime, backed up by a strengthened United Nations system.

The strengthening of multilateralism and of international institutions must be an important part of the process of building a more equitable and democratic international order. This is especially necessary after the experience of the 1980s, which was marked by significant retrogression in the values guiding international relations, in multilateralism and the role of the United Nations system, and in the way in which issues of international development are perceived in the North. The South must lend its full support to rule-based rather than deal-based international arrangements. Clearly, the poor need the protection provided by the rule of law much more than the rich and powerful. The South must therefore take a sustained interest in efforts to improve the working of major international institutions, which now suffer from many weaknesses.

The aspirations of the South will not be fulfilled without a difficult and prolonged struggle. This is a basic message of this Report. If the developing countries are to secure changes in the world system to reflect their needs and to make it more equitable, they must seek to act from a position of strength. This can be attained only through a concerted strategy which spans national development, South-South co-operation, and interaction with the North, including the negotiation of multilateral regimes and their management.

There is no doubt that the twenty-first century will see the emergence of a new international system. However, this could be no more than the adaptation of the present arrangements to new requirements as perceived by the dominant nations of the North. This process has already begun, in that the industrialized countries are defining the areas in which they wish to see change, identifying the changes that their interests demand, and presenting them to the developing countries virtually on a take-it-or-leave-it basis.

By contrast, what is needed is that the world community as a whole should transform radically the institutions and arrangements which arose in a different age—an age of domination, imperialism, and inequality—and which are wholly inadequate to present needs and inconsistent with the goals of democracy, equality, and equity in international relations. This transformation requires the formulation of a vision of a more democratic international structure capable of steering social, political, and economic change in the interests of humanity as a whole, and the adoption of this vision through international agreement.

For its own sake and for the sake of humanity, the South has to be resolute in resisting the present moves by the dominant countries of the North to redesign the system to their own advantage. Containing the great majority of humankind, the South must play its rightful role in the process of fashioning a more equitable and stable system to serve the aspirations of all people.

With this as the objective, the developing countries must:

- Acquire the maximum countervailing power through increased exploitation of the South's collective resources.
- Press for setting in motion a multilateral, democratic process, with the participation of all major interests, to arrive at a global consensus on the new international system, its basic goals, how it should be managed, and the institutions it requires.
- Speak with a united voice in making clear proposals, so as to play a leading role in this process. The proposals should aim at capturing the imagination of the world's people and especially of the young; they should rise above parochialism to articulate a vision of the world as one human family.

In mobilizing all its latent power, the South has first to ensure that its economies are self-fuelling to the maximum extent possible and that their growth is not simply a by-product of growth in the North. The South needs to expand its presence in Northern markets, for which purpose it needs improved access to markets and the roll-back of protectionism, which is now often directed specifically at products of considerable interest to the South in terms of export. But the emerging development patterns of the North clearly suggest that the Northern locomotive economies will not pull the train of Southern economies at a pace that will satisfy its passengers–the people of the South. The locomotive power has to be generated to the maximum extent possible within the economies of the South themselves.

The acute poverty of the South, particularly the low productivity of Southern agriculture, is a pointer to the unexplored potential that exists within the South itself to fuel its growth processes. Sustained rural development, focused sharply on raising the productivity and incomes of small landholders, can be a powerful instrument for the promotion of both growth and equity.

The South as a whole has sufficient markets, technology, and financial resources to make South-South co-operation an effective means for widening the development options for its economies. Intensified South-South co-operation has to become an important part of Southern strategies for autonomous, self-reliant development. The South must build its capacity to sustain a fast pace of growth even if the Northern engine is in low gear.

South-South co-operation is, however, a strategic necessity not only for development within the South but also for securing equitable management of global interdependence. South-South co-operation alone can give the developing countries a collective weight and countervailing power that cannot be ignored by the North. Securing an effective say in the management of the global economy will require this collective strength, backed by unity among the countries of the South, steadfastness in the pursuit of goals, and flexibility in the use of tactics.

The South has additionally to recognize that in the search for new models of international relations, ideas have a critical role, especially ideas rooted in the shared needs and common aspirations of humanity. If these ideas are well supported by research, technically sound, balanced, and reasonable, and if they appeal to the sense of fair play and justice, they will evoke a favourable response from wider sections of the public in Northern societies. An organized and articulate South that advances such ideas will increase its weight in the global debate. Though the equations of power continue to dominate the world, the springs of idealism and human fellowship are not dry. Linking all forces that believe in the shared destiny of humankind under the common banner of an enlightened vision of the global future will in itself be a monumental achievement.

In the final analysis, the South's plea for justice, equity, and democracy in the global society cannot be dissociated from its pursuit of these goals within its own societies. Commitment to democratic values, respect for fundamental rights–particularly the right to dissent–fair treatment for minorities, concern for the poor and underprivileged, probity in public life, willingness to settle disputes without recourse to war–all these cannot but influence world opinion and increase the South's chances of securing a new world order.

Annexe

THE COMMISSION AND ITS WORK

The plans to establish the South Commission were announced at the eighth Meeting of the Heads of State and Government of the Non-Aligned Countries held in Harare, Zimbabwe, in September 1986 by Dr. Mahathir Bin Mohamad, Prime Minister of Malaysia. Dr. Mahathir had headed a steering committee which had been set up, at an international meeting held in Malaysia, to make the preliminary arrangements for the formation of the Commission. He also announced that Julius K. Nyerere, former President of Tanzania, had accepted the invitation to be the Commission's Chairman.

In the months immediately after the announcement, Mr. Nyerere travelled widely in the South to discuss the role of the Commission with people in public life, in the business and academic communities, and in non-governmental organizations. On 27 July 1987, he announced in Dar-es-Salaam the composition of the Commission and the appointment as Secretary-General of one of its members, Dr. Manmohan Singh, Deputy Chairman of the Indian Planning Commission, whom the Indian Government had released for service with the Commission.

The Commission has functioned as an independent body, with its members serving in their personal capacities. Its term was set for three years. Its work has been supported by financial contributions from developing countries. The Commission's Secretariat was established in Geneva with assistance from the Government of Switzerland and started functioning on 1 August 1987.

The Commissioners

Chairman: *Julius Kambarage NYERERE*, Tanzania. Chairman, Chama cha Mapinduzi; President of the United Republic of Tanzania 1964-85; President of Tanganyika 1962-64; Prime Minister from independence in 1961; previously teacher, then nationalist leader.

Secretary-General: *Manmohan SINGH*, India. Deputy Chairman, Indian Planning Commission 1985-87; Governor, Reserve

Bank of India 1982-85; Member-Secretary, Indian Planning Commission 1980-82; Secretary, Ministry of Finance 1976-79; Chief Economic Adviser, Ministry of Finance 1972-76; Professor of Economics, Punjab and Delhi Universities 1962-65 and 1969-70; Chief, Financing for Trade Section, UNCTAD 1966-69.

Ismail Sabri ABDALLA, Egypt. Chairman, Third World Forum; Minister for Planning 1971-75; Professor of Economics and Planning; President, Arab Society for Economic Research; Board member, UNRISD; Member, UN Committee for Development Planning 1980-86.

Abdlatif AL-HAMAD, Kuwait. Director-General and Chairman of the Board of Directors, Arab Fund for Economic and Social Development 1985-; Minister of Finance and Minister of Planning 1981-83; Director-General, Kuwait Fund for Arab Economic Development 1962-81; Member, Brandt Commission; current Chairman of the UN Committee for Development Planning.

Paulo Evaristo ARNS, Brazil. Cardinal 1973-; Archbishop of Sao Paulo 1970-; Auxiliary bishop of Sao Paulo 1966-70; Professor of Theology at Franciscan Institute and Professor of Didactics at Catholic University, Petropolis 1955-65; teacher in a seminary 1953-55; Franciscan priest; recipient of the Nansen Prize from the UN High Commissioner for Refugees.

Solita COLLAS-MONSOD, Philippines. Associate Professor, School of Economics, University of the Philippines; Secretary of Economic Planning and Director-General, National Economic Development Authority 1987-89.

Eneas Da Conceiçao COMICHE , Mozambique. Governor, *Banco de Moçambique* and Member of People's Assembly; previously Vice-Minister of Finance; Chairman of the *Banco Popular de Desenvolvimento*; Member and later Chairman of the *Instituto de Credito de Moçambique* ; Alternate Governor in IMF and Governor in World Bank; Governor in IFAD; Alternate Governor in ADB; has led Mozambican delegations in negotiations with multilateral and regional finance institutions as well as in debt negotiations.

Gamani COREA, Sri Lanka. Chairman of the UN ad hoc Committee for the Preparation of the International Development Strategy for the 1990s; Chancellor of Sri Lanka's Open University and Chairman of the Marga Institute of Development

Studies; Secretary-General of UNCTAD 1974-84; Ambassador to EEC; Deputy Governor of the Central Bank of Ceylon; Head of the Ministry of Planning and Economic Affairs 1965-70; chairman and/or member of a number of UN and UNCTAD expert committees.

Aboubakar DIABY-OUATTARA, Ivory Coast. Currently in private business, engaged in promotion of private investment in Africa; formely Executive Secretary, Economic Community of West African States, and Managing Director, International Bank for West Africa in Abidjan, Ivory Coast.

Aldo FERRER, Argentina. Professor of Economics, University of Buenos Aires; Minister of Economy and Finance, Province of Buenos Aires 1958-60; Minister of Public Works and Services and Minister of Economy and Labour in the Federal Government 1970-71; President, Bank of the Province of Buenos Aires 1983-87; member of the panel of experts of the Alliance for Progress 1967-70; founder and first Executive Secretary of the Latin American Social Science Council 1967-70; author on development issues.

Celso FURTADO, Brazil. Minister of Culture 1986-88; Ambassador to EEC 1985-86; Professor of Economic Development, Sorbonne 1964-85; Research Fellow, Yale University 1964-65; forced into political exile by the military government 1964-85; Minister of Planning 1962-63; first Chairman of the Superintendency for the Development of the Northeast of Brazil 1959-62 and 1963-64; Director, Development Bank of Brazil 1958-59; staff member, UN Economic Commission for Latin America 1949-57.

Enrique IGLESIAS,[*] Uruguay. President, Inter-American Development Bank, 1988-; Foreign Minister 1985-88; Secretary-General, UN Conference on New and Renewable Energy Sources 1981; Executive Secretary, UN Economic Commission for Latin America and the Caribbean 1972-85; President, Central Bank of Uruguay 1967-68; Technical Director, Uruguay National Planning Office 1962-66; Delegate to the Latin American Free Trade Association 1964-67; Professor of Development Economics and Director of the Economics Institute at the University of Montevideo.

---

[*]   Enrique Iglesias was unable to attend the meetings of the Commission.

Devaki JAIN, India. Director, Institute of Social Studies Trust, Delhi and Bangalore; economist-researcher; organized and implemented research programmes on employment, food security, and social movements; founding member, Development Alternatives for Women in a New Era, Third World Women's Network on Development, and Indian Association of Women's Studies; member of advisory committees to the Indian Ministry of Labour, Education, and Rural Development.

Simba MAKONI, Zimbabwe. Executive Secretary, Southern Africa Development Co-ordination Conference 1984-; served successively as Deputy Minister of Agriculture, Minister of Industry and Energy Development, and Minister of Youth, Sport, and Culture 1980-84.

Michael Norman MANLEY, Jamaica. Prime Minister 1989-; Leader, People's National Party, and President, National Workers' Union; Prime Minister 1972-80; Vice-President, Socialist International and Chairman of its International Economic Committee; awarded UN gold medal for contribution to struggle against apartheid.

Jorge Eduardo NAVARRETE, Mexico. Ambassador to China 1989-; Under-Secretary (Economic), Foreign Affairs Ministry 1979-85; earlier Ambassador to Venezuela, Austria, Yugoslavia, United Kingdom, and Ireland; Permanent Representative to UNIDO and IAEA, and Deputy Permanent Representative to the UN, New York.

Pius OKIGBO, Nigeria. Chairman since 1970 of SKOUP & Co. Ltd., a leading Nigerian economic/financial consulting group; former economic adviser to the Federal Government of Nigeria; Ambassador to EEC 1962-67; has served on numerous international committees and commissions, including as Chairman of UN Panel of Experts on the Use of National Accounts in Africa; has also served on various national commissions and other bodies, including as Chairman of the Board of Governors of the Nigerian Institute of Social and Economic Research and of the Presidential Commission on Revenue Allocation.

Augustin PAPIC, Yugoslavia. Senior Fellow, European Centre for Peace and Development, Belgrade, and Council Member, Yugoslav Centre for Strategic Studies; formerly Director-General of Central Bank of Yugoslavia; Alternative Executive Director of the World Bank; Deputy Federal Minister of Foreign Trade;

member of Presidency of Yugoslavia; Ambassador to UN Organizations in Geneva; Ambassador to Egypt; member of Federal Assembly of Yugoslavia.

Carlos Andrés PEREZ , Venezuela. President of Venezuela 1989-; 1980 elected Executive President of the Latin American Association for Human Rights; 1983 elected Vice-President of Socialist International; 1984 elected Vice-President of the Council of Former Chiefs of State; President of Venezuela 1973-78; leader of Parliamentary majority 1964-69; Minister of Interior 1962-64; political exile 1951-58; participated as youth leader in the establishment of *Acción Democrática* political party 1941.

Jiadong QIAN, China. Ambassador; Deputy Director-General, China Centre for International Studies; Member, UN Advisory Board on Disarmament Matters; served successively as Assistant Director, Asian Department, Ministry of Foreign Affairs; Secretary, Office of the Prime Minister of the State Council; Deputy Director, Ministry of Foreign Affairs; Special Research Fellow of the China Institute of International Studies; Ambassador on Disarmament Affairs, and Ambassador-Permanent Representative to the UN in Geneva.

Shridath RAMPHAL, Guyana. Commonwealth Secretary-General 1975-90; Chancellor of University of Warwick, University of the West Indies, and University of Guyana; Chairman, Independent West Indian Commission; former Chairman, UN Committee for Development Planning; Member of Brandt, Palme and Brundtland independent commissions, as well as of the Commission on International Humanitarian Issues; formerly Guyana's Attorney-General, Minister of Foreign Affairs, and Minister of Justice.

Carlos Rafael RODRIGUEZ, Cuba. Vice-President, Council of State, and Vice-President, Council of Ministers, with a long record of ministerial responsibility for economic and international matters; has led Cuban delegations to many international conferences; Dean of the School of Economics, Havana University 1959-62.

Abdus SALAM, Pakistan. Professor of Theoretical Physics, Imperial College (London) 1957-; Director, International Centre for Theoretical Physics (Trieste) 1964-; Founder and President, Third World Academy of Sciences 1983-; Nobel Prize in Physics for research on physics of elementary particles 1970.

Marie-Angélique SAVANE , Senegal. International consultant;
President, Association of African Women for Research and
Development 1977-88; Project leader, UN Research Institute for
Social Development 1979-; Co-ordinator of the study on Food
Systems and Society in Africa 1984-88; Co-ordinator of a
research programme on impact of socioeconomic changes on
women in Africa 1979-83; Editor-in-chief, *Famille et
Développement,* 1974-78; research assistant in a UNESCO study
on education, employment, and migration in Senegal 1972-74.
Tan Sri Ghazali SHAFIE, Malaysia. Chairman, National
Economic Consultative Council; Member, Executive Council,
Pacific Forum, Hawaii; Chairman, Government-owned
Development and Investment Company; Member of Parliament
1971-86; Minister for Planning and Information 1971-73;
Minister of Home Affairs 1973-81; Minister of Foreign Affairs
1981-84; Secretary-General, Ministry of Foreign Affairs 1957-71;
Member, National Operations Council and National
Consultative Council 1969-71; Visiting Professor, National
University of Singapore 1985-88; Chairman, Mara Institute of
Technology 1970-80.
Tupuola Efi TUPUA TAMASESE, Western Samoa.   Deputy
Prime Minister and Minister for Works; Prime Minister 1976-82;
has represented his country at Commonwealth, UN, and South
Pacific Commission meetings.
Nitisastro WIDJOJO, Indonesia. Economic Adviser to the
Government of Indonesia 1983-; Coordinating Minister for
Economic, Financial and Industrial Affairs 1973-1983; Minister
for National Development Planning 1971-1973; Chairman of the
National Development Planning Board 1967-1983; Professor of
Economics, University of Indonesia 1963-present.
Layachi YAKER, Algeria. Coordinator Special Activities to DG
UNESCO; Ambassador to US 1982-84; USSR 1979-82; India
and South Asia 1961-82; VP National Assembly 1977-79; FLN
Central Committee; Minister of Commerce 1969-77; DG
International Co-operation, Foreign Affairs 1962-69;
Vice-Chairman, UNSG Panel on South Africa and Namibia
1985; and UNGA Group of 18 for UN Reform 1986; President
International Ocean Institute; Member, Brandt Commission,
Policy Board Interaction Council, IPC on Agriculture and Trade,
Arab Thought Forum, Exec. Committee Club of Rome.

Hon. Treasurer and Personal Representative of the Chairman: *Amir JAMAL*, Tanzania. Permanent Representative to the UN in Geneva 1985-; Minister of Finance, Minister of Communications and Transport 1977-79; Minister of Finance and Economic Planning 1975-77; Minister of Commerce and Industries 1972-75; Minister of Finance 1965-72; Minister of Economic Planning 1964-65; Minister of Communications and Power 1962-64.

Staff of the Commission

Secretary-General:
Manmohan Singh
Senior Professional Staff:

Carlos Fortin	Abhilash Munsif
Branislav Gosovic	Rohan Ponniah
Charles Gunawardena	Jaime Ros
Henock Kifle	

Chairman's Professional Staff, Dar-es-Salaam:

Jumanne Wagao	Joan Wicken

General Service and Support Staff:
Geneva: Mary-Jane Bennaton, Tudor Jayawardana, Chedra Mayhew, Vasanthan Pushparaj, Guadalupe Quesada, Ayesha Rodrigues, Vibeke Underhill. (Only those who served on contracts of more than one year are listed.) Dar-es-Salaam: Anna Mwansasu, Frank Nyawazwa.

Terms of Reference

The Commission adopted its terms of reference at its second meeting in Kuala Lumpur, 1-3 March 1988.
1. *Analysis of national development experience in the South and elaboration of an integrated perspective and vision of the future*
The Commission will undertake a critical analysis of post-World War II development experience and the lessons it holds for development planning in the future. Having defined development, it will assess the weaknesses and strengths of the developing countries; their development prospects; the constraints they face; the options open to them; and the scope for improved mobilization and utilization of their physical, financial, and human resources.

On the basis of this analysis, the Commission will outline development goals and objectives for the year 2000 and beyond. In doing so, it will take into account the changing demographic, social, and economic conditions in the Third World, and the evolving global environment.

The Commission will also make suggestions for reformulating and updating, wherever necessary, the patterns and strategies of growth to achieve the goals of self-reliance, development, and equity. In doing so it will take into account both the immense promise and potential offered by modern science and technology and the current human and other resource realities. In all its work the Commission will pay special attention to issues relating to poverty and hunger, the satisfaction of basic human needs, human resource development, and industrialization of the Third World.

2. *Analysis of the global environment*

The Commission will analyse and comment on the evolving global environment as this is influenced by political, economic, and technological changes in the North ; it will assess the implications of this evolution for the South and for the planning of development in the South.

It will study: the nature of the evolving interdependence of the world; the impact and effects of the transnationalization process; the interrelationship between development and issues relating to world peace and security; the state of the biosphere, with the challenges this poses to humankind and the management of the global commons. On the basis of these studies the Commission will make appropriate proposals for the equitable management of global interdependence and the building of a new world order.

3. *South-South co-operation for collective self-reliance*

The Commission will carefully assess the role of South-South co-operation in widening the options for development strategies. It will analyse the experience acquired by current and past efforts to achieve such co-operation at every level. It will draw upon this experience to identify weaknesses and obstacles to South-South co-operation, and propose measures that will help to overcome them and to promote a fuller use of the existing potential for collective self-reliance in the South. The Commission will thus seek to foster various modes of South-South co-operation (subregional, regional, interregional, and global) as an essential support to processes of self-reliant national development.

The Commission will examine the need for and the value of a permanent, institutionalized support mechanism for South-South co-operation. It will thus consider whether there is a need for a Third World secretariat and a forum at the global level which, inter alia, would promote greater knowledge of the South by the South, serve as a focus for continuing interaction and mutual consultations among developing countries, carry out research and support their negotiations with the North, and act as a focal point for the exchange of information relevant to development.

4. *South-North relations*

The Commission will assess the state of South-North relations, and analyse their post-war evolution. On the basis of this assessment, and its analysis of the present and probable future global environment, and the imperatives of development, the Commission will examine: the current position of the South in relation to the North, and see how the voice of the South can be strengthened, and its role enhanced in the search for and implementation of greater equity in a new world order.

The Commission will seek to rethink, to update and, where necessary, to reformulate the intellectual foundations, the strategy, and tactics, and the institutional structures of the South in its dealings with the North. The Commission will highlight the close linkages that exist between the international arrangements for money, finance, and trade and their impact on the pace of development in the world economy in general and in the South in particular. It will pay special attention to issues related to a reform of international arrangements for trade, science and technology, money and finance, and intellectual property; the management of transnational actors and processes; the global commons and the human environment; and the future of multilateralism and reform of the United Nations system.

Meetings of the Commission

The Commission held eight plenary meetings:
   First meeting, Mont-Pèlerin, Switzerland, 2-5 October 1987
   Second meeting, Kuala Lumpur, Malaysia, 1-3 March 1988
   Third meeting, Cocoyoc, Mexico, 5-8 August 1988
   Fourth meeting, Kuwait, 10-12 December 1988
   Fifth meeting, Maputo, Mozambique, 27-30 May 1989
   Sixth meeting, New Delhi, India, 11-14 November 1989
   Seventh meeting, Nicosia, Cyprus, 4-8 May 1990
   Eighth meeting, Havana, Cuba, 30-31 July and
   Caracas, Venezuela, 2-3 August 1990
The final meeting of the Commission will be held in Arusha,
Tanzania, 6-8 October 1990.

Working Groups of the Commission

The Commission set up working groups of Commissioners to deal
in depth with certain issues.
Debt. Geneva, 23-24 January 1988, with the participation of
Dragoslav Avramovic, Chandra Hardy, and Carlos Massad.
Uruguay Round of GATT Negotiations. Geneva, 11-12 June
1988, with the participation of Rubens Ricupero, Hani Riad,
Shrirang Shukla, K.G. Anthony Hill, and See Chak Mun as
negotiators of the Group of 77 in the Uruguay Round.
Commodities. Geneva, 28-29 July 1988, with the participation of
Dragoslav Avramovic, Kenneth Dadzie, Peter Lai, and Alfred
Maizels.
South-South Co-operation. Kuwait, 22-24 October 1988, with the
participation of Roderick Rainford.
North-South Issues. London, 29-31 October 1988, with the
participation of G.K. Helleiner.
National Development Issues. Geneva, 2-4 November 1988, with
the participation of Philip Ndegwa and Marc Nerfin.
Science and Technology. Trieste, Italy, 24-25 November 1988,
with the participation of Pablo Bifani and Mohamed H.A.
Hassan.
North-South Issues. London, 2-3 March 1989.
South Secretariat. London, 4-5 March 1989.
Role of the Business Sector. Buenos Aires, 8-10 March 1989.
Draft Report. Kuwait, 17-19 February 1990.

Expert Groups

The Secretariat of the Commission convened several expert groups to assist it in its work.

What South? Nyon, Switzerland, 15 November 1987. Participants: Pablo Bifani, Marc Nerfin, Leelananda de Silva, Michael Zammit Cutajar.

The Reform of the UN System. Nyon, 16 May 1988. Participants: Pablo Bifani, Mahdi Elmandjra, Marc Nerfin, Michael Zammit Cutajar.

Uruguay Round of Trade Negotiations. Geneva, 24-26 May 1988. Participants: Winston Fritsch, Deepak Nayyar, Chakravarthi Raghavan.

The Future of the UN System. Asilah, Morocco, 15-16 August 1988. Participants: Abdellatif Benachenhou, Assia Alaoui Bensalah, Mahdi Elmandjra, Marc Nerfin, together with Commissioners Gamani Corea and Layachi Yaker.

Development Strategies, Policies, and Programmes. Geneva, 26-28 June 1989. Participants: Sukhamoy Chakravarty (Chairman), Abdellatif Benachenhou, Dharam Ghai, Nurul Islam, Elizabeth Jelin, Joseph Ki-Zerbo, Eddie Lee, Enrique Oteiza, Surendra Patel, Vishnu Persaud, Kamal Salih, Ajit Singh, Osvaldo Sunkel.

South-South Co-operation. Geneva, 3-5 July 1989. Participants: Philip Ndegwa (Chairman), Dragoslav Avramovic, Chen Qida, Norman Girvan, Reginald Green, Mahbub ul Haq, Khair El-Din Haseeb, Abdul Jalloh, Wilson Kinyua, Peter Lai, Thandika Mkandawire, Jorge Nef, Surendra Patel, Alicia Puyana.

North-South Relations. Geneva, 11-13 July 1989. Participants: Germánico Salgado (Chairman), Samir Amin, Chen Qida, Stuart Holland, Pedro Malan, Stephen Marris, Carlos Massad, Percy Mistry, Jorge Nef, Surendra Patel, H.M.A. Onitiri, Arjun K. Sengupta, Anton Vratusa.

Development Indicators. Caracas, Venezuela, 31 July-3 August 1989. Participants: Victor Anderson, Gabriel Bidegain, Frank Bracho, Eduardo Bustelo, Meghnad Desai, Antonio Fernández, Dharam Ghai, Hazel Henderson, Manfred Max-Neef, Nancy Angulo de Rodríguez, Sixto K. Roxas, Pedro Sainz, Gustavo Salas, Landing Savané, Luis Thais.

The Future of the UN System. Geneva, 10-12 January 1990. Participants: Diego Cordovez, Ismat Kittani, Marc Nerfin, Graf Alexander York.

Meetings of the Commission with Officials and Intellectuals in the South

Colloquium on South-South co-operation, Kuala Lumpur, 3 March 1988. After its meeting in Kuala Lumpur, the members of the Commission participated in a colloquium on South-South co-operation sponsored by the Malaysian Institute of Strategic and International Studies. The following took part: Khatijah Ahmed, Zain Azrai, B.A. Hamzah, Mohamed Bin Harun, Asmat Kamalluddin, Noordin Sopiee, Hamidah Yusuf.

Meeting with Mexican intellectuals, Mexico, 5 August 1988. Before its meeting in Cocoyoc, the Commission had a working session in Mexico with a group of Mexican intellectuals and officials. Those who took part were: Eugenio Anguiano, Lourdes Arizpe, Manuel Armendáriz Echegaray, Vivian Brachet, Luis Bravo Aguilera, Gerardo Bueno, Mauricio de María y Campos, Antonio Alonso Concheiro, José Córdoba, Pablo González Casanova, Vidal Ibarra Puig, Nora Lustig, Carlos Monsivais, María de los Angeles Moreno, Iván Restrepo, Sergio Reyes Osorio, Jesús Silva Herzog, Rodolfo Stavenhagen, Luis Suárez, Saúl Trejo, René Villarreal, Arturo Warman.

Meeting with intellectuals from the Arab region, Kuwait, 12 December 1988. At the end of its meeting in Kuwait, the Commission held an exchange of views with invited guests Assia Alaoui, Hassan Al Ibrahim, and Khair El-Din Haseeb.

Meeting with Indian academics and experts, New Delhi, 10 November 1989. Before its meeting in New Delhi, the Commission had a discussion with Indian intellectuals and officials. Participants: Isher Judge Ahluwalia, Montek Singh Ahluwalia, J.L. Bajaj, U.S. Bajpai, Shyam Baran, I.K. Barthakur, Krishna Bhardwaj, Rine Bhattacharya, Raja Chelliah, Kamla Chowdhry, C. Dasgupta, Nitin Desai, Biswajit Dhar, Razia Sultan Ismail, Vijay Kelkar, B.V. Krishnamurti, K.S. Krishnaswamy, Nagesh Kumar, Jantesh Mehrotra, Rajesh Mehta, M.G.K. Menon, R.J. Mody, Rakesh Mohan, S.K. Mohanty, V.R. Panchamukhi, Alok Parsad, K.M. Raipurie, V.L.

Rao, Jayanta Roy, Manu Shroff, S.P. Shukla, Ratna M. Sudarshan, M.S. Swaminathan, G.A. Tadas, B.G. Verghese.

Meeting of African policy-makers and experts on the work of the South Commission, Addis Ababa, 22-23 January 1990. African members of the South Commission took part in a meeting with African policy-makers and experts, sponsored by the ECA, OAU and ADB. Participants: Louis Alexandrenne, Aboubakar Baba-Moussa, Abdoul Barry, Makhtar Diouf, A. Haggag, Makonnen Kebret, Jack Kisa, F. Lounes, R.T. N'Daw, Samuel Nnebe-Agumadu, Anthony V. Obeng, Jasper Okelo, D. Ona-Ondo, O. Silla, Siyanbola Tomori, as well as the following members of ECA staff: Adebayo Adedeji, A. Bahri, M. Bongoy, Nancy Hafkin, S. Jack, M. Tchouta Moussa, P. Mwanza, S.C. Nana-Sinkam, Bade Onimode, R. Rakotobe, S. Rasheed, L. Sangare, M. Sarr, Mary Tadesse, A.B. Tall, O. Teriba, W.N. Wamalwa.

Chairman's Contacts and Travel

Before the Commission was formed and during its tenure, the Chairman travelled extensively in the South, meeting Heads of State or Government and other people in public life to discuss issues related to the work of the Commission. He also corresponded with leaders of developing countries on matters related to the Commission's work.

In 1987, the Chairman visited the following countries: India, Venezuela, Peru, Uruguay, Argentina, Brazil, Cuba, Malaysia, Indonesia, Philippines, China, Egypt, Yugoslavia, Algeria, Zimbabwe, Mozambique, and Kuwait.

In 1988, the Chairman visited the following countries: Malaysia, Thailand, Bangladesh, Pakistan, Sri Lanka, Zambia, Zimbabwe, Niger, Ethiopia, Djibouti, Somalia, Kenya, Sudan, Jamaica, Uganda, Nicaragua, Costa Rica, Guayana, Trinidad, Nigeria, Ghana, Gambia, Senegal, Mali, Iran, Iraq, and Syria.

In 1989, the Chairman visited the following countries: Venezuela, Libya, Yugoslavia, Cape Verde, Tunisia, Algeria, Egypt, China, Malaysia, and Indonesia.

Statements and Publications

The Commission has issued the following statements, which were published as booklets:

Statement on External Debt on 3 March 1988

Statement on the Uruguay Round on 8 August 1988 The Commission has also published the following:

The South Commission: Inaugural Statement by Julius K. Nyerere, Objectives and Terms of Reference, List of Commission Members.

Abdus Salam, *Notes on Science, Technology and Science Education in the Development of the South.*

Financial and other Contributions

The work of the Commission was made possible by financial contributions from the South. The following countries contributed:

Algeria ($300,000)
Argentina ($100,000)
Bangladesh ($5,000)
Barbados ($2,000)
Brazil ($135,000)
Botswana ($200,000)
Brunei ($200,000)
China ($400,000)
Cuba ($200,000)
Egypt ($100,000)
Ghana ($100,000)
Guyana ($10,000)
India ($500,000)
Indonesia ($75,000)
Iran ($100,000)
Jamaica ($105,000)
Jordan ($10,000)
Kenya ($100,000)
P. D. R. of Korea ($20,000)
Republic of Korea ($300,000)
Kuwait ($500,000)
Malaysia ($400,000)
Maldives ($5,000)

Mali ($32,700)
Malta ($5,000)
Mexico ($200,000)
Mozambique ($50,000)
Niger ($35,070)
Nigeria ($400,000)
Oman ($225,000)
Pakistan ($20,000)
Philippines ($20,000)
Senegal ($49,000)
Seychelles ($1,000)
Singapore ($50,000)
Sri Lanka ($10,000)
Sudan ($100,000)
Syria ($300,000)
Tanzania ($50,000)
Thailand ($50,000)
Uganda ($100,000)
Venezuela ($596,571)
Yugoslavia ($159,000)
Zambia ($67,769)
Zimbabwe ($300,000).

The following financial contributions were also received: Arab Fund for Economic and Social Development, Kuwait ($355,000), International Development Research Centre, Canada ($46,750), OPEC Fund ($100,000), private sector in Malaysia ($376,900), Third World Foundation, London ($60,000).

Host governments met the local costs of the Commission's meetings in Malaysia, Mexico, Kuwait, Mozambique, India, Cyprus, Cuba and Venezuela. The Government of Tanzania is meeting the local costs of the Commission's final meeting. The Arab Fund for Social and Economic Development met the local costs of two working group meetings held in Kuwait. The Government of Tanzania provided the facilities for the Chairman's Office in Dar-es-Salaam and paid the local costs.

The Federal Government of Switzerland made a contribution of Sfr. 280,000 a year for a period of three years towards the operational expenses, including rent, of the Secretariat in Geneva. The Canton of Geneva provided office furniture and equipment. The Government of Norway provided word processing equipment.

Papers Prepared for the Commission

The Commission benefited from papers contributed by experts from a number of countries, as well as by several institutions. They are listed below:

Amin, S: *National Popular Development, Social and Political Democracy, Delinking.*

Arab Fund for Economic and Social Development: *South-South Co-operation: The Arab Experience.*

Arab Fund for Economic and Social Development: *The Arab Development Group, an Example and a Catalyst in the Process of South-South Co-operation for Development.*

Arab Fund for Economic and Social Development: *Development Emphasis through the Nineties (A Third World View).*

Arizpe, L: *Culture and Knowledge for South Development.*

Avramovic, D: *Debt Problem: What Next?*

Avramovic, D: *External Debt.*

Avramovic, D: *The Debt Crisis of the 1980s: The Beginning of a Wind-Down?*

Balasubramaniam, K: *Health for All Now.*

Barraclough, S: *Towards Improving Food Security.*

Barthakur, I.K: *Quest for Food Security in the Third World.*

Bernal, L.R: *The Brady Initiative: A Lack of Traction.*

Bernal, L.R: *Appropriate Adjustment Policies in Developing Countries.*

Bifani, P: *Science and Technology for Sustainable Development.*

Cassen, R.H: *Mutual Interests Revisited: A Brief Review of the Brandt Commission's Case.*

Chen, Qida: *China's Trade and Investment Relations with other Developing Countries.*

Choi, H.S.C: *Science and Technology Policies in the Industrialization of a Developing Country.*

Economic Commission for Africa: *Creating an Enabling Environment for Intra-African Trade Expansion within the Framework of South-South Co-operation.*

Elmandjra, M., *Human Rights and Development.*

Fritsch, W. and de Paiva Abreu, M: *New Themes and Agriculture in the New Round.*

Ghai, D: *Participatory Development: Some Perspectives from Grass-Roots Experiences.*

Goldemberg, J: *The Role of Science and Technology in the Energy Paths Open to Developing Countries.*

Green, R.H: *Southern Economic Co-ordination/Integration: Concrete Potential or Quest for El Dorado?.*

Griffin, K: *Development Thought and Development Strategies: Four Decades of Experience.*

Griffith-Jones, S: *International Financial and Monetary Reform; A Developing Country Perspective.*

Grlickov, A: *The Perestroika and the Developing Countries.*

Hardy, C: *The Debt Problem in 1988.*

Hardy, C: *North-South Relations: What Next?.*

Helleiner, G.K: *Growth-Oriented Adjustment Lending: A Critical Assessment of IMF/World Bank Approaches.*

Institute for Developing Countries, Zagreb: *Development Redefined.*

INTAL (Institute for Latin American Integration, Inter-American Development Bank): *The Process of Economic Integration in Latin America and the Caribbean, 1985-1988.*

Jha, S: *Biotechnology: Prospects and Problems for the South.*

Jha, V: *Regional Development Banks.*

Maizels, A: *Towards a Viable International Commodity Policy.*

Mann Borgese, E: *Ocean Management.*

Mills-Aryee, D: *Subregional Economic Co-operation in Africa: Problems and Prospects for the Future.*

Mistry, S.P: *A Review of Relations between North and South, Retrospect and Prospect.*

O'Brien, P. and Giger, A: *Privatisation: Scope and Implications for Development in the 1990s.*

Parikh, J.K: *A North-South Perspective for Capital Goods for the Power Sector.*

Parikh, K.S: *Food Security in Developing Countries.*

Patel, S: *South Commission, Main Lines of its Action.*

Peña, F: *Working Together: Latin American Journey Toward Economic Integration.*

Raghavan, C: *Improving the Capacity of the South.*

Raghavan, C: *The Midterm Review of the Uruguay Round.*

Raghavan, C: *The South in the Uruguay Round.*

Rainford, R: *Some Reflections on Lessons to be Learnt from Economic Co-operation in the Caribbean Community and Common Market.*

Saigal, J: *Some Reflections on the Development Perspective for the South.*

Samuel, W.A: *Regional Co-operation in the Caribbean.*

Searwar, L: *North-South Negotiations: Institutions and Processes.*

Sharan, H.N: *South-South Co-operation in the Energy Sector: New Approaches for Effective Partnerships.*

Singer, H.W: *Lessons of Post-War Development Experience, 1945-1988.*

Singh, A: *The World Economic Crisis and Industrial Development in the South in the 1980s: Analytical and Political Issues.*

Sobhan, R: *Creating International Liquidity within the South.*

Sobhan, R: *Restructuring the International Financial Institutions.*

Sobhan, R: *South-South Co-operation in Higher Education.*

Sobhan, R: *South-South Co-operation: The Logic of Experience.*

Sobhan, R: *The Changing Dynamics of South-South Co-operation.*

Stare, M: *South-South Co-operation in Trade with Special Emphasis on GSTP Implementation.*

Svetlicic, M. and Cabric, M: *Critical Assessment of Economic Co-operation among Developing Countries (ECDC) and Decisions and Recommendations for its Promotion.*

Swaminathan, M.S: *China and the World in the Nineties, Sustainable Food and Nutrition Security for the 1990s.*

Szentes, T: *Changes and Transformation in Eastern Europe: International Implications and Effects on the South and East-South Relations.*

Taylor, A.B: *The African Debt Crisis.*

Thomas, H.C: *The Implications for Developing Countries' Export Earnings Growth of an Increase in the Share of Imports by Developing Countries from Each Other: A Simulation Analysis.*

UNFPA (United Nations Fund for Population Activities): *Population and Human Resource Development: Problems, Priorities and Forward-Looking Strategies.*

Verbic, M: *How to Overcome the Information Gap.*

Wignaraja, P: *Participatory People-Centred Development.*

Yu Yongding: *The Evolving Trends of the World Economy Towards the Year 2000.*

Acknowledgements

The Commission could not have done its work without relying on the advice, knowledge, and work of many individuals in both South and North, including those who spared the time to take part in its working groups or prepared papers for its use. To them all the Commission expresses its sincerest appreciation.

The Commission also wishes to acknowledge with gratitude the assistance received from many institutions in different parts of the world and organizations and departments within the UN system. Special thanks are due to the UNCTAD Secretariat whose staff were throughout available for advice and consultation.

The Commission benefited from contacts with the following institutions:

African Development Bank, Abidjan, Ivory Coast.
African, Caribbean and Pacific Secretariat, Brussels, Belgium.
Afro-Asian Peoples' Solidarity Organization, Cairo, Egypt.
Arab Fund for Economic and Social Development, Kuwait.

ASEAN Secretariat, Djakarta, Indonesia.

Asian and Pacific Development Centre, Kuala Lumpur, Malaysia.

Asian Development Bank, Manila, Philippines.

Asociación de Economistas de América Latina y el Caribe , Havana, Cuba.

Asociación Latinoamericana de Integración, Montevideo, Uruguay.

Association of Caribbean Economists, Kingston, Jamaica.

Association of Development Research and Training Institutes of Asia and the Pacific, Kuala Lumpur, Malaysia.

Atwater Institute, Montreal, Canada.

Bangladesh Institute of Development Studies, Dhaka, Bangladesh.

Caribbean Community Secretariat, Georgetown, Guyana.

Central African Customs and Economic Union, Bangui, Central African Republic.

Centre for Development Studies, Trivandrum, India.

Centre for Applied Studies in International Negotiations, Geneva, Switzerland.

Centre for Arab Unity Studies, Beirut, Lebanon.

Centre for Economic Studies and Planning, School of Social Sciences, Jawaharlal Nehru University, New Delhi, India.

Centre for International Co-operation and Development, Ljubljana, Yugoslavia.

Centre for Our Common Future, Geneva, Switzerland.

Centre for Policy Research, New Delhi, India.

Centre for the Study of Administration of Relief, New Delhi, India.

Centro de Investigación y Promoción Agrícola Ambiental, Managua, Nicaragua.

Centro Regional de Estudios del Tercer Mundo, Bogotá, Colombia.

China Institute of Contemporary International Relations, Beijing, China.

Commission on Health Research for Development, Boston, USA

Commonwealth Secretariat, London, UK.

Communauté économique de l'Afrique de l'Ouest, Ouagadougou, Burkina Faso.

Cooperation Council for the Arab States of the Gulf, Riyadh, Saudi Arabia.

Corporación de Investigaciones Económicas para Latinoamérica, Santiago, Chile.

Council for the Development of Economic and Social Research in Africa, Dakar, Senegal.

Dag Hammarskjöld Foundation, Uppsala, Sweden.

Development Alternatives, New Delhi, India.

Development Alternatives with Women in a New Era, Rio de Janeiro, Brazil.

Economic Community of Central African States, Libreville, Gabon.

Economic Community of the Great Lakes Countries, Gisenyi, Rwanda.

Economic Community of West African States, Lagos, Nigeria.

European Centre for Peace and Development, Belgrade, Yugoslavia.

Friedrich-Ebert Stiftung, Bonn, Federal Republic of Germany.

German Foundation for International Development, Berlin, Federal Republic of Germany.

Indian Council for Research on International Economic Relations, New Delhi, India.

Indian Institute of Foreign Trade, New Delhi, India.

Indian Institute of Technology, Bombay, India.

Indira Gandhi Institute of Development Research, Bombay, India.

Institut panafricain de relations internationales, Geneva, Switzerland.

Institut universitaire d'études du développement, Geneva, Switzerland.

Institut universitaire de hautes études internationales, Geneva, Switzerland.

Institute for African Alternatives, London, UK.

Institute for Development and International Relations, Zagreb, Yugoslavia.

Institute for East-West Security Studies, New York, USA.

Institute for International Economics, Washington DC, USA.

Institute for Social and Economic Change, Bangalore, India.

Institute for World Economics, Budapest, Hungary.

Institute of Developing Economies, Tokyo, Japan.

Institute of Development Studies at the University of Sussex, Brighton, UK.

Institute of International Studies, Beijing, China.

Institute of Social and Economic Research, University of West Indies, Kingston, Jamaica.

Institute of Social Studies Trust, New Delhi, India.

Institute of Strategic and International Studies, Kuala Lumpur, Malaysia.

Institute of World Economics and Politics, Chinese Academy of Social Sciences, Beijing, China.

Instituto para la Integración de América Latina, Buenos Aires, Argentina.

Inter-Parliamentary Union, Geneva, Switzerland.

Inter-American Development Bank, Washington DC, USA.

International Association of State Trading Organisations of Developing Countries, Ljubljana, Yugoslavia.

International Center for Public Enterprises in Developing Countries, Ljubljana, Yugoslavia.

International Centre for Theoretical Physics, Trieste, Italy.

International Council for Adult Education, Toronto, Canada.

International Development Centre, University of Oxford, UK.

International Development Research Centre, Ottawa, Canada.

International Food Policy Research Institute, Washington, DC, USA.

International Foundation for Development Alternatives, Nyon, Switzerland.

International Institute for Applied Systems Analysis, Laxenburg, Austria.

International Organization of Consumers Unions, Penang, Malaysia.

International Rice Research Institute, Manila, Philippines.

Interpress Service, Rome, Italy.

Marga Institute, Colombo, Sri Lanka.

National Institute of Urban Affairs, New Delhi, India.

Nigerian Institute of Social and Economic Research, Ibadan, Nigeria.

North-South Institute, Ottawa, Canada.

North-South Roundtable, Society for International Development, New York, USA.

OECD Development Centre, Paris, France.

OPEC Fund for International Development, Vienna, Austria.
Organization for Social Science Research in Eastern Africa, Addis Ababa, Ethiopia.
Overseas Development Institute, London, UK.
Pakistan Institute of Development Economics, Islamabad, Pakistan.
Preferential Trade Area for Eastern and Southern African States, Lusaka, Zambia.
Research and Information System for the Non-Aligned and other Developing Countries, New Delhi, India.
Secretaría Permanente del Tratado General de Integración Económica, Guatemala, Guatemala.
Shanghai Institute for International Studies, Shanghai, China.
Sistema Económico Latinoamericano , Caracas, Venezuela.
Social Science Council of Nigeria, Ibadan, Nigeria.
Society for International Development - Switzerland Chapter, Geneva, Switzerland.
Southern Africa Development Co-ordination Conference, Gaberone, Botswana.
Southern African Universities Social Science Council, Dar-es-Salaam, Tanzania.
Tata Energy Research Institute, New Delhi, India.
Technology for the People, Geneva, Switzerland.
Third World Forum, Dakar, Senegal.
Third World Foundation for Social and Economic Studies, London, UK.
Third World Network, Penang, Malaysia.
Third World Network of Scientific Organizations, Trieste, Italy.
Vienna Institute for Development and Co-operation, Vienna, Austria.

The Commission was also helped by contacts with the following organizations and departments in the UN system:
Department of International Economic and Social Affairs, New York, USA.
Office of the Director-General for Development and International Economic Co-operation, New York, USA.
Economic Commission for Africa, Addis Ababa, Ethiopia.
Economic Commission for Europe, Geneva, Switzerland.
Economic Commission for Latin America and the Caribbean, Santiago, Chile.

Economic and Social Commission for Asia and the Pacific, Bangkok, Thailand.

Economic and Social Commission for Western Asia, Baghdad, Iraq.

Food and Agriculture Organization, Rome, Italy.

General Agreement on Tariffs and Trade, Geneva, Switzerland.

International Fund for Agricultural Development, Rome, Italy.

International Labour Office, Geneva, Switzerland.

International Monetary Fund, Washington DC, USA.

International Research and Training Institute for the Advancement of Women, Santo Domingo, Dominican Republic.

International Trade Centre UNCTAD/GATT, Geneva, Switzerland.

The World Bank, Washington DC, USA.

United Nations Children's Fund, New York, USA.

United Nations Conference on Trade and Development, Geneva, Switzerland.

United Nations Development Programme, New York, USA.

United Nations Educational, Scientific and Cultural Organization, Paris, France.

United Nations Environment Programme, Nairobi Kenya.

United Nations Institute for Disarmament Research, Geneva, Switzerland.

United Nations Industrial Development Organization, Vienna, Austria.

United Nations Institute for Training and Research, New York, USA.

United Nations Fund for Population Activities, New York, USA.

United Nations Research Institute for Social Development, Geneva, Switzerland.

United Nations University, Tokyo, Japan.

World Food Council, Rome, Italy.

World Food Programme, Rome, Italy.

World Health Organization, Geneva, Switzerland.

World Institute for Development Economics Research, Helsinki, Finland.

World Intellectual Property Organization, Geneva, Switzerland.

World Meteorological Organization, Geneva, Switzerland.

Index

Diaby-Ouattara, Aboubakar, 291
diarrhoea, 101
dictatorships, 46,48
disarmament
  gains momentum, 5,220
  North-South relations, 265
discrimination, 13
  against women, 81,128
diseases, 99,101
double taxation agreements, 184
drugs
  illicit traffic, 7,51,155,266-7
  use by the South, 46

East African Economic Community,
  144
East Asia
  economic growth in 1980s, 66
  growth of industry, 96
  population growth, 104
  poverty, 84
  rural industry, 93
  education, 103
East Caribbean Common Market, 144
East-West relations
  easing of tensions, 4,20,
    153,220
Eastern Europe
  consequences for the South
    of reforms, 20,153,220
  market for petroleum, 263
  North-South negotiations,
    4,20
  participation in the IMF,
    World Bank and GATT, 221
EC *see* European Community
Economic Co-operation among
  Developing Countries (ECDC),
  169,181
Economic Community of Central
  African States (CEEAC), 146,156
Economic Community of West African
  States (ECOWAS), 146,156,197,199
economic growth
  achievements, 32-4
  decline in 1980s, 61
  in developed countries, 56
  indispensable for South's
    development, 12,80,82,272
economy
  macroeconomic management,
    114,118-20
  market forces, 114,275
  State involvement, 48,113-6
  see also world economy
ecosystems
  common resource management, 194
ECOWAS *see* Economic Community
  of West African States

education
  children, 278
  distance, 104,163
  expenditure cuts, 68
  girls, 282
  inadequate infrastructure, 26
  primary and secondary, 102-3
  progress, 74
  South-South co-operation, 160-3
  university, 104,161-2
  see also schools; literacy
education and training
  in-house training, 111
  science and technology, 39-45,
    81,104,110-11,191
  South-South co-operation,
    160,163,191
  technical and vocational, 163
Egypt
  Arab Co-operation Council, 156
  Tripartite Agreement, 145
elections, 12
employment, 15
  creation, 94
  off-farm, 90,93
  see also labour
energy, 195
  conservation, 280
  international regime, 262-3
entrepreneurs, 122
  role of State as entrepreneur,
    114-5
  see also business sector
  South-South co-operation, 164
environment
  adverse effects due to pattern
    of development, 39
  agricultural, 88
  causes of stress, 134-8
  challenge to the South, 134-41
  degradation, 6,82
  North-South co-operation, 218,
    224,258-60
  protection, 138-41,213,280-1
  South's responsibilities, 280
  South-South co-operation, 193-4
erosion, 39,136
Euro-currency markets, 55
European Community
  Common Agricultural Policy, 243
  COMPEX scheme, 248
  Lomé Convention, 156,243
  monetary union, 237
  Multi-Fibre Arrangement, 243
  protection against imports, 242
  single market, 5,242
  STABEX scheme, 248
European Monetary System, 237